Break into English

STUDENT'S BOOK 2
Michael Carrier & Simon Haines

HODDER AND STOUGHTON

LONDON   SYDNEY   AUCKLAND   TORONTO

Contents

		Structure	*Function*	
UNIT 1 Nottingham Today **Topic:** Living in a City **Small Talk:** Where do you live?		Revision of Present Simple Revision of Present Continuous Revision of Numbers	Asking for information Giving personal information	1
UNIT 2 The History of Nottingham **Topic:** The past and the present **Small Talk:** Where were you born?		Revision of Past Tense Time phrases in the past	Making comparisons	7
UNIT 3 Leisure **Topic:** Leisure, holidays, pastimes **Small Talk:** Talking about your family		Revision of Present Continuous with future meaning Present Simple with future meaning	Making invitations	13
UNIT 4 Working Life **Topic:** Health, jobs & work **Small Talk:** At the chemist		Conjunctions 'when', 'until', 'as soon as', Revision of 'going to' future 'Have got'	Relating events in the past Making plans and arrangements Describing illness	19
Language Study 1				25
UNIT 5 Accidents **Topic:** Biographies, the recent past **Small Talk:** Physical appearance		Present Perfect with 'yet' and 'just' Duration with 'since' and 'for'	Narrating past events Describing duration	27
UNIT 6 Women's Work **Topic:** Jobs **Small Talk:** Personal qualities		Contrast between Present Perfect & Past Use of 'ago' and 'ever' Use of 'remember' + infinitive/ + gerund	Describing past events	33
UNIT 7 Problems **Topic:** Money & other problems **Small Talk:** Talking about fears & worries		Revision of modals: must, have to, could, can, need to Word order: already/just/yet/never	Talking about obligations Talking about problems	39
UNIT 8 Predictions and Promises **Topic:** The future **Small Talk:** Starting conversations		Future with 'will' 'Shall' in offers	Making predictions Making offers Making promises	45
Language Study 2				51
UNIT 9 Tourism **Topic:** Travel & tourism **Small Talk:** Asking for directions		Comparatives & superlatives: as...as, more/less than... 'Don't mind' + gerund	Describing statistics Making comparisons Giving opinions Making a point	53
UNIT 10 Town and Country **Topic:** Living in the country **Small Talk:** Describing houses		Use of Gerund + Infinitive So + adjective, such + adjective/noun	Expressing likes & dislikes Qualifying statements, opinions	59

	Structure	Function	
UNIT 11 Eat better, feel better **Topic:** Health & nutrition **Small Talk:** Asking for permission	Conditional 1 Modals: should, ought to, you'd better Countable/uncountable: less/fewer	Giving advice Suggesting actions	65
UNIT 12 Conservation **Topic:** Looking after the environment **Small Talk:** It's not allowed	Use of Gerund + Infinitive 'By': time and quantity	Agreeing/disagreeing Giving an opinion	71
Language Study 3			77
UNIT 13 In the News **Topic:** Immigration **Small Talk:** At the restaurant	Past continuous Use of all/most/both/a few/a little Past tense of 'must' & 'can' Connectors: because/when/while	Narrating Describing past events	79
UNIT 14 Life begins at forty **Topic:** Employment, youth **Small Talk:** Moods and feelings	Used to Verb + gerund and/or infinitive Question tags (negative tag)	Describing past habits	85
UNIT 15 Music **Topic:** Different kinds of music **Small Talk:** Complaining in a shop	Like/want 'I'd rather' + verb Enough	Expressing preferences Agreeing/disagreeing	91
UNIT 16 Radio Trent **Topic:** Local radio **Small talk:** On the telephone	Reported speech Modals: ought to/should	Reporting what people say Obligations	97
Language Study 4			103
UNIT 17 Arts and Entertainment **Topic:** Entertainment **Small Talk:** Suggestions	Relative clauses Conditionals: unless/whether Modals: irregular future	Describing conditions and consequences Specifying and clarifying information Giving warnings	105
UNIT 18 Living in the City **Topic:** Problems of city life **Small Talk:** Money	Present perfect continuous While/during Question tags (positive tags) Relative clauses (that)	Describing duration in the past Confirming details Clarifying & explaining	111
UNIT 19 Britain and the USA **Topic:** Life in Britain and the USA **Small Talk:** Asking for help with words	Causatives Say/tell + that (reported speech) Still & yet	Getting things done Reporting instructions Clarifying information	117
UNIT 20 Magazines **Topic:** Writing & working for a magazine **Small Talk:** Hobbies & interests	Word order Although Reported speech	Reporting what is said	123
Language Study 5			129
Appendices			131

UNIT 1   Nottingham Today

PRESENTATION

1 Before you read, answer these questions.
- What is a city?
- What is your town or city like?
- What can you say about the city of Nottingham?

FACTS AND FIGURES ABOUT NOTTINGHAM AND ITS AREA

		1981	(1971)
POPULATION	Nottingham (city)	272,141	(300,630)
	Nottinghamshire (county)	985,283	(974,573)
AGE-GROUPS	0 – 15 years old	22.3%	
	16 – 65 " "	59.4%	
	over 65 " "	18.3%	
HOUSING IN THE CITY	People in their own house	37.5%	
	People in council houses	49.8%	
	Others (e.g. renting flats)	12.7%	
	Single person households	25.9%	
	Single parent households	3.1%	
	Non-British households	4.4%	
	Households without cars	55.5%	
EMPLOYMENT	People without jobs	13.1%	

2 Read about Kathy.

This is Kathy Baker. She is the manager of the Job Centre in the middle of Nottingham. She lives in a flat in the city, but soon she is going to buy her own house. Kathy really likes Nottingham; she thinks it is a great place to live. But there are many people with serious problems. Every day she has to work with unemployed people. She tries to find jobs for them. New industries are coming to Nottingham, so things are getting better, but only very slowly.

My name's Charlie Bloom. I work at the Raleigh Bicycle Factory. It's a huge place. I started work here when I was only 14 years old. That's 45 years ago, but I like my work, and I know I'm lucky to have a job. We make really top-class bikes—the best in the world, I think.

Now listen to some more Nottingham people. They are talking about themselves and their work.

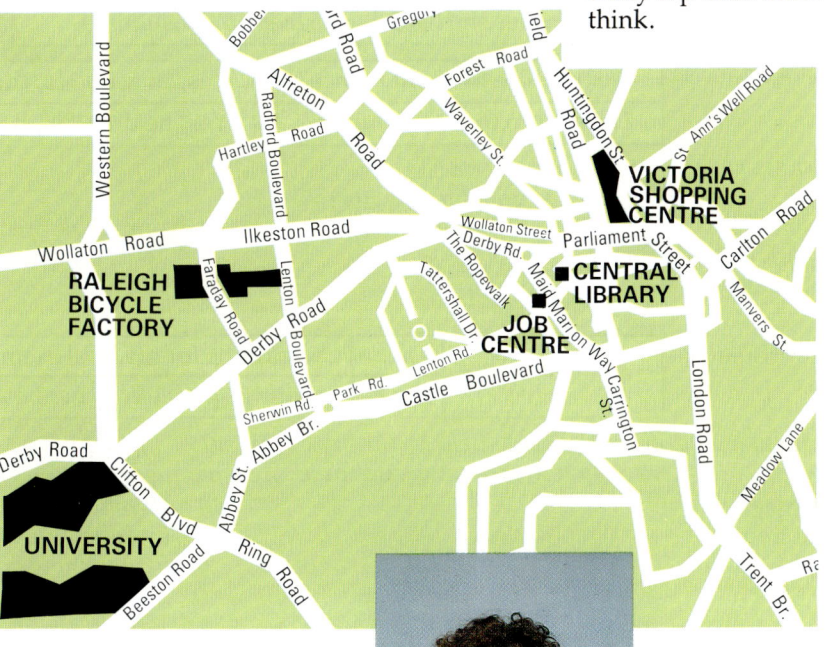

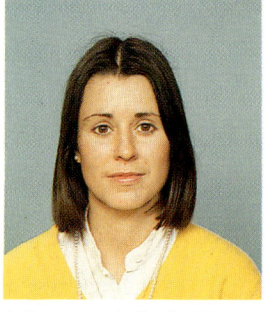

My name's Judy Kingston, and I work in the Central Library—that's right in the middle of the city. I think Nottingham's a wonderful place. It's full of interesting people. I actually work in the Local Studies section of the library.

My name's Alan Elston. I'm 22, and I'm a student in my last year at Nottingham University. I live in a small flat with four friends. At the moment I'm working hard for my final exams—I'm studying to be a teacher. Next year? Well, who knows?

My name's Harsha Khan. My family comes from Pakistan, but now we live here in Nottingham. I've got a stall in one of the markets in the Victoria Shopping Centre—it sells all kinds of Asian food. In my spare time I work for the Pakistan Centre.

3 Now answer these questions about Alan, Charlie, Judy and Harsha.

1 Why is Alan worried about getting a teaching job in a Nottingham school?

2 What is Charlie Bloom going to do when he retires next year?

3 What is there in the Local Studies part of the library where Judy works?

4 How does the Pakistan Centre help the Asian people in Nottingham?

Check!
Look at Facts and Figures about Nottingham on page 1. Now tick the correct statements.
1 The population of the city of Nottingham is bigger than it was in 1971. ☐
2 The population of the county of Nottinghamshire is bigger than it was in 1971. ☐
3 Most households in Nottingham have a car. ☐
4 Nottingham has a small non-British population. ☐

UNIT 1

Language Focus

The Present Simple:

I / We	live	in a small flat in the city centre.
Judy	works	at the Central Library.

ORAL EXERCISE *example:* Where do you work?
                you: I work at the Raleigh Factory.

1 you live?/large house
2 you work?/supermarket
3 Alan live?/small flat
4 Judy work?/centre of Nottingham
5 Ahmed work?/market
6 they live?/little village

Question Forms:

What do you do?	I work in a bank.
Where does she live?	She lives in the suburbs.
Do they like living in France?	Yes, they do/No, they don't.
Does he go to work by train?	Yes, he does/No, he doesn't.

ORAL EXERCISE *example:* You/live/a city
                you: Do you live in a city?

1 you/live/a city
2 they/work/a bank
3 he/watch/television
4 she/speak/Spanish
5 you/like/chocolate
6 he/study/university

The Present Continuous:

At the moment	I'm	working	for my final exams.
	she's	writing	a letter to her boyfriend.

ORAL EXERCISE *example:* Can I speak to Mr Price, please?
                you: I'm sorry, he's not here. He's having a meeting.

1 have/a meeting
2 work/at home
3 work/in London
4 have/lunch
5 interview/new secretary
6 inspect/new factory

SMALL TALK

Where do you live
A Have you got your own house?
B No, we live in a flat, but we're moving next year. What about you?
A We bought our house last year.

Find out where your partner lives. Is it a house or a flat? Has it got a garden, a garage, etc?

PRACTICE

1 How do these people travel to work in the morning? Match these phrases with the pictures.

by car   by bike   on foot   by bus   by train

Mike

Wendy

Brian

Ahmed

Alison

Now write sentences like this: Alison travels to work by train.

3

2 Now look at the pictures again and make conversations with your partner like this.
Student A—Alison   Student B—bike/there's a rail strike.
A   Do you always go to work by train, Alison?
B   Yes, but I'm going by bike today because there's a rail strike.

Student A	Student B
Alison	bike/there's a rail strike
Mike	bus/it's raining
Wendy	foot/my car needs repairing
Ahmed	bike/the buses were full
Brian	taxi/I'm late for a meeting

3 Many British students leave home to go to university. Alan for example, comes from Bristol, but he is at university in Nottingham. Here is some information about Alan's flatmates. None of them comes from Nottingham.

DUNCAN
Name: Gerald Duncan
Home address: 73, Queen's St., Glasgow, Scotland
Subjects: Physics and Maths
University Year: 1st

ALPINE
Name: Richard Alpine
Home address: The Old Cottage, Cambridge
Subjects: Modern Languages
University Year: 2nd

TRAVIS
Name: Amy Travis
Home address: 172 Forest Road, Liverpool 16
Subjects: Education
Year: 3rd

HARRIES
Name: Sue Harries
Home address: 89 Star Street, Liverpool 8
Subjects: Music
University Year: 2nd

This is part of a letter from Alan to his parents. He is telling them about his new flatmates. Fill in the missing words.

"...... my new flatmates. Anyway I'll tell you a bit about them all. It's quite strange none of them actually comes from Nottingham. I share a room with Richard. He's studying _____ and he comes from _____. Amy Travis and Sue Harries are in the downstairs room. Amy ___ from _____ and she's doing _____ like me. Sue is really nice. She's _____ music and she ___ _____ Liverpool. Last of all there's _____ _____ He's a first year student. He's ___ ___ and _____. He _____"

4 Now work in pairs. You are talking about the students you have met. Ask about their home towns.
A   Where does Alan come from?
B   He's from Bristol.
A   Is that a big city?
B   Yes, quite big. It's got a population of over 387,000.
A   How far is it from Nottingham?
B   About 151 miles, I think.
A   What is there to see there?
B   Well, it's got two football grounds, there's a university, and of course there's the famous Clifton Suspension Bridge.

Now you: Use the information from this table.

1 mile = 1.6 kilometres. Now fill in the distances in kilometres.

Town	Population	Distance from Nottingham	Interesting features
Bristol	387,977	151 miles _____ km	two football grounds, a university, the Clifton Suspension Bridge
Cambridge	90,440	90 miles _____ km	a market, excellent bookshops, the university
Glasgow	762,298	281 miles _____ km	a famous football team, 70 public parks, the modern underground railway
Liverpool	510,306	99 miles _____ km	two famous football teams, two cathedrals, the Cavern Club (home of the Beatles)

UNIT 1

TRANSFER

1 Work in groups of four.
Fill in identity cards like this one for each of your three partners.

Name: ....
Address now: ....
....
Home town/city: ....
Occupation: ....

Now find out more about your partners' home towns or cities. Fill in a chart like this.

	City	Population	Distance from capital city	Interesting features
Partner 1				1 2 3
Partner 2				1 2 3
Partner 3				1 2 3

2 WRITING
Now write about the home town/city of *one* of your partners. Use the information in the chart.

3 DISCUSSION   Work in pairs. Try to answer these questions.

1 What is a city?
    What is the difference between a city, a town and a village?

2 What makes a city a good place . . .
    . . . for people who live there?
    . . . for people who work there?
    . . . for tourists and visitors?
    . . . for business people?

3 What makes a city a bad place . . .
    . . . for people who live there?
    . . . for people who work there?
    . . . for tourists and visitors?
    . . . for business people?

4 LISTENING
Listen to this description of New York and tick these words (√) as you hear them.
chief ☐; commercial ☐; skyscrapers ☐; statistics ☐; employs ☐.

Listen to the cassette again, and fill in the gaps in these sentences with the correct number. Write figures.
• Nearly _____ people live in New York.
• There are _____ schools in the city.
• New York has _____ radio stations and _____ television stations.
• _____ policemen and _____ teachers work in New York.

Now answer these questions.
• What are Brooklyn, the Bronx, and Manhattan?
• How many hospitals are there in New York?
• What is the common name for New York?

What else do you know about New York? Write down five other things about the city.

5 SOUNDS

Word stress
Listen to the cassette and repeat these words.

Nóttingham/phótograph/begínning/impórtant/internátional/personálity

Notice where the stress is.
Now listen again to the description of New York. Tick these words as you hear them and put the stress in the right place.

population ☐   commercial ☐   galleries ☐

universities ☐   skyscraper ☐

particularly ☐   headquarters ☐

industries ☐   statistics ☐   hospitals ☐

technical ☐   policemen ☐   television ☐

SKILLS

1 READING

Before you read
* Look back at the first two pages of this unit.
* What do you already know about Nottingham?
* What sort of a city is it?
* Where is it in England?
* What sort of jobs do the people have?

Now read this text, find out more about Nottingham.

Nottingham, in the East Midlands, is a large, commercial centre and the home of important national industries and multi-national corporations. Boots, Raleigh Bicycles and the John Player Tobacco company all have their headquarters here. They employ thousands of Nottingham people in their offices and factories. Nottingham is also the centre of one of Britain's most important coal-mining areas.

The city has a long and interesting history. Today it is a fascinating mixture of the old and the new.

Look back at the questions in *Before you read*.
What more can you say about Nottingham?

2
Here are some more places of interest in Nottingham. Match these photographs, with the correct caption and description.

* This 19th Century theatre is in the centre of the city. Recent repairs and redecorations cost the city £5m. (Photo _____)

* The city has two of the most modern indoor shopping centres in Britain. Much of Nottingham's central shopping area is for pedestrians only. (Photo _____)

* To make life easier for the people of Nottingham, there is a free bus service. It is called 'Cityline'. (Photo _____)

* You can still do your shopping in one of the old street markets. (Photo _____)

* This is the ultra-modern, 2,500 seater concert hall. It cost £12m to build, and has an impressive, all-glass front. (Photo _____)

* This outlaw is Nottingham's most famous historical character. He 'robbed the rich and gave to the poor.' His statue stands near to the walls of the Castle. (Photo _____)

CAPTIONS
* Sneiton Market
* The Royal Concert Hall
* Cityline, the free bus service
* The Theatre Royal
* Robin Hood Statue
* Broad Marsh Indoor Shopping Centre

3 Words
* Which words helped you to match the captions, descriptions and photos?

* Find words in the descriptions which mean about the same as:

  personality, criminal, very new, well-known, walkers

* Find words in the descriptions which mean the opposite of:

  rich, outdoor, more difficult, old-fashioned

6

UNIT 2   The History of Nottingham

PRESENTATION

1
- Is your town industrial? What sort of industry does it have?
- Why do some towns and villages grow into cities?

❓ When was the Norman Invasion of Britain?

❓ What was the population of Nottingham at this time?

❓ Where did people move from during the Industrial Revolution?

❓ Why did so many people have to live in slums?

❓ How many people moved into Nottingham in the 19th century?

❓ Why did the population fall in the 20th century?

The History of Nottingham

In 1068, two years after the Normans invaded Britain, William the Conqueror came to the small town of Nottingham. To the north of the town he built a castle. At that time most of the town's 6500 people worked in local trades: making cloth, iron or beer, farming, or coal-mining.

During the next three centuries many more people came to live in Nottingham to work in the newer industries: glass-making, brick-making and pottery. This was the beginning of the Industrial Revolution. All over England people moved from the country to the cities. The population of Nottingham grew too quickly. There were not enough houses for everyone, and many people had to live in terrible, overcrowded slums. The Industrial Revolution brought large factories and new housing for working families, but there was still great poverty. Many people died before the age of 25.

In the 19th century the city grew outwards. The population increased from 28,000 to 250,000, as Nottingham became more important as a centre of industry and coal-mining. Between the 1930s and the 1960s Nottingham Council pulled down the worst slums, and many people moved to new houses outside the city. The population stopped increasing, and actually started falling, as more people moved out of the city centre.

COAL-MINING

GLASSMAKING

BRICKMAKING

POTTERY

SLUMS

2 Make up some more questions on this text.

When . . .?   Where . . .?   What . . .?   Why . . .?   How many . . .?

Ask your partner these questions.

3 LISTENING

Listen to Harry Shepherd and his wife Sally. In 1960 they moved out of the poor area of Old Radford, in the centre of Nottingham, to the new Broxtowe Estate on the outskirts of the city. They are describing the differences between Broxtowe and Old Radford.

- Are they happier than they were? Listen.

Check!

Listen to the cassette again, and then tick (✓) the correct boxes in this chart.

FEATURES	OLD RADFORD	BROXTOWE
older houses	✓	☐
1 larger houses	☐	☐
2 friendlier people	☐	☐
3 a dirtier area	☐	☐
4 a healthier place	☐	☐
5 a happier place for Harry and Sally	☐	☐

Language Focus

The Simple Past:

In 1068	the Normans	came	to Nottingham.
In the 19th Century	Nottingham	grew	outwards.
In the 1930s	they	built	the Broxtowe Estate.

When	did	Harry and Sally	move to Broxtowe?
Where	did	they	live until 1960?

They	moved	there in 1960.
	lived	in Old Radford.

Did	the Normans invade Britain in 1068?
	the city grow in the 19th Century?

No,	they didn't.
	they invaded Britain in 1066.

Yes,	it did.
	the population grew to 250,000.

ORAL EXERCISE *example:* Did the Normans invade Britain in 1068?/1066
you: No, they didn't. They invaded Britain in 1066.

1 Did the Normans come to Nottingham in 1066?/1068
2 Did he arrive here yesterday?/at the weekend
3 Did they move to Manchester?/Nottingham
4 Did she work in London?/Manchester
5 Did they pull the slums down in the 1920s?/1930s
6 Did they move from Old Radford in 1950?/1960

Comparing:

The people	were	friendlier than	they are here.
The shops	are	more modern than	they were there.

ORAL EXERCISE *example:* streets/narrow
you: The streets were narrower than they are here.

1 people/happy
2 air/clean
3 streets/dirty
4 houses/small
5 neighbours/helpful
6 people/hardworking

Time phrases with the past:

In	1960	**At** that time
	the 19th Century	**Between** 1930 and 1960
	those days	**During** the next three centuries

UNIT 2

SMALL TALK

Where were you born?
A Were you born in Manchester?
B No. I was born in London, actually.
   We moved here in 1978.

Ask your partner where he was born.   Ask when he moved.

PRACTICE

1 Work with a partner. Ask each other about population changes in British cities between 1750 and 1801. These were years of great industrial change.

STUDENT A
Student B cover this

**POPULATION DISTRIBUTION
1750**

STUDENT B
Student A cover this

**POPULATION DISTRIBUTION
1801**

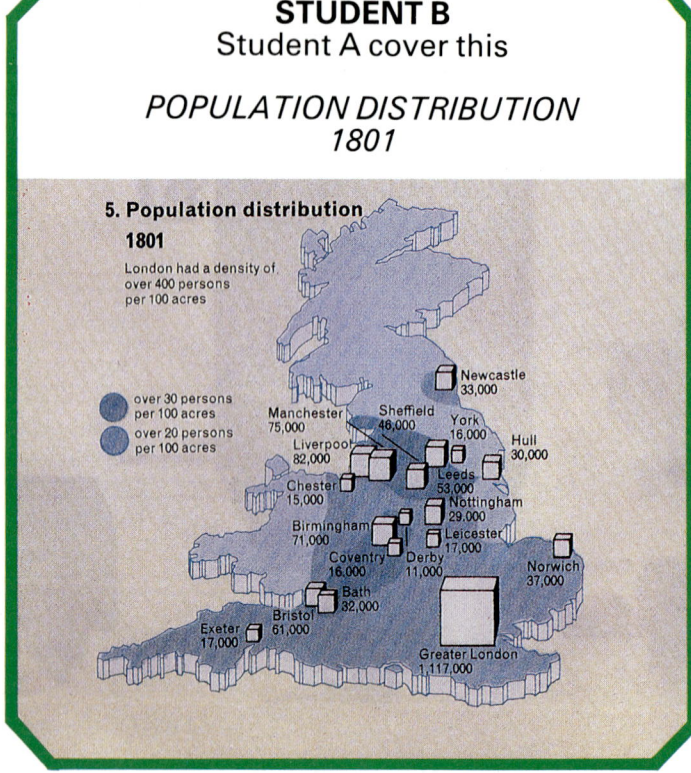

Ask each other questions like this.
example: Nottingham/1750

B How many people lived in Nottingham in 1750?
   or
   What was the population of Nottingham in 1750?
A Fifteen thousand.
B Really? In 1801 it had 29,000 inhabitants.

Now write down your partner's answers so you have the information for both years.

Questions for A to ask B
1750
- London/1801 . . .
- Hull/1801 . . .
- Birmingham/1801 . . .
- Manchester/1801 . . .

Questions for B to ask A
1801
- Bristol/1750 . . .
- Leeds/1750 . . .
- Liverpool/1750 . . .
- Sheffield/1750 . . .

2 WRITING
Write three or four sentences to describe the differences in the cities between 1750 and 1801.

3
Look at Monica's diary. Ask questions like this:
A What did Monica do on Monday morning?
B She worked at home.

Monday
a.m. work at home / phone dentist
p.m. bank for money – meet Peter, lunch
evening Football 7.30 – write to Pamela

Tuesday
a.m. Cambridge (visit Paul + John)
p.m. London for lunch – write notes for conference
evening evening classes – French / wash hair

Wednesday
a.m. Day off work – YIPPEE!!
p.m.
evening Dallas 8.00 (I love J.R.)

Thursday
a.m. Sales conference

Friday

Saturday

Sunday

Next week

Make a diary for yourself for last week, like this.
Fill in what you did each day.

Ask each other questions about how you spent last week, like this.
A What did you do on Monday?
B I worked all day, and in the evening I went to the cinema to see *Gandhi*.
Write down your partner's answers on a blank diary page.

4 WRITING
Think about what you did last week.
- Where did you go?
- Who did you see?
- What did you talk about?
- What did you eat?

Now write ten sentences about what you did in the week.

UNIT 2

TRANSFER

1 Look at these two pictures of factory workers. The first shows an 18th century Sheffield factory. The men are making cutlery, that is knives, forks, spoons etc. Picture two shows young men learning how to operate machines in a modern workshop.

Describe picture 1 using the simple past and picture 2 using the present simple.

DESCRIBE	USE SOME OF THESE WORDS
the factory	hot, dark, big, crowded, old
the workers	strong, tired, dirty, poor, unhappy
the working day	long, tiring

DESCRIBE	USE SOME OF THESE WORDS
the factory	modern, clean, light, warm
the workers	young, relaxed, clean, well-paid, happy
the working day	short

With your partner make up five sentences. Compare the two factories, the workers and their working day.

2 Find out about your partner's town or the area where he/she lives now.
- First write some questions about the people, the buildings, the workplaces.
- Ask your partner these questions. Write down his/her answers.

Now ask if your partner has moved house. If he/she has, then ask:
—Was the old house bigger than the new one?
—Which town was bigger?
—Were the people in X friendlier than the people in Y?
How many other questions can you ask?

Write five sentences about your town, comparing the past and the present.
- In 1800 the city built a new cathedral.
- In 1600 the city was richer than it is now.
- There was more industry in the town in the 1960s.

3 🎧 LISTENING

Listen to this man. He is talking about his first job—in the 1920s. As you listen, try to decide the answer to this question.
     Did he enjoy his first job?

Test your memory
1 How much money did he earn a week?
2 How much did the farmer give him?
3 When did he finish work on Sundays?

Times
Fill in the gaps in these sentences with times. Use numbers.
- From Monday to Saturday he worked from _____ to _____. Altogether he worked for _____ hours. He had _____ hour for lunch.
- On Sunday he worked from _____ to _____. Altogether he worked for _____ hours.

SKILLS

1 READING

Read this letter. In it Anne is telling her friend, Sue, about a day she had in Nottingham. It is mostly in the simple past.

Anne thanks Sue.

She explains what she is doing at the moment.

A description of past events.

What happened yesterday.

Details of the day.

A list of all the things she did and saw.

An invitation to Sue to stay.

> 17, Thornton Rd.
> Oxford,
> OX2 5BU
>
> 16th April, 1986
>
> Dear Sue,
>
> Thank you for your letter. It ___ good to hear from you again. I'm on holiday this week, so at last I've got time to write to you.
> I must tell you about my day in Nottingham yesterday. It ___ great! ___ my first visit for about five years. It really ___ back memories.
> I ___ to go on a coach trip round the city to see all the famous sights. I ___ the coach at the bus station. First we ___ a marvellous day. I ___ the historical parts of the city, like the Castle, the Theatre Royal, the Trip to Jerusalem (that's a pub). We ___ past several old markets, and then we ___ into the outskirts of Nottingham. The old, industrial areas of the city ___ quite fascinating. At several places on the route the driver ___, and everyone ___ out and ___ photos. I must show you them the next time we meet.
> Would you like to come and stay for a weekend soon? We've got so much to talk about. I'm looking forward to that.
>
> Love,
> Anne

Now fill in the gaps in the letter with these verbs.

| caught | stopped | saw | was | had | went | got | decided | was | were | brought | took | drove |

2 WRITING

Last week you were on holiday. You spent a day in London, your first for six years. Write a letter to a friend saying what you did and saw.
Look at the leaflet for ideas for your trip.

DON'T FORGET
- your address and the date.
- to thank your friend for his/her last letter.
- to tell your friend what you are doing at the moment.

ALSO
- describe what you did yesterday, in general, and then in detail.
- end your letter with a suggestion about meeting your friend again.
- you can finish your letter with any of these phrases:
  "See you soon,"
  "Love,"
  "Best wishes,"
  "Yours,"

UNIT 3   Leisure

PRESENTATION

1 What kinds of entertainment do you like? Do you like sport, films, concerts?

🎧 Listen to this announcement about tomorrow's football match in Nottingham. Where do you think the announcement is from?

Queens Park Rangers are travelling to Nottingham tomorrow for their match against Notts Forest. Forest are currently seventh in the First Division. . . .

2 🎧 Now listen to this conversation between two men. They are talking about the match.

Mike Are you coming to the match tomorrow afternoon, Dave?
Dave Sorry, Mike, I can't, I'm buying a new car tomorrow.

3 🎧 Now listen to some more conversations. People are arranging their future entertainment.

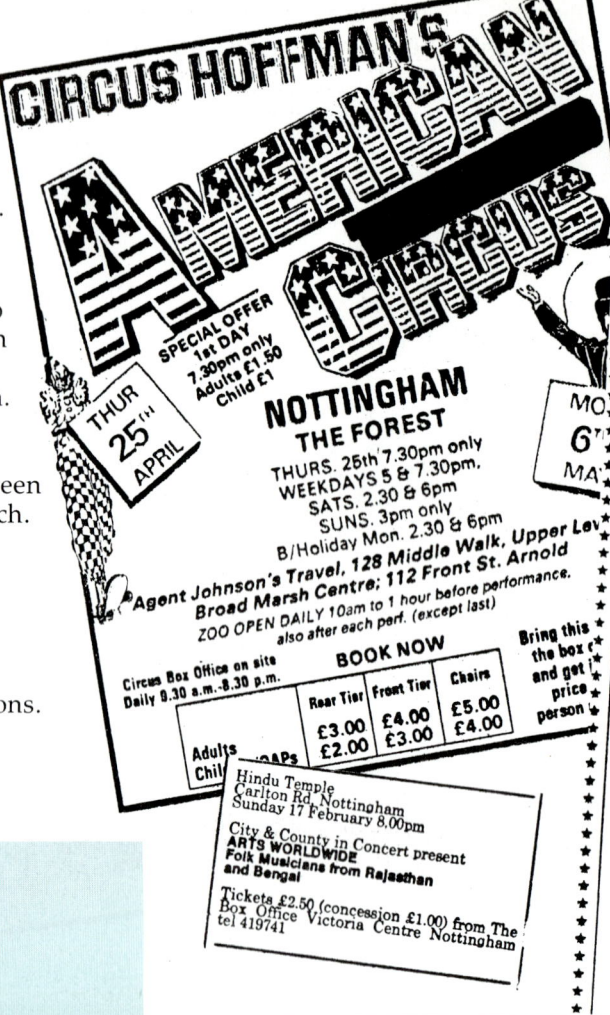

Anita Hello, Jenny. Anita here. Are you doing anything tomorrow evening?
Jenny No, I don't think so. Why?
Anita Well, we're all going to the American Circus. Would you like to bring your kids along? It starts at 7.30.
Jenny That's a great idea. Thanks.
Anita That's okay. See you there then.

Andy Do you know, there's a concert of folk music from Rajasthan and Bengal at the Hindu Temple?
Jane Really? I'd love to go. When is it?
Andy Sunday. It starts at 8 o'clock, and only costs £2.

Anne Hi, Mary. This is Anne. Paul and I are going to the theatre in a few weeks time. Do you and Mark fancy coming along?
Mary We'd love to come. What's on?
Anne It's a musical called *Are you lonesome tonight?* It's about Elvis Presley.
Mary That sounds great, Anne. When exactly is it on?
Anne It starts the week of June 17th. I'm phoning the theatre on Monday to book our tickets.

Check!
Match the beginnings and endings of these sentences.

1 Dave can't go to the match
2 Anita and her family are going to
3 The concert of folk music is
4 *Are you lonesome tonight?*
5 It's a musical about

a starts on June 17th.
b at the Hindu Temple.
c the life of Elvis Presley.
d the American Circus.
e because he's buying a new car.

13

Language Focus

Present Continuous:
future plans and intentions

| Are you doing anything | at the weekend? |
| Where are you going | tomorrow evening? |

| I'm | going | to the circus | tomorrow. |
| We're | moving | house | on Saturday. |

ORAL EXERCISE *example:* What are you doing on Friday evening?/play tennis
 you: I'm playing tennis on Friday evening.

1 What are you doing for your holidays?/go to France
2 When are you having your party?/Saturday night
3 What are you doing at the weekend?/drive to Paris
4 When are you buying your new TV?/tomorrow
5 When are you going on holiday?/next Friday
6 What are you doing tomorrow morning?/going shopping

Present Simple: timetables,
programmes of events

| The circus | starts | at 7.30. |
| The gates | open | at 2 o'clock. |

ORAL EXERCISE *example:* When does the match start?/three o'clock
 you: It starts at three o'clock.

1 When does the film finish?/7.15
2 When does the concert start?/8.00
3 When does your train leave?/3.17
4 When do your parents arrive?/6.00
5 When does the show end?/5.30

SMALL TALK

Talking about your family

A Do you come from a large family?
B No, I'm an only child unfortunately.
   My mother couldn't have any more children.
   What about you?
A I've got a brother and two sisters.

Find out about your partner's family
   Do you have a large family?
   How many brothers and sisters have you got?

PRACTICE

1 Here is John Miller's diary for next week.

```
Mon 22   meet bank manager
Tues 23  have lunch with directors/exhibition in London
Wed 24   fly to Munich/Heathrow 3.20 supper with Gerhard
Thurs 25 meet German clients/sales conference
Fri 26   fly to Heathrow/10.15 take car to garage
Sat 27   sailing with Jack/Theatre 7.30
Sun 28   lunch at mother's/Jeremy's party
```

Ask and answer questions like this.
   What's John doing on Monday?
   On Monday he's meeting his bank manager.

2 Here is part of your year planner. Fill it in with dates and times of some more business trips for the next six months. You are also going to Madrid, Paris, Cairo, and Peking.

Date	Destination	Airport	Flight time
January 2nd	Edinburgh	Heathrow	16.30
January 5th	London	Edinburgh	17.45
January 24th	Belfast	Heathrow	
January 27th	London	Belfast	
March 16th			
March			20.15

Now tell your partner about your trips.
   I'm travelling to Edinburgh on January 2nd. The flight leaves Heathrow at half-past four in the afternoon.

UNIT 3

3 Look at the advertisements for different kinds of entertainment and then talk to your partner like this.

A Would you like to come to the wrestling with me?
B Yes, I'd love to. When is it?
A It's on Thursday. It starts at 7.45.
B Great! How much does it cost?
A It's £2 or £2.50.

> You can also use the very informal: 'Are you coming . . .?'

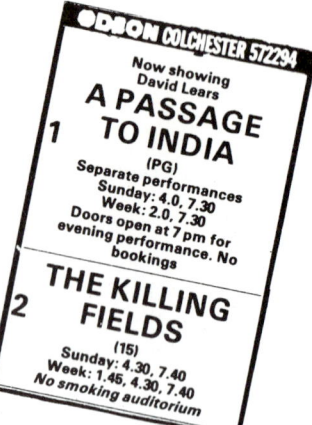

4 WORDS

Arrange these words under these three headings.

police	kids	football	concert	player	film	parents	squash
circus	tennis	theatre	party	musical	skiing	farmer	

How many more words can you add?

PEOPLE	SPORT	ENTERTAINMENTS

TRANSFER

1
You and your partner are going on a study visit to the USA in the summer.
You booked a holiday last winter. But now there are some changes to the original programme.

STUDENT A

This is the original visit programme. Your partner receives a letter from the travel company. It contains the details of the changes.
Check the arrangements, dates, times, etc with your partner.

Use questions like this.
- What time does our flight arrive?
- What are we doing on the twenty-second?
- Are we still having the lecture on American lifestyles?

Write out a new programme as your partner answers your questions.

Study Tours

Offer you this exclusive 10-day study holiday to the States
June 17–June 26

Day 1 Arrive Boston Airport 11.30 am. Coach to host family meeting, then car to individual host families.
Evening: Welcome party/barbecue at a host family home.

Day 2 Introduction to study programme by teacher–leader.
Afternoon: Trip to Stoneham Zoo.

Day 3 *Morning:* Lecture on American lifestyles.
Afternoon: Sightseeing—the City of Boston.

Day 4 All-day excursion to Cape Cod.

Day 5 *Morning:* Lecture on American Government.
Afternoon: Tour of Boston City Hall with Mayor.

Day 6 *Morning:* Lecture on American Education System.
Afternoon: Tour of Harvard University Campus.

Day 7 Free day with Host Family.

Day 8 *Morning:* Lecture on American Family Life.
Afternoon: Picnic at Forest River Park.

Day 9 *Morning:* Lecture on American Sports.
Afternoon: Bowling at Sunnyside Bowling Alley.
Evening: Farewell Party at a host family home.

Day 10 *Morning:* free time for packing and shopping.
Afternoon: by coach to Boston Airport Leave on 19.15 flight.

DON'T MISS THIS CHANCE OF A LIFETIME!!

UNIT 3

STUDENT B

This is the letter you receive from the travel company. It gives details of all the changes to your study trip to the USA. Phone your partner and tell him/her about these changes. Answer your partner's questions with sentences like this.
- Our flight arrives in Boston at 3.20 in the afternoon.
- We're having a welcome party on the second evening.

Study Tours Ltd
17 Bridge Street, London WC1

Mr J. Edwards,
72 Manor Road,
Colchester,
Essex.
                                17.5.86

Dear Mr Edwards,

We are sorry to have to inform you that the arrangements for your forthcoming holiday to USA have been changed. (Tour STL 27). The circumstances of this change are beyond our control, but we can assure you that your American tour remains excellent value for money. We apologise most sincerely for any inconvenience this may cause. Please let us know immediately if we can be of any further assistance.

Yours faithfully,

P. Mann

P. Mann (Managing Director Study Tours Ltd.)

ITINERARY

June 17 — Arrive Boston Airport 3.20 pm.* Coach to host family meeting, then car to individual host families.

June 18 — Introduction to study programme by teacher–leader. *Evening: welcome party/barbecue at home of a family.

June 19 — Morning: Lecture on American lifestyles. *Afternoon: guided trip to typical shopping centre.

June 20 — All-day excursion to Cape Cod.

June 21 — *Morning: Lecture on American Education system. *Afternoon: Tour of Harvard University campus.

June 22 — Morning: Lecture on American Government. *Afternoon: Tour of Boston City Hall with Mayor.

June 23 — *Morning: Lecture on American Sports. Afternoon: bowling at Sunnyside Bowling Alley.

June 24 — *Free day with host families.

June 25 — *Morning: American family life. Afternoon: sightseeing—the City of Boston. Evening: Farewell party at a host family's home.

June 26 — Morning: free time for packing and shopping. Afternoon: by coach to Boston Airport. Leave on 19.45 flight.*

*denotes a change of time or activity

SKILLS

1 READING

New England Homestay

A structured 2 or 3 week programme staying with American host families. Centred close to Boston, PGL Homestay programmes have been designed to provide British youngsters with a carefully planned insight into contemporary American life and customs.

Boston, the capital of Massachusetts, is both an enjoyable city to visit and historically of great importance. The famous 'Freedom Trail'—a 1½ mile signposted walk—is the easiest way to trace the history of Boston on foot. Other places of interest in Boston include Beacon Hill, with its steep, gas-lit streets and old town houses, the Museum of Science and the Boston Museum of Fine Arts.

THE HOMESTAY Your party will be accommodated, normally in pairs, with carefully chosen American families. Selection of the families is coordinated locally by American International, a respected American organisation specialising in educational travel. Groups are normally placed in residential communities within easy access of a metropolitan area, introducing students to a wide range of American life in a concentrated period of time. The homestay is based on half board accommodation on excursion days and full board when with host families.

QUESTIONS

1. How long are these homestay holidays?
2. Who are they for?
3. What is the purpose of homestay holidays?
4. What state of America is Boston in?
5. What is the Freedom Trail? How long is it?
6. What are the names of two of Boston's museums?
7. Do the young people stay on their own in American families?
8. Who chooses the families in Boston?

2 LISTENING

Listen to this phone conversation between Paul and his friend Annie. They are arranging a holiday.

Annie Hello, 62943.
Paul   Hello, is that you Annie? This is Paul.
Annie Paul! How lovely to hear from you. How is everything?
Paul   Not too bad, thanks. Listen. Are you going away for your summer holidays this year?
Annie No, I don't think so. Why?
Paul   I just thought we might go somewhere together. How about it?
Annie That's a great idea, Paul. Where are you thinking of?

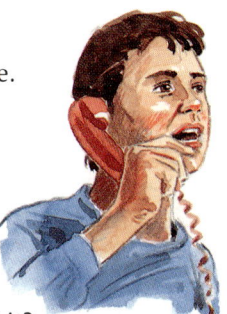

Now listen to the rest of their conversation. Paul makes several suggestions for their holiday together. He gives places, dates, costs and means of travel. Listen carefully to Paul and fill in the gaps in this chart.

Listen again to the second half of the conversation and make a note of Annie's responses to Paul's suggestions:
   Why can't she go to Rome?

SUGGESTED PLACE	DATES	PRICE	TRAVEL
1 Crete			by plane
2	5 June 26 June		
3		£250	
4			

3 WRITING

You are writing to your friend, explaining about your holiday next month. Describe where you are going, what you are going to do and see.

4 SOUNDS — How many stresses?

In Annie's phone conversation, she said:

   That's *ter*ribly ex*pen*sive. (2 stresses)

Listen and repeat these sentences. How many stresses do you hear? Mark them.

   That's very nice of you.
   Why don't I meet you tomorrow?
   Is that Bill's new car over there?
   What a beautiful baby, Mary!
   Is this the right road to London, please?
   I'd like a green sweater, not a blue one.
   College starts again on the third of September.

UNIT 4 Working Life

PRESENTATION

1

Dear Sir
I had to visit my doctor last week. Do you know, I had to wait outside the surgery for 45 minutes. Finally I went in. The doctor spent 3 minutes with me, wrote me a prescription, and said: 'Come back next week'. Now doctors are asking for more money. Are they really worth it?
Yours faithfully,
P.G.Slater (Mr)

Check!
1 Who is Mr Slater writing to? How do you know?
2 How much time did the doctor spend with him?
3 Does he think doctors should get more money?

2

- Why was the car driver in pain?
- Why did Dr Fleet have no breakfast?
- How many people did he see at the Centre?
- What was wrong with Mrs Freeman?
- How many old people did he visit?
- Why did the police come to the Centre?

LETTERS TO THE EDITOR

Dear Sir,
May I reply to Mr Slater's letter about doctors — The Gazette 31st March. Let me tell him and other readers about a typical doctor's day. Last Monday was a good example.
My phone rang at 5 o'clock in the morning. I had to get to a serious accident on the motorway. The police could not get the driver out of one of the cars. He'd got a broken leg and was in great pain. I gave him an injection, and then waited until they cut him free. I had no time for any breakfast.
I hurried back to the Health Centre for my morning surgery. Between 9.30 and 11 o'clock I saw twenty patients. Some needed tablets or medicine, but some were not really ill at all — like Mrs Freeman. She was just worried about her husband, who has bronchitis, and had no-one to talk to.
At 11 o'clock I started my home visits — to see people who could not get to the Centre. I saw several children with flu, three old people who spent all their time in bed, and two mothers with very young babies.
At midday I thought about lunch, but as soon as I got back to the Centre, the police arrived — they wanted to ask me some questions about the motorway accident.
Am I worth more money, or not?

Yours faithfully,

Dear Sir,
In reply to a letter in last week's paper, I would like to protest

Check!
1 At what time did the doctor's phone ring?
2 How many patients did he see that morning?
3 Why did the police come to see him?

3 LISTENING

Listen to the cassette. Mrs Philips goes to the Health Centre to see Dr Fleet.

As you listen, find out what is wrong with Mrs Philips and how Dr Fleet tries to make her better.

Check! Answer these questions
1 What is wrong with Mrs Philips?
2 When did she start to feel ill?
3 Why does Dr Fleet say 'Open your mouth'?
4 What does Dr Fleet do to make Mrs Philips better?

Language Focus

Simple Past: relating two events

I	waited	until	they	cut him free.
The police	came	as soon as	I	got back.
I	got up	when	the phone	rang.

ORAL EXERCISE Complete the sentences with one of these words—when/until/as soon as
example: He got up/the alarm rang
you: He got up as soon as the alarm rang

1 Jane waited/her friend arrived
2 He got on the bus/it came
3 They phoned the police/they heard the explosion
4 I rang/I heard the terrible news
5 John worked/he finished the job

Going to: future plans and intentions

I'm going to	examine	you.
	take	your blood pressure.
	write	a prescription.

ORAL EXERCISE example: There's a new Bond film at the cinema./see
you: I'm going to see it tomorrow.

1 There's a new Bond film at the cinema./see
2 Your car's terribly dirty./wash
3 You need a new watch./buy
4 My brother's arriving from America./meet
5 Hamlet is on at the National Theatre./see
6 My bicycle's got a puncture./mend

Saying what is wrong with you:

I've got	a headache.
	a broken leg.
	a virus.

ORAL EXERCISE example: He/headache
you: He's got a headache.

1 Jane/stomach ache
2 I/broken arm
3 She/pain in her shoulder
4 He/broken finger
5 They/virus
6 I/chest pains

SMALL TALK
At the chemist

A Have you got anything for a sore throat?
B Yes, certainly. I've some tablets or some medicine.
A Have you got penicillin?
B No, I'm afraid not. You need a doctor's prescription for penicillin.

Ask your partner for something for a headache/sunburn/an insect bite.

PRACTICE

1 WORDS
Find words in the Presentation under these three headings:

PEOPLE	PLACES	MEDICAL

Now put these words under the headings
headache   surgery   police
chemist   motorway   driver
flu   hospital   baby   patient
medicine   Health Centre   injection
pain   doctor   tablet   children

UNIT 4

2 Other people, as well as doctors, have busy lives. Read about what Adrian March, Tony Hill and Amanda Gibson did yesterday morning.

Adrian March
Dispatch Rider

I got up at 5 o'clock, and drove to an office in Central London. I arrived at half-past six and collected my first package. I delivered it to another office in Birmingham at 9 o'clock. Between then and midday I delivered five important packages to offices all over the South of England.

Tony Hill
Milkman

I got up at half-past four and went by bike to the depot. As soon as I got there, I put twenty crates of milk on to my van and left. Between half-past five and half-past eight I delivered 500 pints of milk to people's homes. Then I drove back to the depot and collected some more milk.

I got up at half-past six and caught the bus to the hospital. As soon as I arrived I took breakfast to the patients in my ward. Then I made their beds, and gave them their injections and medicine. Between half-past nine and midday I took the doctor round the ward and got two patients ready for operations.

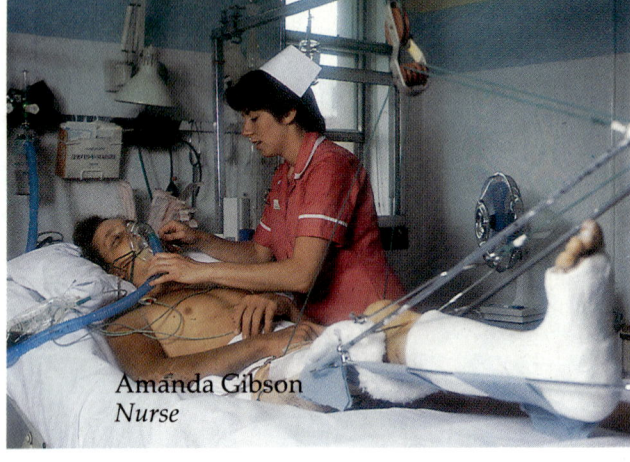

Amanda Gibson
Nurse

Complete this conversation with your partner.
A What time did you _____ up yesterday, Tony?
B I got up at _____.
A And how did you get to work?
B I went by _____.
A What did you do when you _____?
B The first thing I did was put _____ on to my van.
A What else did you do _____ morning?

Now make more conversations like this with Adrian March and Amanda Gibson.

3 **WRITING**
Write a description of the busy day that Adrian, Tony or Amanda had. Add some new information if you like.

4 Doctor A saw these six patients this morning. He is talking to his colleague Dr B. about them. They have conversations like this.

B What was wrong with Mrs Bellamy, then?
A She had a broken arm.
B So what did you do?
A I sent her to the hospital for an X-Ray.

Now make more conversations like this with your partner.

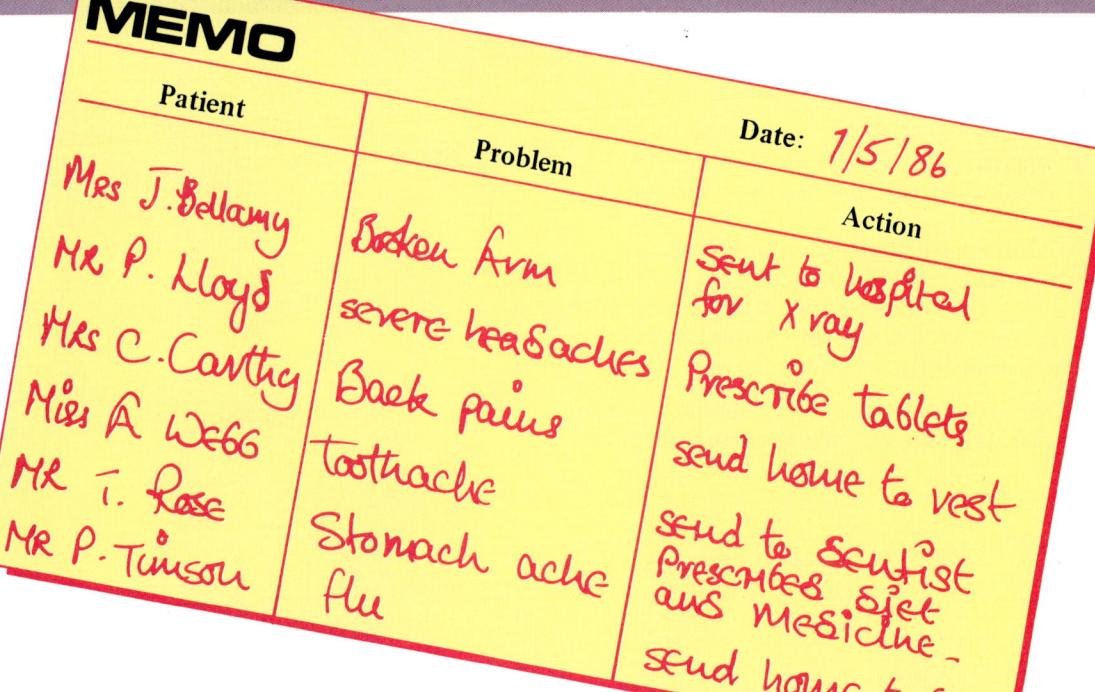

MEMO   Date: 1/5/86

Patient	Problem	Action
Mrs J. Bellamy	Broken Arm	Sent to hospital for X ray
Mr P. Lloyd	severe headaches	Prescribe tablets
Mrs C. Carthy	Back pains	send home to rest
Miss A. Wegg	toothache	send to dentist
Mr T. Rose	Stomach ache	Prescribe diet and medicine
Mr P. Timson	flu	send home to bed.

5 Talk about this picture with your partner.

That car's going to crash.
The painter's going to fall.

Now write sentences about the picture.

hair
eyes
nose
mouth
chin
ears
beard
moustache
lips
face

Frank

Richard

Joe

6 Look at these faces.
Describe these people to your partner.
Use the words in the picture.

Frank's got curly blond hair and a beard

long
short
small
big
curly
straight
blond
dark
wavy
black

Anne

Carol

Christine

22

UNIT 4

TRANSFER

1 WRITING

Think about all the things you did last year.
What was the busiest month? Make a calendar.
Fill in the things you did and then ask your partner what he/she did and fill in the calendar again.

Now read your partner's calendar for your year. Is it correct? Talk about any mistakes.

JANUARY	FEBRUARY	MARCH	APRIL	MAY	JUNE
JULY *went to Crete on holiday. Met Jo and Alison*	AUGUST	SEPTEMBER	OCTOBER	NOVEMBER	DECEMBER

2 LISTENING

Pete and Jenny are at a New Year's Eve Party. At this time of year many people make *New Year Resolutions*, which means they decide to do something or to stop doing something in the New Year. Listen to their conversation and then fill in this chart.

Now it's your turn. Make a resolution. Plan what you are going to do, and how you are going to do it.

Work in pairs. Find out about your partner's resolution. What is it? How is your partner going to do it?

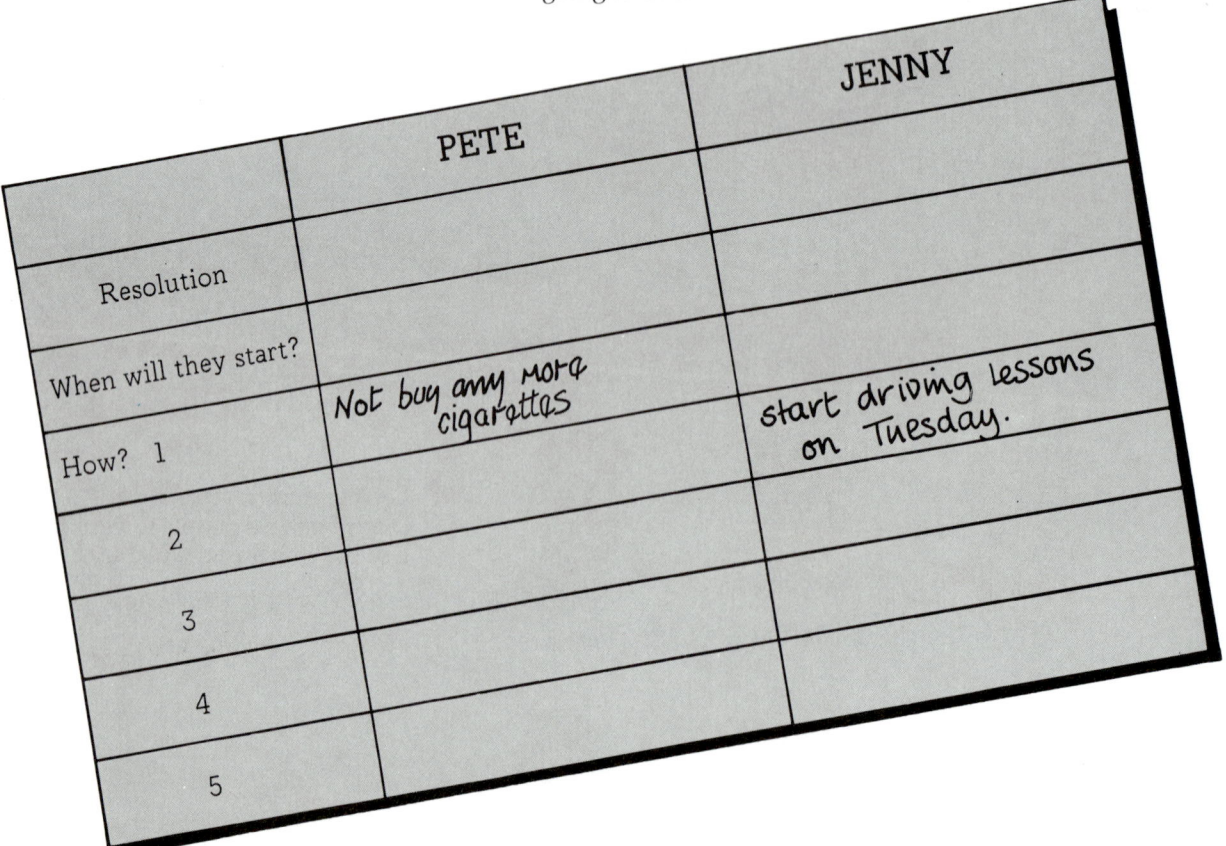

	PETE	JENNY
Resolution		
When will they start		
How? 1	Not buy any more cigarettes	start driving lessons on Tuesday.
2		
3		
4		
5		

23

SKILLS

1 READING
Read about the life of D. H. Lawrence. When did he leave Nottinghamshire? When did he come back to Eastwood?

2 Now read the text again—this time more slowly. Answer some more When Questions
- When did D. H. Lawrence start school?
- When did he leave school?
- When did he go to university?
- When did his book *The White Peacock* come out?
- When did he get married?

3 What do you find surprising or unusual about the life of D. H. Lawrence? Write down anything you find surprising, and give a reason.

D. H. Lawrence in Eastwood
Arthur Lawrence was a coal miner. He lived at 8A Victoria Street in Eastwood with his wife Lydia. The Lawrences had five children: two daughters and three sons. The youngest son was born on 11th September 1885. He was called David Herbert Richard Lawrence.

1892 Lawrence started school at the age of 7. He had five unhappy years at this first school.

1898 Lawrence moved to Nottingham High School. He was not a very good pupil here. In English he was 13th out of 21.

1901 He left school and got his first job. He did boring office work. That year he was very ill and nearly died. He also met Jessie Chambers, a farmer's daughter. He wrote about her in many of his books.

1906 Lawrence started at the University of Nottingham. He studied to become a teacher.

1908 He finished at the University and left Nottinghamshire. He worked as a teacher in a school in South London.

1911 He had to stop teaching because he became ill again. His first book, *The White Peacock* came out.

1912 He returned to Eastwood. That same year he met Frieda Richthofen, the wife of his old University professor of French. He visited Germany with her. They fell in love.

1914 Lawrence and Frieda Richthofen were married. He never went back to Eastwood.

4 Now look at the map of Eastwood. Where did the Lawrence family live between 1885 and 1911. Write the four addresses with the right dates.

Date	Address
1885–	
–	
–	
–1911	

5 Also on the map find the names of:
- Lawrence's school from 1893–1898
- Two pubs (public houses) in Eastwood.
- The village church.
- One of Lawrence's books—a novel.

6 Write eight important dates in your life. Write notes about what happened, or what you did at these times.

Language Study 1

Talking about the present   There are *two* present tenses in English:

Use the Present Simple to talk about routines:
- What do you do at weekends?
- Does he always go to work by train?
- We usually go to the theatre.
- Yes, he does.
- No, he doesn't.

Time phrases to use with the Present Simple:
- always, often, sometimes, never, usually, every morning

Use the Present Simple to talk about normal states or situations:
- Great Britain has a population of about 57 million people.
- Water boils at 100°C.
- English people love animals.

Use the Present Continuous to talk about something that is happening now – at the time of speaking, or something that is not finished:
- Are you having a good holiday?
- What are you doing?
- Yes, I am. I'm really enjoying myself.
- I'm listening to the radio.

Time phrases to use with the Present Continuous:
- now, at the moment, this week, this year

Talking about the past   Use the Past Simple to talk about events in the past which are finished, events which happened at a particular time in the past:
- When did the Normans arrive in Nottingham?
- Where did the Sheperds live before 1961?
- They arrived in 1068.
- They lived in Old Radford.

Time phrases to use with the Past Simple:
- last night, yesterday, last week, in 1983, 20 years ago

Note   Many common verbs are irregular in the Past Simple:
- come – came; go – went; have – had; see – saw; be – was

There is a full list of irregular verbs on page 133 of this book.

Talking about the future   You now know three ways of talking about the future:

Use the Present Continuous to talk about definite plans and arrangements:
- What are you doing next weekend?
- I'm flying to Greece.

Use **going to** to talk about your immediate intentions:
- We've got a puncture; what are we going to do?
- I'm going to buy a new tyre.

and for predictions
- Look at those clouds, it's going to rain

Use the Present Simple to talk about fixed programmes of events or timetables:
- When does the match start?
- When does the London train leave?
- It starts at 7.30.
- It leaves in ten minutes.

Time phrases to use with the future:
- this evening; tomorrow, next week, in the summer, in 1995

Invitations   Inviting somebody to do something
- Would you like to come to our party on Saturday?
- Do you fancy seeing the new James Bond film?

Accepting an invitation
- Thanks, I'd love to.
- That's very kind of you, thanks.

Refusing an invitation
- I'm sorry, I can't. I'm going away for the weekend.
- No, sorry. I don't like James Bond films.

Don't forget, English people often say 'Thanks' ('Thank you') and (I'm) Sorry.

Talking about your health   With most names of illnesses we do not use a/an. Common exceptions are a cold/a headache.
- What's the matter?
- What's wrong with you?
- I've got a headache.
- I've got toothache.
        measles.
        pneumonia.

And this is the most useful question to use at a chemist shop:
- Have you got anything for a headache?

Pronouns   Pronouns can be the subjects of verbs: (*I,you,he,she,we,they*)
- I love Italy.
- Where did he go last week?

They can also be the objects of verbs: (*me,you,him,her,us,them*)
- David loved her.   (*her* is a direct object)
- Anne sent me a birthday card. (*me* is an indirect object)

Possessive adjectives show possession: (*my,your,his,her,our,their*)
- Was David your boyfriend?
- That's my new motorbike.

Possessive pronouns (mine, yours, etc) also show possession:
- That car is mine.

Pronouns
Subject	Object
I	me
You	you
He	him
She	her
We	us
They	them

Possessives
Adjectives	Pronouns
my	mine
your	yours
his	his
her	hers
our	ours
their	theirs

Comparing
- The houses here are bigger than they were there.
- People are friendlier here.
- Food is more expensive than it was.

EXERCISES

TALKING ABOUT THE PRESENT

Present Simple
- What do you do in the evenings?
- How do you get to school/college?
- Ask five questions about English people.
- Write five sentences about English people.

Present Continuous
- Look round the classroom. Write about your friends. What are they doing?

TALKING ABOUT THE PAST
- What did you do last weekend?
- What did you do in these years: 1982, 1983, 1984, 1985?
- Ask ten questions about the past eg Did you watch TV last night? What did you do on Monday?

TALKING ABOUT THE FUTURE

Present Continuous
- What are your plans for the weekend? Write 3 sentences.
- Now ask your partner.

Going to
- What are you going to do immediately after this lesson?
- What are you not going to do?

Present Simple
- When does the next lesson start?
- What time does school finish today?

INVITATIONS   In writing accept and refuse these two invitations:
- Would you like to come and stay for the weekend?
- Do you fancy going to the disco on Saturday night?

HEALTH
- When did you last have a headache?
- When did you last have stomach ache?

PRONOUNS   Read about Kim Wilde. Then draw a circle round the object pronouns ○; a square round all the subject pronouns □; and underline the possessive adjectives —:

Kim Wilde made her first record when she was only 20 years old. In her first 4 years as a singer she sold 10 million records worldwide. Until recently she lived with her parents and her brother Ricky. They all give her a lot of help. Ricky writes some of Kim's songs, and produces her records. 'I'm lucky to come from a musical family,' says Kim. 'Music is the centre of my life – it is my first love.'

26

UNIT 5 Accidents

PRESENTATION

1 Read these Stop Press items of news from an evening paper.

DC10 Disaster—100 dead

Plane crash near Heathrow. 100 people die in DC10 crash. At least seven survivors. Telephone for information: 01-529 0472

MOTORWAY PILE-UP IN FOG

Police close M1 motorway south of junction 25.
39 vehicles in accident in thick fog.
Seven dead, dozens injured.
Police warning: *'Slow down in fog!'*

2 Now listen to these two News Flashes.

Check!

	MOTORWAY ACCIDENT	PLANE CRASH
1 How many people are dead?		
2 How many people are injured?		
3 What was the cause of the accident?		
4 Where was the accident?		
5 What 'vehicles' were in the accident?		

3 Now listen to this interview. David Grant is asking an official of the airline about the DC10 crash.

Grant Have you spoken to any of the survivors yet?
Official No, I haven't. It's really too early. They're still suffering from shock.
Grant Have the crew said anything about the minutes just before the crash?
Official No, they haven't. The pilot, co-pilot and head steward are all dead. The rest of the cabin staff are on their way to hospital now.
Grant And what about the flight recorder? Have you found that yet?
Official Yes, we have, and of course we're hoping that it contains all the information we need.
Grant Thank you.

4 VOCABULARY
Listen to the **News Flashes** again. Tick these words or phrases when you hear them.

1 *multiple accident* ☐
2 *completely blocked* the M1 ☐
3 an *on-the-spot* interview ☐
4 but *amazingly* ☐
5 with *minor injuries* ☐
6 the *emergency services* at work ☐
7 out of the *wreckage* ☐
8 on a *stretcher* ☐

Now guess the meanings of these words or phrases.

Language Focus

The Present Perfect:

	Regular verbs	*Irregular verbs**
I've (I have)	**recovered** (recover)	**seen** (see)
You've (You have)	**rushed** (rush)	**been** (be)
He's (He has)	**worked** (work)	**done** (do)
She's (She has)	**heard** (hear)	**had** (have)
We've (We have)	**crashed** (crash)	**brought** (bring)
They've (They have)	**died** (die)	**found** (find)
		taken (take)
		given (give)
		spoken (speak)

*There is a full list of irregular verbs on page 133.

ORAL EXERCISE   Saying what you have **just** done. (very recently)
example: arrive at Heathrow
   you: I've just arrived at Heathrow.
1 find my glasses
2 hear the doorbell
3 rush home from London
4 see my brother
5 speak to my father on the phone
6 do my homework

Now say what you have **never** done.
example: drink/champagne
   you: I've never drunk champagne.
1 work on Sundays
2 take drugs
3 hear so much noise
4 speak to a policeman
5 have a car accident
6 see the president

Talking about what you have done:

Have you	spoken to the survivors yet?		No,	I haven't.
	found the flight recorder?		Yes,	we have.

Saying how long:

I've	worked	on the motorway	**for** ten years.
I've	been	here	**since** 4 o'clock.

ORAL EXERCISE   *example:* work here/ten years
   you: How long have you worked here?
          I've worked here for ten years.

1 live here/1983
2 be in England/3 years
3 study English/5 years
4 teach at this school/15 years
5 play the piano/1984

SMALL TALK

Physical appearance

A   Have you seen my brother around?
B   What does he look like?
A   He's tall and thin with long, dark hair and he wears glasses. He looks like me, but he hasn't got a beard.

Ask your partner about two people in your class.
   What does . . . look like?

UNIT 5

PRACTICE

1 What has happened to these people?

Make sentences about these people. What have they just done?

He's just fallen off his horse.

Now work with a partner. Point to a picture and ask a question, like this.

Have they just seen a film?
Yes, they have.
No, they haven't. They've just arrived at the airport.

2 These three students have spent six months in Britain. Now they are telling each other what they have done since they came here.

	George	**Maria**	**Gina**
London sights	Buckingham Palace Oxford St.	Madame Tussauds Houses of Parliament	Westminster Abbey National Theatre
Visits to other towns	Oxford Bristol	Brighton Cambridge	York Edinburgh
Sports	football match	Wimbledon tennis	horse racing at Ascot
Food	fish & chips marmalade	roast beef custard	steak & kidney pie black pudding
Drinks	beer whisky	lager orange squash	tea beer

Work in pairs. Talk about what these people have done.

A Has George been to Oxford St.?
B No, he hasn't but he's been to . . .
A Where has . . .?

3 Talk about these people with your partner. Like this.

A What's your name?
B Jimmy Crowther.
A And what do you do?
B I'm a shopkeeper.
A How long have you been a shopkeeper?
B For about six years.
A But you've lived in Nottingham for longer than that, haven't you?
B Yes, I have. I've lived here since 1957.

TRANSFER

1 Compare past experiences.
Work in pairs and then change partners.

FIRST MAKE A LIST OF THESE THINGS:	example
• the five most interesting places you have visited in the last two years.	– Egypt and the Pyramids – New York – Red Square in Moscow
• two of the best things you have ever done.	– met the Pope – seen the Space Shuttle
• two of the worst things you have ever done.	– been in a train crash – fallen out of a window

Now ask your partners about these places and these experiences.

  Have you been to New York?

Make a note of his/her answers and answer his/her questions.

30

UNIT 5

2 WRITING

Write a letter to a friend you have not seen for several years. Tell him/her some of the things you have done since your last meeting. Write about your personal life, your job or your studies, your holidays etc.

Start like this.

> Dear _____,
> I'm sorry I haven't written for so long. I've been so busy. I just haven't had the time. Let me tell you some of the things I've done in the last three years ....
>
> Yours,
>
> ....

Your address _____
Date _____

3 GAME Work in groups.

1 When you have finished writing, put all the letters into a pile.
2 Take any letter (but not yours).
3 Talk to the person who wrote it, like this:
   I understand you've started a new job.
   Have you really . . .?
4 Tell the rest of the group about the letter you have read.

4 DISCUSSION

You and your partner are looking for a youth leader to take a party of young people on a tour of Europe for two months during the summer holidays. You put this advertisement in the local newspaper.

You receive these three application forms. Decide who is the best person for the job. Discuss them with your partner.

> He looks very good. He's worked as a Youth Club leader.
> Yes, but he hasn't passed his driving test.

GOOD WITH YOUNG PEOPLE?
HAVE YOU . . .
. . . worked with young people before?
. . . been a Youth Club Leader?
. . . travelled to more than three European countries?
. . . passed exams in foreign languages?
. . . passed your driving test?
. . . driven a minibus?
. . . got a clean driving licence?
More than 5 YES answers?
Then write to us for an application form.
You may be the person for us!!

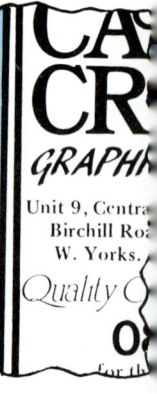

Name: Graham Brown
Date of Birth: 16.5.67
Address: 13, Manor Rd,
Redhill, Surrey
Work with young people? Yes/No
Youth Club Leader? Yes/No
Travel Guide? Yes/No
Countries visited: France, Germany, Spain, Russia
Languages? French, Spanish, Russian
Can you drive? Yes/No
Have you driven minibus? Yes/No
Clean licence? Yes/No
Driving test date: 20.10.85

Name: Stuart Fox
Date of Birth: 20-12-65
Address: 25 Beaconsfield Road, Loughborough, Leics
Work with young people? Yes/No
Youth Club Leader? Yes/No
Travel Guide? Yes/No
Countries visited: Denmark, Sweden, Germany
Languages? German, Spanish
Can you drive? Yes/No
Have you driven minibus? Yes/No
Clean licence? Yes/No
Driving test date: 28-11-84

Name: Pat Manchester
Date of Birth: 9.2.66
Address: 46, Long St, Bath, Avon
Work with young people? Yes/No
Youth Club Leader? Yes/No
Travel Guide? Yes/No
Countries visited: Italy, Spain, Yugoslavia
Languages? French, German
Can you drive? Yes/No
Have you driven minibus? Yes/No
Clean licence? Yes/No
Driving test date: 6.6.84

SKILLS

1 LISTENING

Last week you listened to a radio interview with Caroline Faber, a famous film star of the 1950s. She was sixty last Wednesday. As you listened you made notes, but you did not write all the details.

Listen again and fill in the gaps in your notes:

> **Caroline Faber Interview**
>
> (a) <u>Very full life</u>
> Married ___ times. Husband now called ___
> Married for ___ years.
> Lived in Hollywood for ___ years.
> But: No children. Why? Too ___
>
> (b) <u>Career</u>
> 1. Made more than ___ films.
> 2. Star of about ___
> 3. Starred with E.G. Robinson, James ___, ___ Newman, and Rob___ R___
>
> (c) <u>Personal Life</u>
> 1. Dinner with every President
> 2. Holidays with P___ ___, and H. Hughes.
> 3. Travel: would still like to see ___
> 4. Future: wants to act on the ___ stage.

2 WORDS

Match these words from the interview with a word or phrase which means about the same.

interview	meanings
my *current* husband	the most famous names in films
your *career*	personal
I've co-starred with *the greats*	working life
your *private* life	violent, rough, exciting
That's been very *stormy*	present
That's my *affair*	business, concern

3 SOUNDS

Intonation

Listen and repeat these sentences:

I'm buying a car next Tuesday.
Are you getting a new one?
Yes, a Ford, or maybe a Fiat, . . .

Now listen and repeat these sentences. Mark the intonation.
I was at work yesterday.
Oh, did you see Peter?
No, he wasn't there.
Well, who did you go with?
I got a lift with Brian.
Is he a friend of yours?
Yes, and Joe, Sam, . . .

32

UNIT 6 Women's Work

PRESENTATION

1 🔊 Orbis Airways have their Head Office at East Midlands Airport, just outside Nottingham. I went there last Thursday morning and met First Officer Anne Peacock—one of the two women pilots at Orbis. I asked Anne about her job.

Interviewer How did you become a pilot, Anne? It's an unusual job for a woman, isn't it?
Anne Yes, I suppose it is. Well, I always wanted to fly, so I went to an Air Training College in Oxford.
Interviewer And then?

Check! Listen to the interview again and then put these events in Anne's career into the right order.
- She left Jersey Airlines.
- She got her pilot's licence.
- She has flown all over the world.
- She got a job with Jersey Airlines.
- She was out of work for several months.
- She got a job with Orbis Airways.
- She went to Air Training College.

2 Now read these Case Studies about girls who want to do *men's work*.

Case Study 1

Diana has always wanted a job in engineering. When she was at school, her teachers laughed at her and gave her no help. Since she left school, she has written letters to all the engineering firms in her home town. Many have not even replied. Last July, she eventually got an interview with a local company. The interview lasted twenty-five minutes. The main question was 'How do you feel about working with men?' A boy from her old school also had an interview. His interview lasted forty-five minutes and he got the job.

Case Study 2

Lesley is fifteen. When she leaves school next year, she wants to be a motor mechanic. During the last two years, she has often worked in her uncle's garage and has helped to repair dozens of cars. Last week she even repaired her father's car. Her teachers at school have given her no real help at all. They have suggested an office job or factory work. At her last interview with the careers teacher, the advice was 'Why don't you get a job as a secretary or a hotel receptionist? Motor mechanics is a boy's job, Lesley.'

head office	central office	dozen	12
firm	company	suggest	give an idea
eventually	in the end, finally	advice	ideas to help you

Language Focus

Simple Past or Present Perfect?

| When | did you come | to Orbis? |
| How long | have you worked | for Orbis? |

| I came here | **in** 1982. |
| I've worked here | **since** 1982. |

ORAL EXERCISE *example:* When/see him *you:* When did you see him?
How long/work here. *you:* How long have you worked here?

1. when/meet her
2. how long/live here
3. how long/smoke a pipe
4. when/see the film
5. when/arrive from London
6. how long/wear glasses

Have you ever . . . ?

| Have you ever been to Brazil? |
| When did you go there? |

| Yes, I have. |
| I went there 10 years **ago**. |

ORAL EXERCISE *example:* Have you ever been to Mexico?/9 years
you: Yes, I have. I went there nine years ago.

1. Have you ever been to Spain?/10 years
2. Have you ever been to Canada?/3 years
3. Have you ever seen the President?/5 years
4. Have you ever met the Queen?/2 years
5. Have you ever watched Dallas?/a week
6. Have you ever been to London?/6 months

Simple Past and Present Perfect:

| Since she left school, she has written dozens of letters. |

ORAL EXERCISE *example:* come here/meet lots of people
you: Since I came here, I've met lots of people.

1. see you / travel all over the world
2. leave London / have three jobs
3. arrive here / do nothing
4. buy my new car / have 2 accidents
5. go to university / make lots of new friends
6. get that record / listen to it a hundred times

Remembering the past:

| I can remember | walking | into the offices of Jersey Airlines. |
| | writing | a lot of letters. |

ORAL EXERCISE *example:* I met you in London.
you: I can remember meeting you in London.

1. I took out my keys.
2. I unlocked the door.
3. I went into the building.
4. I got into the lift.
5. I went up to the fourth floor.
6. I shouted for help.

SMALL TALK

Personal qualities

A What's your new flatmate like?
B Jane? She's really nice.
A She always seems rather quiet and shy to me, even a bit dull.
B She isn't at all dull when you get to know her. She isn't the outdoor type, but she's talkative and interesting. Great fun to be with.

Ask your partner about two people in your class.
What is . . . like?

UNIT 6

PRACTICE

1 WORDS

Match these words from the Presentations with their correct meanings.

licence / straightaway / joke / eventually / repair

- something funny, something to laugh at
- immediately, without waiting
- after some time
- permit
- mend, make work again

2 These people all had good jobs, but now they are out of work. Here they explain what they do to save money or make money.

I TYPE LETTERS FOR PEOPLE AND DELIVER NEWSPAPERS.

I PLAY MUSIC IN THE STREET AND LOOK AFTER OTHER PEOPLE'S CHILDREN.

I MAKE MY OWN BEER AND I GROW VEGETABLES IN THE GARDEN.

I GIVE PEOPLE DRIVING LESSONS AND I REPAIR MY OWN CAR.

JANE 1982   **MIKE 1984**   **PAUL 1983**   **JOHN 1985**

Now talk to your partner about these people, like this.

A   When did Jane lose her job?/How long has Jane been out of work?
B   She lost her job in 1982./She has been out of work since 1982.
A   And what has she done to make money?
B   She's typed letters for people and she's delivered newspapers.

3 Work with a partner. Imagine you *have* been to all these countries. Make conversations like this.

A   Have you ever been to France?
B   Yes, I have.
A   When did you go there?
B   I went there in 1975/10 years ago.

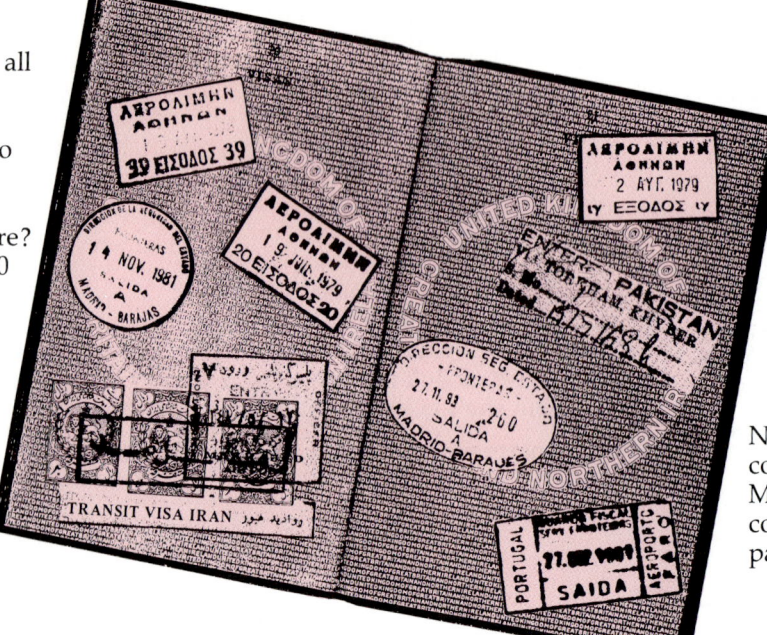

Now make a list of the countries you have visited. Make two more conversations with your partner (about yourselves).

4 When you got home last night, your wallet with £50 and your credit cards in it was not in your pocket. It was there in the morning. These pictures remind you what you did during the day.

Tell your partner what you did yesterday, like this.
- A I can remember leaving the house.
- B What time was that?
- A About 8 o'clock.
- B What's the next thing you can remember doing?

TRANSFER

1 🎧 LISTENING
19-year-old Susan Mann is from London. She has just finished her first year at Bristol University, where she is studying medicine. Listen to what she has done during her first year.

Susan uses these phrases. What do you think they mean?
- I've enjoyed *every minute* of my first year here.
- *Much as I love my family*, it's done me good to get away.
- I've learned *to stand on my own two feet*.
- I'm not so *well-off*.
- *All in all* it's been a great year.

Now answer these questions.
1 How has Susan saved money in Bristol?
2 How has she kept herself healthy?
3 How has she spent her free time?

2 Work in groups of 3 or 4.
Talk about the advantages and disadvantages of leaving home and living away from your parents. Make sentences like this.
- You can stay out late.
- You have to do your own shopping.

3 Since she came to Bristol, Susan Mann has become more independent.
Make a list of some of the ways in which *you* have become more independent during the last year.

Now find out what your partner has done. You can ask questions like this.
- What have you done during the last year?
- How have you become more independent?

36

UNIT 6

4 MEMORIES

Compare memories with your partner. You can talk about some of these memories.
- Being a baby or a young child
- Your first day at school
- Your first job or your first party
- Your wedding day or your first boyfriend or girlfriend.

You can ask questions like this.
- What's the first thing you can remember about . . .?
- What can you remember about . . .?

I CAN REMEMBER GOING FOR A WALK WITH MY GRANDFATHER

I CAN REMEMBER WALKING THROUGH THE SCHOOL GATE AND SEEING HUNDREDS OF NEW FACES

5 WRITING

Write about when you were a child.
Describe your life then, and what you remember doing.

6 GAME

Each member of the group writes down or thinks of an unusual and interesting experience he/she has had.
The other members of the group have to discover the secret.
They can only ask twenty questions.
example:
Secret: I've flown to America on Concorde. (A)
Questions:
Have you met a famous person? (B)
   Was this person a film star? (C)
   Was this person a politician? etc. (D)
Have you visited an interesting place? (B)
Have you seen something exciting? (C)
   Was it dangerous? (D)
   Was it frightening? (B)
Have you made an interesting journey? (C)
   Was it by train? (D)
   Was it by road? (B)
   Was it by plane? (C)
   Was it on Concorde? (D)

7 INTERVIEW

Make your own questionnaire to find out what interesting things your partners have done in their lives. Make a chart like this and write your own questions.

Question	Student 1	Student 2	Student 3
Have you ever ………?			
…… been to Paris?			
…… swum at midnight?			
…… eaten frogs legs?			
…… seen a flying saucer?			
……			
……			
……			
……			
……			

SKILLS

WRITING
Applying for a job.
Here are four advertisements for jobs.
They are all from local newspapers.

JOINER REQUIRED

Small busy workshop needs another hard working joiner
Must be able to plane, machine, and hand joint furniture from start to finish
Interesting work building individual pieces and restoring antiques, for which further training will be given

John Moore Antiques,
Nethergate Street,
Laverham,
Suffolk
Laverham 277510

OFFICE JUNIOR/ ASSISTANT

A varied and interesting position with a good telephone manner, accurate typing, pleasant personality and lots of common sense.

If you are 16 to 19 then send hand-written details to:

Mr. B.K. Graves,
H.G. White,
Whitehall Road
Peterborough

ELECTRONIC ENGINEER

Required, micro-computer experience, driving licence essential
Salary negotiable

Telephone: Ipswich 431260, P K Electronics, Stoughton House, Stoughton, Ipswich, Suffolk

---

A YOUNG PERSON WANTED

To assist in the selling of Austin Rover cars in Clacton.
Apply in writing only to:
Mr B A Carter,
Jones Garage,
Old Road,
Clacton

---

17 Earlham Road
Norwich
Norfolk

A J Electronics
Sproughton House
Sproughton
Ipswich
Suffolk

19 May 1985

Dear Sir,

I am writing to apply for the post of Electronic Engineer. I saw your advertisement in the Essex County Standard of 17 May.

For the last two years I have worked as a computer engineer in the Norwich area of Norfolk. I have worked with all kinds of computers, including micros. I have driven a car for six years now, and I have never had an accident.

Please send me further details of the advertised job. I look forward to hearing from you.

Yours faithfully,

W. Edwards

William Edwards (Mr)

62, Maldon Road,
Colchester,
Essex.

Michael Moore Antiques,
Nethergate St.,
Clare,
Suffolk.

25th May 1985

Dear Sir,

I would like to apply for the job of joiner in your workshop. I saw your advertisement in the Essex County Standard of 17th May.

For the last eight years I have worked as a joiner for a small company here in Colchester. I have made all kinds of furniture, including chairs, tables and cupboards.

I am very interested in antiques, and have always wanted to restore old furniture.

Please send me further details of this job. I look forward to hearing from you.

Yours faithfully,

David Panther.

Mr David Panther

These are replies to three of the advertisements.
Match the letter with the right advertisement.
Then write a letter of application for the fourth job. Don't forget to
- give your address.
- write the address of the person you are writing to.
- write the date.
- explain why you are writing and where you saw the advertisement.
- describe what you have done (Have you passed any exams?/What other jobs have you done?).
- end your letter with your signature and your full name.

---

28 Spring Road
Tiptree
Essex

Mr B K Ashman
H G Wallace Ltd
Whitehall Road
Colchester

28 June 1985

Dear Mr Ashman

I am interested in the job of Office Junior/Assistant. I saw your advertisement in the Essex County Standard of 17 May.

I am 18 years old and I have just left the Thurstable School in Tiptree. I have just passed 'O' level exams in English, Maths, Geography and Shorthand and Typing. For the last two years I have done holiday work with my father's office. I have made telephone calls and typed letters for him. I have also just passed my driving test.

I look forward to hearing from you.

Yours sincerely

Susan Harris

Susan Harris

UNIT 7 Problems

PRESENTATION

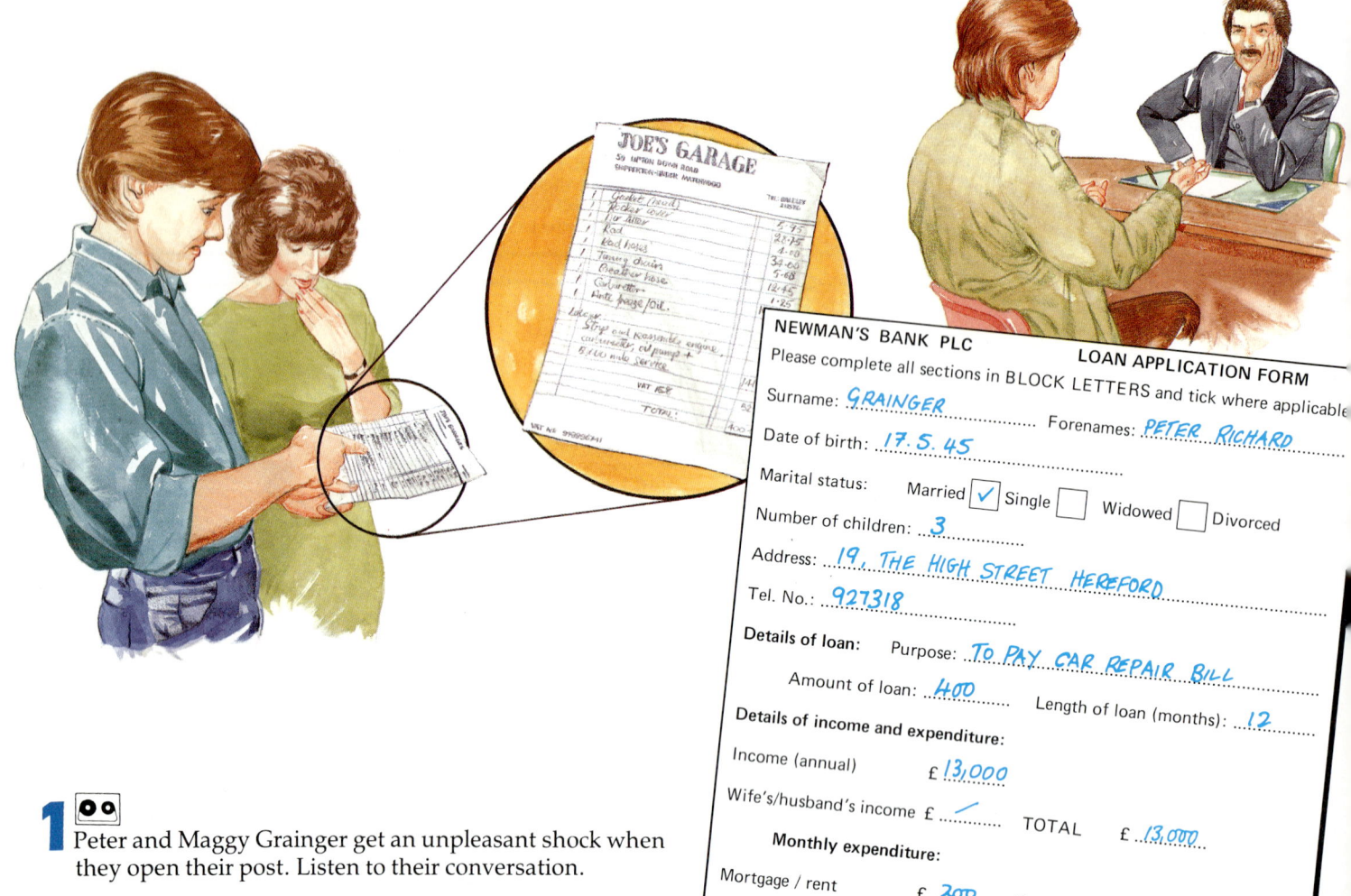

1 Peter and Maggy Grainger get an unpleasant shock when they open their post. Listen to their conversation.

Pete Oh no! This is terrible!
Maggy What is it? What's the matter?
Pete It's the bill from the garage. The repairs to the car are going to cost £400.
Maggy What? Four hundred pounds? But we haven't got . . .
Pete What's worse we've got to pay it by the end of the month.
Maggy Oh, Pete. How can we pay £400? We haven't got any money in the bank.
Pete Let me think. I know, you could get a part-time job.
Maggy But I've already tried, Pete. There aren't any jobs.
Pete I suppose we could get a bank loan.
Maggy Yes, that's it. You must go and see the manager today.

NEWMAN'S BANK PLC — LOAN APPLICATION FORM
Please complete all sections in BLOCK LETTERS and tick where applicable

Surname: GRAINGER   Forenames: PETER RICHARD
Date of birth: 17.5.45
Marital status: Married ✓ Single ☐ Widowed ☐ Divorced ☐
Number of children: 3
Address: 19, THE HIGH STREET HEREFORD
Tel. No.: 927318

Details of loan: Purpose: TO PAY CAR REPAIR BILL
Amount of loan: 400   Length of loan (months): 12

Details of income and expenditure:
Income (annual) £ 13,000
Wife's/husband's income £ —   TOTAL £ 13,000

Monthly expenditure:
Mortgage / rent £ 200   Food £ 200
Other regular payments £ 50   Access ✓ Visa ☐ £ 30
Telephone (approx) £ 15   Diners ☐ American Express ☐
Electricity (approx) £ 10

Signed: P R Grainger   TOTAL £ 505
Date: 29.9.86

2
Manager Good morning, Mr Grainger. What can I do for you?
Peter Good morning. Well, you see, I need to borrow £400.

Check!

1 What is the bill for?
2 Who sent the bill?
3 When has Peter got to pay the bill?
4 Why can't Maggy get a job?
5 What did Peter and Maggy spend their savings on?
6 What has Peter got to do first, to get a loan?

Language Focus

Suggesting answers to a problem: could

How can we get £400?	You could	get a part-time job.
	We could	get a bank loan.

Rejecting a suggestion:

but I can't get a part-time job.

ORAL EXERCISES

example: How can I save money?/buy cheaper food
you: You could buy cheaper food.

1. How can we make driving safer?/lower the speed limit
2. How can I keep fit?/take more exercise
3. How can he make some money?/start his own business
4. How can we make new friends?/join a sports club
5. How can we afford a holiday?/work hard and save money
6. How can I keep slim?/go on a diet

Describing obligations: must & have (got) to

You You	must	go and see the bank manager today. fill in a loan application form.

We've got to pay the bill by the end of the month.

ORAL EXERCISE

example: I'd like to see the doctor, please./make an appointment.
you: You must make an appointment.

1. I'd like to see the manager, please./make an appointment
2. My flatmate's very ill./phone the doctor
3. I'd really like that job./come for an interview
4. Someone has stolen my car./phone the police
5. I've just bought a television./get a licence for it
6. I haven't seen my parents for months./write them a letter

Describing needs: need/need to

I	need	£400. a new car.

I We	need to	borrow £400. know your financial position.

ORAL EXERCISE

example: She doesn't earn much money./find a new job
you: She needs to find a new job.

1. I'm getting very fat./take more exercise
2. She can't breath./fresh air
3. He never knows what the time is./new watch
4. I can't see very well./buy some new glasses
5. I'm always late for work./get up earlier
6. I don't know his telephone number./telephone directory

Already/just/yet/never:

I've **already** done that.
He's **just** been there.
We've **never** seen him before.
I haven't seen it **yet**.

SMALL TALK

Talking about fears and worries

A What's wrong. Is something worrying you?
B No, not really. I'm just not looking forward to walking home.

A You aren't scared of the dark, are you?
B Of course not . . .
But you hear of so many attacks on people late at night, and that frightens me.

Is your partner frightened of spiders/growing old/the dark/high buildings/losing a job?

40

UNIT 7

PRACTICE

1 WORDS

Match these words from the Presentation with their correct meanings.

details	first name	post	money lent
position	yearly/every year	shock	great surprise (not pleasant)
annual	facts/full information	bill	money not spent
forename	situation	loan	account/demand for payment
income	money earned	savings	letters/mail

2 These people have important meetings in London today but they have missed the train. What can they do to get to the meeting on time? Look at these pictures and then talk to your partner, like this.

A I've missed my train, what can I do?
   or
   I'm going to be late for my meeting, what can I do?
B You could hitch-hike to London.

taxi

hitch-hike

bicycle

bus

phone

wait

3 You and your partner have just moved into a new house. There are a lot of things wrong with it.
Look at the picture(s) and then make conversations like this.
A What are we going to do about the broken windows?
B Yes, they look terrible. We must replace them.
   or
   Yes, they're dangerous. We must replace them.
Use some of these words.

   repair   replace   repaint   rebuild
   redecorate   clean (up)   tidy (up)

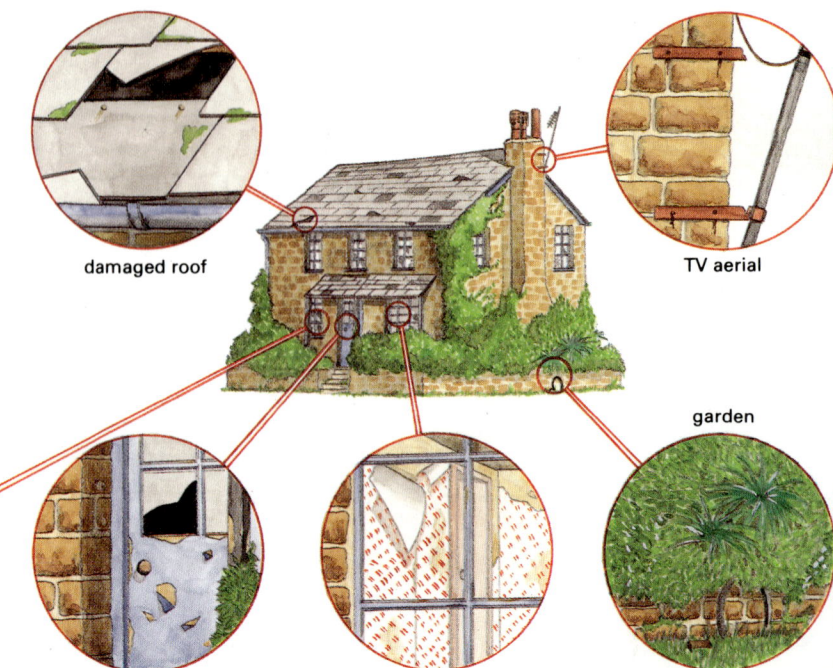

damaged roof

TV aerial

broken windows

doors and windows

living-room

garden

4 You and your partner have now repaired everything in your new house and you are planning to give a house-warming party. Of course you want it to be a success.

Use these pictures to help you to talk about what you need (to do).

Now talk to your partner, like this:

A   What about food for the party?
B   Well, we need lots of different kinds of food.
    or
    Well, we need to buy plenty of food.

Write out a list of the things you need to do.

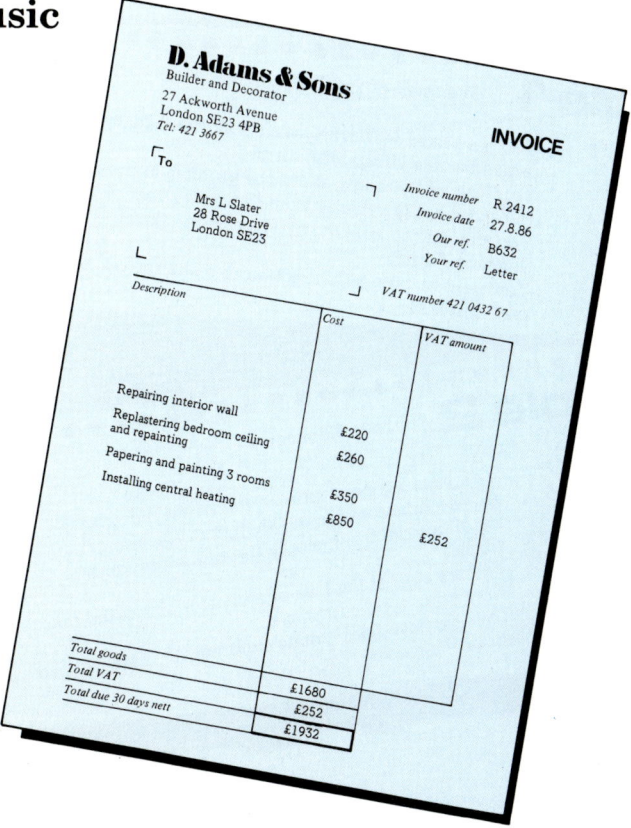

lots of drinks   **lots of people**

good food   **decorations**   **music**

TRANSFER

1 DISCUSSION

You have received this bill for redecorations and repairs to your flat. Discuss how you are going to pay it. You have no savings.

Other problems to discuss.

- You've lost the key to your house and cannot get in.

- You've been to London for the evening and have missed your last train home. You have no money.

D. Adams & Sons
Builder and Decorator
27 Ackworth Avenue
London SE23 4PB
Tel: 421 3667

INVOICE

To
Mrs L Slater
28 Rose Drive
London SE23

Invoice number   R 2412
Invoice date   27.8.86
Our ref.   B632
Your ref.   Letter

VAT number 421 0432 67

Description	Cost	VAT amount
Repairing interior wall		
Replastering bedroom ceiling and repainting	£220	
Papering and painting 3 rooms	£260	
Installing central heating	£350	
	£850	£252
Total goods	£1680	
Total VAT	£252	
Total due 30 days nett	£1932	

42

UNIT 7

2 ROLE PLAY

The situation:
- A busy main road runs through the middle of Maybridge, a pretty little Sussex village with narrow streets and charming old buildings. The road is one of the main routes to the Channel port of Newhaven.
- Year by year more and more heavy vehicles—lorries and coaches—are using the road.
- In the past five years there have been twenty-three accidents in the village. Seven people have died—four of them children.
- The people of the village have set up an action group to decide what to do about this problem.
- Their main worries are the safety of the people of Maybridge—especially the children and old people, and their beautiful, historical buildings.
- There have been many ideas. Here are some of them:
  —a bypass round the village.
  —a ban on heavy vehicles (with an alternative route).
  —a wider street.
  —making the old buildings stronger.
  —a ban on parking in the main street.
  —a reduced speed limit in the village.

Discuss the problem and some of these ideas. You can think of your own ideas as well. You are villagers, and want to send some suggestions to your local council.
Here are your characters:

Role 1 Chairman of the Action Committee
* You have lived in Maybridge all your life. You can remember the village without traffic.
* You feel very strongly about the problem and want to ban all heavy vehicles from the main street.
* You suggest the building of a bypass to take all this heavy traffic
* You want to take serious action to make the council take notice.

Role 2 Village shopkeeper
* You have a general store in the village high street. All the villagers use your shop, but you also get a lot of custom from people travelling through the village.
* You are against the idea of a bypass; this could take away your extra customers.
* You also have three young children. You are worried about their safety.

Role 3 Young mother
* You have two young children – John, 7 and Tom, 5 They have to walk to the village school every morning along the High Street. The pavements are very narrow and the traffic is very busy at 9 o'clock in the morning.
* You have very strong feelings about the danger, and you want a bypass.

Role 4 Pub Landlord
You are the owner of the only pub in the High Street of the village.
Your pub is a very beautiful old building. In the last ten years three lorries have crashed into your front wall. The damage has been very expensive, and you are afraid that the building is now very weak.
You want to ban heavy lorries from the village, but many of your best customers are people who are travelling through Maybridge.
You are against the idea of a bypass because you don't want to lose money, but you don't want your pub to fall down.

After your discussion write a list of suggestions to send to the local council.

Use sentences like this in your discussion and your written suggestions.
- We could suggest a bypass.
- We must have a bypass.
- We need a bypass.

SKILLS

1 READING

Match these newspaper headlines with the extracts of the reports.

hunt vanish/ disappear	... At 6pm on February 10, Kevin left his school after basketball practice. He hasn't been seen since. A huge police *search* has come up with nothing: ... About 2,000 children *go missing* in San Francisco each year, but none has ever stayed in the headlines for so long.
help	Band Aid leader, Bob Geldof, who has visited the scene of the famine in Ethiopia: 'Western governments say they are sending in masses of *aid* but when I was there I couldn't see it anywhere—all I saw was 15 bags of flour for 25,000 people.'
causing pain crime	'The Royal Society for the Prevention of *Cruelty* to Animals prosecuted 1,932 people last year. ... Of last year's convictions, 22 resulted in prison sentences ... Cruelty to dogs was the most frequent *offence*.'
only just	'Single parent Helen Smith and her daughter Natasha froze to death because they could not afford to heat their council flat ... Although the family had an electric fire, and two paraffin heaters in case the gas central heating broke down, none were in use when police officers broke into the flat on Friday. They found the mother, 31, and daughter, 13, on a bed. Michael, 11, was in the same room, *barely* alive.'
people who can work	'Unemployment in Britain is at a record level ... The number of people out of work rose to 3,340,958 in January. ... That's 13.9% of the *workforce*.'

AMERICAN ALARM OVER VANISHED CHILDREN

It's Just Not Enough

KILLER COLD: INQUIRY INTO MOTHER'S DEATH

RECORD CONVICTIONS BY RSPCA

Jobless Total A Record

Now choose one of these problems and write about possible solutions.

2 SOUNDS

Linking

Listen and repeat this sentence.
   I want to stop smoking
Two sounds are linked.
Now listen and repeat these sentences.
Mark the sounds that are linked.

I'm a bit tired.
Where are all his suits?
He stopped to tell me to phone Nigel.
I'm meeting him at five forty-five.
Stop pushing me, please.
Please slow down, I'm tired.

UNIT 8 Predictions and Promises

PRESENTATION

1 People have always been interested in the future. We can never be absolutely certain about the future. We have to predict and promise. Listen to this conversation between Ian and Jane.

| Predicting certainties |
| Predicting |
| Promising |

Ian Jane, I've got two tickets for the concert on Friday. Would you like to come?
Jane I'd love to, Ian, but I won't be here. I'll be on a beach somewhere in the South of France on Friday.
Ian Oh, that's a shame. Perhaps another time then? Have a good holiday.
Jane I will. And thanks for asking me. I'll send you a postcard from France. Bye.

Check!
1 What does Ian invite Jane to do?
2 Why can't she go with him?
3 What does she promise to do while she is in France?

2 Most of the future is unpredictable. A lot of people earn their living by predicting the future.

YOUR STARS ☆ By Mary Pluto ☆

There will be changes at work and in your personal life. You won't find these easy to deal with, but don't worry, things will return to normal next week.

21st March – 20th April

Love is in the air this week. On Saturday you'll meet someone very important to you and your future.

21st April – 20th May

TODAY'S BIRTHDAY!!
Today will be a real day to remember! Your luck is changing! Next year will be one of the most successful of your life!

THIS EVENING THE SOUTH-EAST OF THE COUNTRY WILL HAVE HEAVY SHOWERS, BUT THESE WILL CLEAR BEFORE DAWN. TOMORROW WILL BE SUNNY AND HOT AGAIN. TEMPERATURES WILL REACH 22° CELSIUS

3 Other people earn their living by making promises. Listen to this politician. He is talking about the party's new election manifesto. As you listen tick off the points on this Election Leaflet. What does he talk about that is not in the Manifesto?

LIBERAL DEMOCRATIC PARTY
ELECTION MANIFESTO

● **Schools:** More Teachers – Smaller classes

● **Jobs:** Money for new businesses in your area

LIBERAL DEMOCRATIC PARTY

● **Transport:** No cuts in bus services
Bus and Rail services for all

● **Health:** Cheaper medicines

Language Focus

Making Predictions: certainties

I'll	be on the beach in the South of France on Friday.
I won't	be here.
The South East will	have heavy showers this evening.

Making Predictions: guesses

On Saturday you will	meet someone very important to you.
Next year will	be one of the most successful of your life.

ORAL EXERCISE example: I/London/tomorrow
you: Where will you be tomorrow?
I'll be in London.

1 I/New York/next week
2 He/hospital/on Saturday
3 They/Moscow/next winter
4 I/on holiday/for the whole of June
5 I/Paris/during the first week in December
6 She/South of France/on Friday

Making promises:

We will	employ	thousands of people on important community projects.
We won't	cut	rural bus services.

ORAL EXERCISE example: What will you do when you take power?/cut taxes
you: When we take power we'll cut taxes.

1 cut taxes
2 build more schools
3 employ thousands of people
4 not cut bus services
5 not increase taxes
6 give everyone a week's holiday

The Future with WILL:

I		I'll
You		You'll
He		He'll
She	will	She'll
It		It'll
We		We'll
They		They'll

| There | will | There'll |

Suggestions and offers with SHALL:

| Shall | I / we | phone you next week? / meet you at the airport? |

SMALL TALK

Starting conversations

1 A I hear you're starting a new job on Monday. Congratulations.
   B Thanks. I'm really looking forward to it. What are you doing these days?

2 A Did you see that old film on television last night?
   B Yes. Wasn't it wonderful. I can remember seeing it at the cinema when I was about seven.

Start a conversation with your partner.

Did you see . . .?
I hear that you're going . . .?

UNIT 8

PRACTICE

1 WORDS
Match the weather symbols with the correct words & phrases.

Symbol	Noun	Phrases
	cloud	It's snowing / It's snowy
	rain	It's foggy
	snow	It's sunny / The sun's shining
	sun	It's cloudy
	(thunder)storm	It's seventeen degrees
	fog	It's raining / It's rainy
	temperature	It's stormy / There's a thunderstorm

2
Finish these conversations, using the correct form of the future.

1. *Sue* Dave, I'm going to a party on Saturday night. Would you like to come?
   Dave I'd love to, Sue, but I _____ _____ here. I' _____ _____ on holiday in the Algarve. But thanks for asking.
   Sue Have a nice time in Portugal.
   Dave I _____ .

2. *Pete* Hello, Debbie. It's me.
   Debbie Pete! Where are you?
   Pete I'm at King's Cross Station. I'm catching the 7 o'clock train. I' _____ _____ home at about midnight.
   Debbie _____ I come and pick you up at the station?
   Pete That'll be great. I' _____ wait outside the main entrance.

3
Match the descriptions of the weather with these three summary charts.

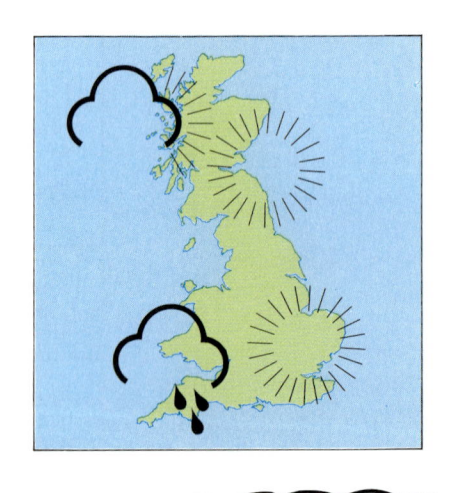

"Most of the country will be hot and sunny, but in the West it will be cloudy with sunny intervals. Maximum temperature will be 20°C."

Wednesday midday

"In the North of England it'll be cloudy with occasional showers of rain. In the South it will be mainly sunny. Temperatures will reach 17°C."

Thursday midday

"It will be cloudy over most of the country, but there will be sunshine in the South East of England when the fog has cleared. Maximum temperature will be 19°C."

Friday midday

Now make conversations with your partner, like this.

A I'm going to Manchester on Thursday. Can you tell me what the weather will be like?
B It'll be rainy all day on Thursday.
A And the temperature?
B It won't be more than 19°C.

1. Cornwall / Friday
2. Brighton / Wednesday
3. South Wales / Friday
4. London / Thursday
5. Newcastle / Thursday
6. Scotland / Wednesday

4 Look carefully at this information about some of England's football teams.

	Played	Won	Lost	Drawn
Everton	8	7	0	1
Liverpool	8	3	4	1
Newcastle	8	6	1	1
Southampton	8	8	0	0
West Ham	8	1	5	2
Chelsea	8	2	4	2
Birmingham	8	4	4	0
Manchester United	8	3	3	2
Ipswich	8	7	1	0
Leeds	8	5	1	2

This week's matches:
- Liverpool v Newcastle United
- Ipswich v West Ham United
- Leeds v Chelsea
- Birmingham v Manchester United
- Southampton v Everton

Who do you think will win? Make conversations like this.

A Liverpool are playing Newcastle United on Saturday. Who do you think'll win?
B I think Liverpool will beat Newcastle easily.

5 You are coming to live in England for a year. It will be your first time away from home and your parents. Your mother and father are worried about you. You have to make a lot of promises.

A (Parents) Promise you'll write to us.
B (Child) Okay. I'll write twice a week. I promise.
I won't stay out late, I promise. I'll be home before midnight.

1. Write/Twice a week 
2. Telephone/Every weekend 
3. Come home/December and April
4. Get into trouble/Very good 
5. Waste money/Only £20 a week 
6. Stay out late/Before midnight

UNIT 8

TRANSFER

1 GROUPWORK
Work in groups of 3 or 4

Fill in this chart for your partners and yourself.

Predict what your life and theirs will be like in twenty years' time. Then discuss in pairs.

Compare your predictions.

Places	Partner 1	Partner 2	Partner 3	Myself
Living House / Flat Country / Town				
Work Job Own country / abroad Indoor / Outdoor Money				
Personal Married / Single Children Rich / Poor				

A I think you'll be married with three children. You'll be quite rich, and you'll live in a flat in the centre of a busy city.
B Do you think so? I certainly won't live in a city, but I'll probably be married and have children. But I won't have three. Two will be quite enough.

2 Read this extract from an election manifesto. Then make up election speeches. Promise people what you will do when you win the election.

Labour – The Way Ahead for Essex

Education – the best investment
- Labour wants more pre-school places immediately.
- Labour wants more teachers and smaller classes.
- Libraries are important. We need more books and more mobile libraries.

A Plan for Jobs
- We need to bring new industries into the area.
- Local people must get jobs in these new industries.

Transport – don't miss that bus
Cheap public transport helps everyone.
- Labour has plans for a free transport scheme for old and disabled people.
- We don't want small Essex villages to die, so we will keep bus services in the country areas.

Planning for People
- We will spend more money on roads and pavements.
- We will open new country parks and other recreation places.

Take Care of Our County   Vote Labour May 2

Vote Labour

3 WRITING
How will the stories end?
- Read these two story beginnings.
- Discuss possible endings with your partner.
- Write your favourite ending.

Today Jeremy Baker will try to break the land speed record in his enormous rocket-powered car FIREBIRD. I can see him now. He's walking towards the car—he's climbing in and strapping himself in. He's started the engine. There's a deafening noise. Firebird is moving. . . .

Last week a team of the world's best divers discovered the wreck of the Magnet, the famous luxury liner which disappeared in a storm off the coast of Ireland thirty years ago. The crew and 500 passengers drowned in the tragedy. Today the divers have brought special equipment and are going to explore the inside of the Magnet. . . .

SKILLS

1 LISTENING

We asked people the question *What will life be like in the year 2500?* Here are their answers. Which of the speakers thinks that the future will be better than the present?
Whose ideas are these?

Idea	Paul	Margaret	John
The Earth will be colder			
People will not have private cars			
Food will be difficult to get			
The sun will heat people's houses			
Ice will cover Europe			
People will live longer			
Robots and computers will do all the work			
People will not have to work			

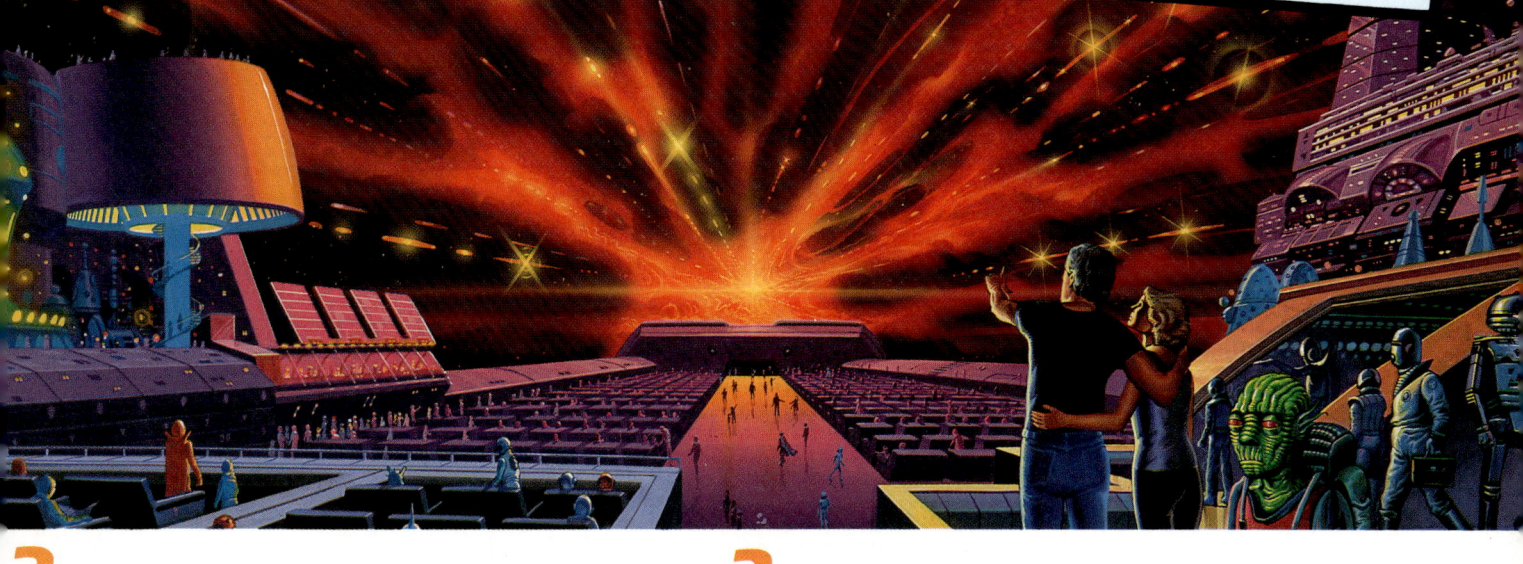

2 WORDS

Match these words with their meanings

ice	human beings
hunger	mechanical people
optimistic	costing a lot of money
mankind	hopeful
illness	frozen water
alive	need for food
robots	disease
expensive	living, not dead

3 WRITING

Listen again to John's answers and make a list of all the positive and negative things he thinks will happen.
Finish these phrases.

NEGATIVE
- No-one will . . .
- Petrol will be . . .
- People won't be able . . .

POSITIVE
- People won't have to . . .
- Robots and . . .
- Heating for our homes . . .

4 DISCUSSION

Work in groups.
What do you think life will be like in the year 2500?
Use some of these phrases.

- I think that . . .
- Probably . . .
- I'm sure that . . .
- It's not certain that . . .

50

Language Study 2

Talking about the past   You now know how to use past tenses in English:

Use the Past Simple to talk about actions and events which are finished, events which happened at a particular time in the past:
- The fire started at 10 o'clock last night.

Use the Present Perfect to talk about finished actions and events (at no particular time) . . .
- Have you (ever) seen the President?
- Have you finished that book yet?
- Yes, I have.
- No, I haven't.

. . . and to list experiences:
- He's flown to America on Concorde, he's met the President, and he's been to Disneyland.
- I've often been to London, but I've never seen the Queen.

. . . and to link actions or situations which started in the past and are not finished:
- How long have you worked here?
- I've worked here for 10 years.
- I've worked here since 1958.

Use the Past Simple and the Present Perfect together:
- I came here in 1973 and I've worked here since then.
- Since I left college, I've done six different jobs.

Time phrases to use with the Present Perfect:
Questions: yet, ever
Statements: never, since (1958), for (10 years)

Note Many common verbs are irregular in the Present Perfect:
- see – have seen; do – have done; leave – have left.

There is a full list of irregular verbs on page 133.

Use **can remember + -ing** for memories:
- I can remember driving into town and parking my car. After that I can't remember anything.

Talking about the future   You now know four ways of talking about the future. Look back to page 25 to remind yourself about:

The Present Continuous	• I'm flying to Athens next weekend.
going to future	• I'm going to buy a new car.
The Present Simple	• The train leaves at 6.45.

Use the Future **will** to predict certainties . . .
- I won't be here next week. I'll be in America.

. . . and to make guesses about the future:
- 1995 will be my lucky year. I read it in the newspaper.

. . . and to make promises:
- I'll buy you a new guitar tomorrow.
- I won't be late, I promise.

Modal verbs   Use **can** or **could** to talk about problems, and suggestions for answers to problems:
- How can I save money?
- You could stop smoking.
- You know I can't stop. I've tried before.

Use **must** to talk about obligations and necessities:
- The window's broken. We must mend it straightaway.
- You must phone your mother. She's waiting by the telephone.

Note Don't forget, you can use **have (got) to** . . . for obligations too.

Use **need (to)** to talk about necessities and needs:
- What do we need for our journey?
- We need food, drinks and some warm clothe[s]
- What do we need to do before we leave?
- We need to lock the doors, shut the windows and turn off the lights.

Describing people   Describing their appearance:
- What does she look like?
- She's short and slim with long blonde hair.

Describing their personality:
- What's he like?
- He's a serious person, but he's very friendly.

51

EXERCISES

TALKING ABOUT THE PAST

Past Simple
- What did you do yesterday evening?

Present Perfect
- Which foreign countries have you visited?
- Have you ever seen or met any famous people?
- Write about some of the things you have never done (but would like to do).
- Check the Present Perfect of these verbs: bring; drink; eat; find; go; read; take.
- Write ten questions about the past.

Remembering
- What can you remember doing yesterday afternoon?

Past Simple & Present Perfect
- What have you done since you got up this morning?
- How long have you lived here?
- How long have you spoken English?

TALKING ABOUT THE FUTURE

Present Continuous
- What are your plans for this evening?

going to future
- What are you going to do tomorrow?

Present Simple
- What classes do you have tomorrow?
- What time do they start and finish?

will future
- Where will you be this time tomorrow?
- Guess what the weather will be like at the weekend.
- Make two promises (things you will do)
- Make two promises (things you won't do)
- Write ten questions about the future.

MODAL VERBS

can/could
- Suggest answers to these problems:
  'What can I do to lose weight?'
  'What can I do to earn more money?'

must
- What must I do? . . .
  . . . I want to get to work early tomorrow morning
  . . . I'm going for an important job interview this afternoon.

need
- You are going on a camping holiday. What do you need to take?
  What do you need to do before you go?

DESCRIBING PEOPLE
- Write a description of two of your friends.
  Write about their appearance.
  Write about their personalities.

UNIT 9 Tourism

PRESENTATION

1 Tourism in Britain is big business. During the last 10 years, the number of tourists coming to Britain has increased enormously. This has created a large number of new jobs.

Nearly **1½ million people** throughout the whole of Britain depend, directly or indirectly, upon tourism for their livelihoods. Not only does tourism employ **four times** as many people as the motor car industry in Britain, it earns **four times** more foreign currency.

Britain's **biggest** single market for overseas visitors is Western Europe. Over **seven million** European visitors came here in 1982. They spent **£1,158 million** within the country. The **largest** single contingent of European visitors in 1982 came from France. There were **1,518,000** of them. They spent **£176 million** within the country. After Europe, the USA provides the **most** visitors to Britain each year. In 1982 **1,726,000** Americans spent **£564 million** within this country.

Visitors list these main reasons for coming to Britain: to meet the people... to see the countryside... historic associations... old buildings... colourful pageantry... the English language... the theatre... the arts... business conferences... exhibitions... sporting events... sporting facilities... shopping for world-famous British products.

The estimated breakdown of expenditure by overseas visitors in 1984 was:

	£ million
Shopping	1,500
Accommodation	1,150
Eating and drinking out	620
Internal transport	480
Entertainment	190
Services and others	254
Fares paid to British air and shipping lines on travel to and from Britain	1,125
	5,319

Check!

1. Where do most tourists to Britain come from?
2. How many people's jobs depend on tourism?
3. What did foreign visitors spend most money on?
4. Which is bigger, the car industry or the tourist industry?
5. Which country sends the largest number of tourists to Britain?
6. List three reasons tourists give for visiting Britain.

2 INTERVIEW

Cambridge is one of the biggest tourist attractions in Britain. Approximately 4 million tourists visit Cambridge every year—that's 11,000 people every day, or 33 tourists for every member of the population of Cambridge. People living in this tourist centre don't have the same feelings about tourists as people in a city like Nottingham.

> We don't get that many tourists in Nottingham, but they're very welcome. They're mostly interested in Robin Hood or the university, so they don't affect me. They bring more money to the city, so that's a good thing. I think we should make the city more interesting for tourists—perhaps we can create more jobs that way.

> What I don't like about the tourists is the way they take the town over. In the summer you can't get in the shops, you can't park your car, and the streets are full of noisy people.
> A lot of them are rude, too. They push you in the street, they don't say 'please' or 'thank you' in the shops and pubs, and they always seem to be shouting. I'm glad when the winter comes. I'm afraid they'll spoil the city with more development for the tourists.

Check!

1. Give two of the reasons why the Cambridge woman doesn't like tourists.
2. What does the Nottingham woman feel the city should do to help tourists?
3. What are visitors to Nottingham interested in?
4. In what way are tourists rude, according to the Cambridge woman?
5. Why do people in Nottingham have different feelings about tourists?
6. Calculate how many people live in Cambridge.

Language Focus

Talking about numbers & statistics:

> It's **more than before**.
> This year's number is **34% lower than** last year's.
> **Over 4 million** tourists visited Cambridge last year.
> **Nearly 1.5 million** jobs depend on tourism.
> Visitors spent **approximately £1,500 million** on shopping.
> Tourism employs **4 times as many people as** the car industry.
> That's **twice as much as** the aircraft industry.

ORAL EXERCISE *example:* The government created 500,000 jobs./nearly
you: The government created nearly 500,000 jobs

1. 11 million tourists visited the palace./over
2. People on holiday spent £300m on hotels./approximately
3. The government employs more people than the business world./10 times as many
4. Tourism earned more money than the car industry./4 times as much
5. This year's income is lower than last year's./29%
6. There are more jobs in this industry than before./over 30%

Comparing/superlatives:

> Britain's **biggest** market is Western Europe.
> The **largest** group came from France.

> **The most expensive** shop is Harrods.
> That's **the most comfortable** chair.

> **The least expensive** shop is Woolworths.
> That's **the least comfortable** chair.

ORAL EXERCISE *example:* That's an expensive chair./see
you: That's the most expensive chair I've seen.

1. This is a comfortable sofa./sit on
2. That's a beautiful picture./see
3. That's a clever idea./hear
4. That's a strong perfume./smell
5. This is a sweet cocktail./taste
6. That's a quiet motorbike./ride

Giving opinions/making a point

Negative:
> I don't think we should . . .
> I'm afraid . . .
> What I don't like is . . .

Positive:
> I don't mind us bringing in more tourists . . .
> Spending by tourists is . . .
> In fact they bring extra work . . .

ORAL EXERCISE *example:* I don't think they should build a new road.
you: I don't mind them building a new road.

1. I don't think we should build a new sports centre.
2. I don't think they should close down the theatre.
3. I don't think they should develop the shopping centre.
4. I don't think we should allow more tourists to come here.
5. I don't think he should employ foreign workers.
6. I don't think we should talk about him.

SMALL TALK

Asking for directions

A Can you tell me the way to the University?
B Sure. Go straight along here until you come to the taxis. Carry on past the bus station. Then you take the first right and it's on your left.
A Thanks

Ask your partner the way to the station / the bus station / the airport.

UNIT 9

PRACTICE

1 Discuss these statistics with your partner.

Use these phrases.
BTA tourist figures show that . . .
58% of the tourists . . .
In 1981 the tourists spent . . .
The most popular place to visit was . . .

TOURISM IN ENGLAND BY BRITISH RESIDENTS
Most tourist trips in England are by British residents. The table below describes the volume and value of tourism by British adults and children accompanying them.

Millions	Trips	Nights	Spending
1979	97	415	£3,025
1980	106	435	£3,525
1981	104	415	£3,675
1982	101	400	£3,600
1983	110	435	£4,300

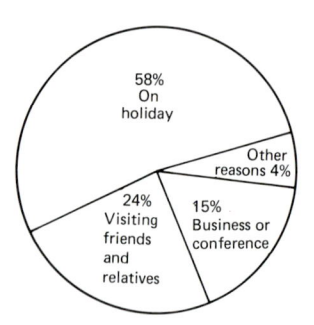

1983 Visits

Historic buildings and gardens
- Tower of London 2,182,000
- Kew Gardens 1,038,000
- Roman Baths, Bath 798,000
- State Apartments, Windsor Castle 707,000
- Stonehenge 605,000
- Warwick Castle 512,000
- Hampton Court Palace 504,000

Museums and art galleries
- Science Museum 3,346,000
- National Gallery 2,897,000
- British Museum 2,844,000
- Natural History Museum 2,500,000
- Victoria & Albert Museum 1,818,000

Zoos
- London Zoo 1,239,000
- Chester Zoo 801,000
- Chessington Zoo 668,000

Other attractions
- Blackpool Pleasure Beach 6,700,000
- Madame Tussaud's 1,996,000
- Alton Towers 1,600,000
- Wicksteed Park 1,250,000
- Thorpe Park 820,000

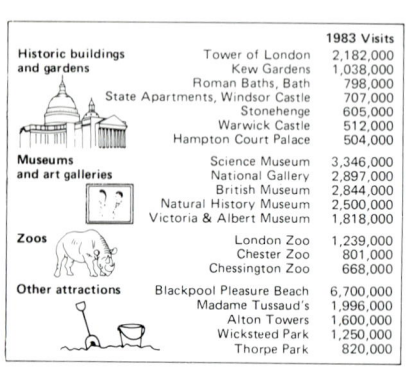

TOURISM IN ENGLAND BY OVERSEAS VISITORS
In 1983 there were 12.5 million visits by overseas residents to the UK. An estimated 11.4 million of these tourist trips were to England, where they spent £3,300 million.

Millions	Trips	Nights	Spending
1979	11.5	135	£2,525
1980	11.1	130	£2,675
1981	10.4	120	£2,700
1982	10.7	120	£2,850
1983	11.4	130	£3,300

- 58% On holiday
- 24% Visiting friends and relatives
- 15% Business or conference
- Other reasons 4%

Base: All Tourist Trips in England, 1983

2 These are the sales figures for the Alma Cola Company.

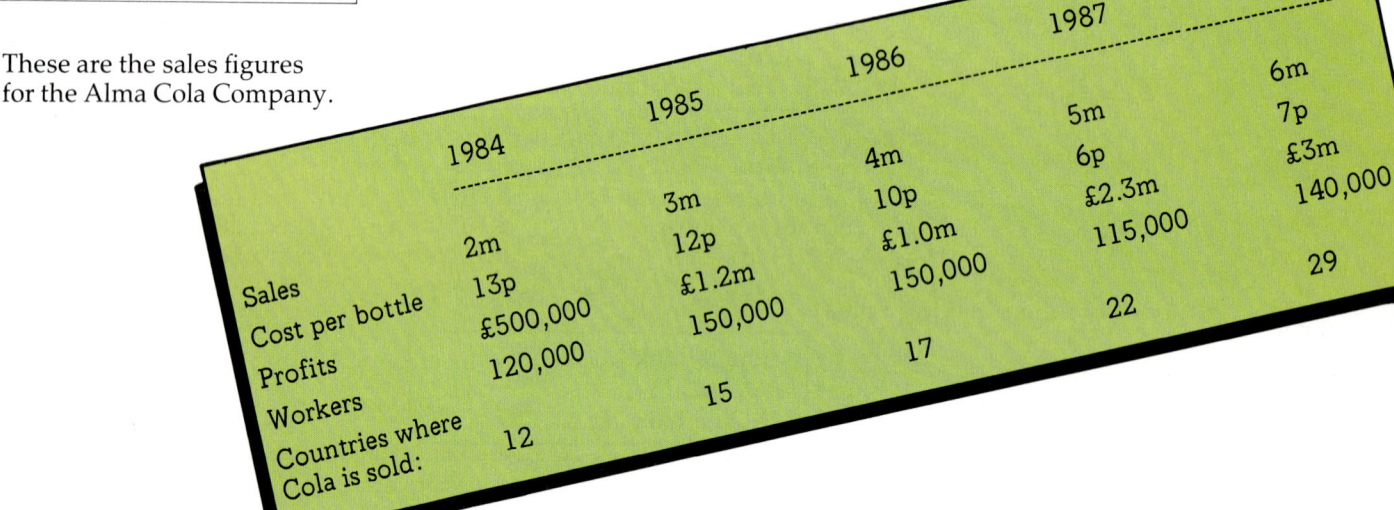

	1984	1985	1986	1987	1988
Sales	2m	3m	4m	5m	6m
Cost per bottle	13p	12p	10p	6p	7p
Profits	£500,000	£1.2m	£1.0m	£2.3m	£3m
Workers	120,000	150,000	150,000	115,000	140,000
Countries where Cola is sold:	12	15	17	22	29

1 Describe the sales for the 5 years like this
   Sales in 1985 were more than . . .
   less than . . .

2 Describe the profits like this.
   Profits for 1985 were nearly . . .
   over . . .

With your partner, write a short text about the changes in the figures for *Workers* and *Countries*.

3 Give an opinion about these things/ideas.

POSITIVE
I don't mind . . .
I'm in favour of . . .
I'm not bothered about . . .

Be positive about:
   eating fish
   living in your country
   punk fashions
   sportsmen & women getting paid

NEGATIVE
I'm not happy about . . .
I'm against . . .
I don't think people should . . .

Be negative about:
   people who smoke
   tourists
   journalists
   violence in cities

4

STUDENT A
(Student B cover this!)
You are visiting the C&H warehouse. Ask for directions from Warrior Square station. Make a map like this and draw the way you must go. Mark the position of the warehouse.

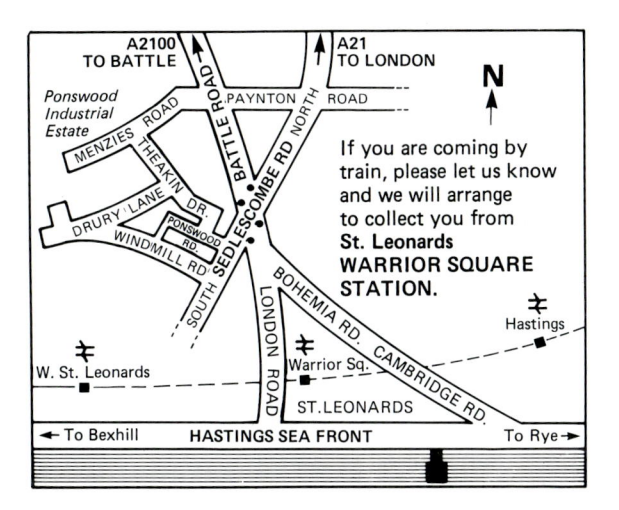

STUBENT B
(Student A cover this!)
Your partner wants some directions. You have a map.
Answer the questions and explain how to get to the destination.

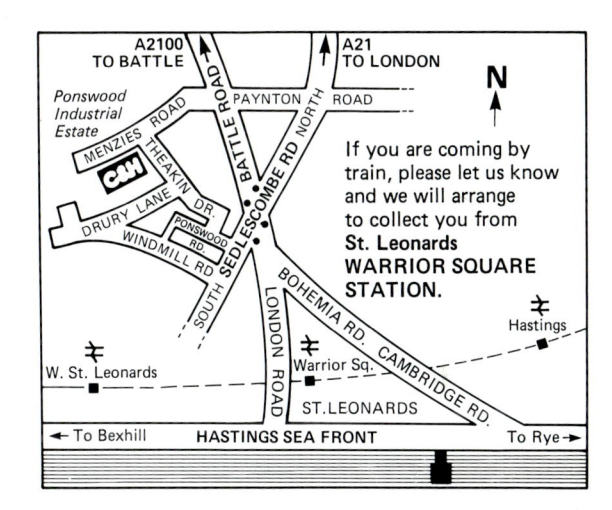

TRANSFER

1 TOURISM

Work with a partner. You have the results of some interviews about people's feelings towards tourists. You want to find out the information which is missing from your box. Your partner has all the missing information. Ask questions like this.

- How many people said tourism brings money to the town?
- What percentage of people think there are too many crowds?

Student A:

ADVANTAGES:	
brings money to town	_____
provides more jobs	7%
better leisure facilities for local people	_____
can meet interesting people	5%
get better roads	_____
don't know	_____
DISADVANTAGES:	
traffic jams	_____
too many crowds	18%
too much litter	_____
too much noise	_____
parking problems	3%
hooliganism & bad behaviour	_____

Student B:

ADVANTAGES:	
brings money to town	67%
provides more jobs	_____
better leisure facilities for local people	8%
can meet interesting people	_____
get better roads	5%
don't know	8%
DISADVANTAGES:	
traffic jams	38%
too many crowds	_____
too much litter	16%
too much noise	4%
parking problems	_____
hooliganism & bad behaviour	2%

UNIT 9

2 DISCUSSION

Does tourism make people better? Do people understand a country better if they visit it as a tourist?
Are there any disadvantages in tourist travel? Can it damage international understanding?
Talk to your partners about:

- your experiences as a tourist.
- your experiences of tourists from other countries.

3 ROLEPLAY

Imagine you live in a tourist town. You and your colleagues have to decide whether to allow a development of the tourist facilities in your town. This means building extra hotels, car parks, opening new restaurants and bars, etc. It will bring extra jobs to the area, but will also cause traffic jams, noise, crowds and problems for people looking for hotel rooms.

Tourist board officer:
You are in favour of the scheme
You think it will make the town more interesting

Councillor:
You are against the scheme
You don't like foreigners

City centre residents:
Give your own opinions

Police chief:
You are against the scheme
Tourists cause trouble

Business-person:
You are in favour of the scheme
Tourists spend a lot of money

Proposals to discuss.
a turn the river into a boating area, rent out small boats and motorboats.
b build a helicopter pad on top of a store.
c allow the shops to open on Sundays.
d allow the bars & pubs to open at any time.
e stop people parking in the centre of the city.
f close certain streets and make them shopping-only streets.
g raise money by charging a 'tourist tax' on hotels, restaurants, etc.

SKILLS

1 READING

The great forest of Sherwood to the north of Nottingham once covered a huge area. It was here Robin Hood robbed the rich merchants and tax gatherers. Today, the forest is considerably smaller but it still retains much of its age old atmosphere. Near Edwinstowe, where Robin was married, stands the famous Major Oak with a girth of 30 feet and over 1,000 years old. The outlaws in Lincoln green could well have hidden in its hollow trunk.

In the village churchyard at Blidworth is the grave of Will Scarlet, one of Robin's most trusted followers. The remains of Little John lie in the churchyard at Hathersage, about an hour's drive away from Nottingham in the Derbyshire Peak District.

In the past twelve years Nottingham has opened two of the finest indoor shopping centres in Europe. Coupled with the traditional shopping centre around the city's Old Market Square, they offer the shopper a tremendous choice of goods and services.

The shopping areas are all linked by a system of traffic free streets and a free bus service called Cityline.

Everything in fact has been done to make shopping in Nottingham a pleasant experience.

No one should be at a loss to find somewhere in Nottingham to enjoy themselves. Night clubs, discos, cinemas and theatres abound. There are all kinds of restaurants and dozens of traditional inns and public houses. Indeed, Nottingham is well known for the quality of its locally brewed ale and one of its pubs, the Trip to Jerusalem, claims to be the oldest in the country.

Vocabulary

merchant	businessman
tax gatherer	tax collector
to retain	to keep
oak	a type of tree
girth	distance around the outside
outlaws	men who fight against the law
Lincoln green	the colour of their clothes
trunk	the middle of a tree

2 LISTENING

Listening to Roger talking about tourists in Cambridge. Find out what he thinks. Complete the two phrases beginning:

We find it's . . .
Yes, it's . . .

Now listen to Roger again and find out what foreign students find *strange* in England. Why is it strange?

Listen to that section again and fill in the missing words in this text:

They find the nightlife a bit . . . in England. They can . . . at 11 o'clock at night and stay out until 4 o'clock in the . . ., but in England they . . . at 11 o'clock at night. That's a bit strange for . . ., but apart from that I think they quite . . . England, most people, . . . from the weather.

Check!

1. What types of shopping centre can you find in Nottingham?
2. Where did Robin Hood rob rich people?
3. Where is Hathersage?
4. What is Cityline? What is it for?
5. Which is the oldest pub in the country?
6. Where is Little John buried?
7. What is the name of the old shopping centre in Nottingham?
8. Name 4 things you can do in the evenings in Nottingham.

SOUNDS

Listen to this conversation and repeat each sentence
 A He's going to Moscow on Saturday.
 B Where?
 A To Moscow.

Now listen and repeat these conversations and write down B's questions and A's answers.

3 WRITING

More formal letters
When you are writing to someone you don't know, you need to write in a more formal way.
A formal letter starts like this:

Dear Sir,
or Dear Madam,
or Dear Mr Johnson,

And ends like this:

Yours faithfully,
  (If you started with 'Dear Sir')
or Yours sincerely,
  (If you started with 'Dear Mr Johnson')

TASKS

A Read this letter to the newspaper. Write an answer—but be polite and formal!

††††LETTER'S PAGE††††
Dear Sir,
These foreigners are getting on my nerves. Why can't the council stop them coming here and making a mess of the city? They're noisy, rude, unfriendly, they don't wait in queues, and they don't spend much money here.
They make this town a terrible place to live in. I think we should get rid of them.
Yours faithfully,

B You are going to stay in a hotel in Nottingham. Write and explain what sort of room you want. Be formal.

Your letter should look like this:

address
date
Dear Sir,
———
———
yours faithfully
W. Williams

UNIT 10 Town and Country

PRESENTATION

1 🎧 Listen to Joan and Peter. They are talking about where they live.

Joan We really love living in the country, don't we, Pete?
Pete Yes, everyone's so friendly, and there's such a relaxed atmosphere in the village.
Joan It's all very different from city life.

Check!
1 Where do Peter and Joan live now?
2 Do they prefer the town or the country?
3 How did Peter get to work?
4 How does he get to work now?
5 Where does Joan work? What does she like about it?

2 🎧 Now listen to what Judy and Dave think about living in the same village.

Judy I'm really sick of living here, Dave. It's so dead. There's nothing to do at the weekends. We always end up going into town, and then it's so expensive getting back here late at night. I'd really love to move somewhere with a bit more life.
Dave Look, Judy, we've been through all this before.

Check!
1 Where do Dave and Judy live?
2 Are they happy here?
3 Why don't they move? (Give the *main* reason)
4 What does Judy dislike about the place?

3 Read this text about changes in the population of Nottingham.

Trends

The main reason for the fall in the City's population in recent years has been the movement of families out of the city centre. This is particularly true of young families who have moved to rural areas to the south and east of Nottingham. The City's population now has an increasing proportion of older residents. In 1983, it was estimated that 18.1% of Nottingham's population were pensioners, including 3% aged over 80.

Check!
1 Why has the population of Nottingham fallen?
2 What sort of people have moved out?
3 Where have most of them moved to?
4 Is the population of the city getting younger or older?

VOCABULARY

atmosphere	*feeling, mood (of a place)*		
a bore	*something uninteresting, boring*	rural	*in the country*
a chat	*a talk, conversation*	increase	*get bigger*
to relax	*to rest, to enjoy yourself in a lazy way*	estimated	*calculated (but not precisely)*

Language Focus

Likes and dislikes:

				Strength of feeling
I	like	living	in the country.	+
We	enjoy	meeting	people.	++
	love	working	in the village pub.	+++

I	don't mind	looking	for jobs in Nottingham again.	

I	don't like	living	here.	–
	hate	sitting	in front of the television.	– –
	can't stand	driving	to work every day.	– – –

I'm	sick of	living	in the middle of nowhere.	– –
	fed up with			– –

ORAL EXERCISE *example:* He lives in the middle of London. (+)
  you: He likes living in the middle of London.

1 We go to France for our holidays. (++)
2 Don't you listen to classical music? (–)
3 I go to discos. (+)
4 They go for camping holidays. (+++)
5 He drives to work. (– – –)
6 She works late on Tuesdays. (– –)

Other uses of the -ing form:

We	end up	going	into town at the weekends.
We'll	start	saving	again.

It's	expensive	getting	back here late at night.
It's	difficult	finding	work these days.

Qualifying—so, such as:

Everyone's	so	friendly here.
It's		dead here.

There's	such a	pleasant atmosphere here.
It's		bore here.

ORAL EXERCISE *example:* (a) People here are friendly.
  you: People here are *so* friendly.
  (b) This is a quiet place to live.
  you: This is *such a* quiet place to live.

1 Food is expensive these days.
2 That was a boring film.
3 I've just read an interesting book.
4 It's been a lovely summer.
5 I'm pleased with my new car.
6 I feel fit after my holiday.

SMALL TALK

Describing houses

A What's your flat like?
B It's a third floor flat in the middle of town.
   It's got two bedrooms.
A What's your house like?
B It's a three-bedroomed house on the outskirts of Cambridge.

Find out about your partner's house.

60

UNIT 10

PRACTICE

KEY
+ = like
++ = enjoy
+++ = love
− = don't like
− − = hate
− − − = can't stand

1 These people all live in Nottingham. You read about them in Unit 1. Here are lists of what they like and dislike about living in Nottingham.

	Likes		Dislikes	
Kathy Baker	Live/Nottingham	(+)	Drive/work	(−)
Job Centre Manager	Work/Job Centre	(++)	Live/small flat	(− −)
	Meet/People	(+++)	Tell/people there are no jobs for them	(− − −)
Alan Elston	Teach/children	(+)	Be/poor student	(−)
Student Teacher	Live/City centre	(++)	Work/weekends	(− −)
	Go/concerts	(+++)	Take/exams	(− − −)
Charlie Bloom	Meet/friends at pub	(+)	Cycle/in rain	(−)
Factory Worker	Relax/in front of TV	(++)	Work/nights	(− −)
	Work/garden	(+++)	Go/shopping	(− − −)
Judy Kingston	Work/library	(+)	Repair/damaged books	(−)
Librarian	Read/books about Nottingham	(++)	Sit/in boring meetings	(− −)
	Talk/local people	(+++)	Work/Saturday mornings	(− − −)

Talk to your partner about these people.
A Does Kathy Baker like working at the Job Centre?
B Yes, she does. She enjoys it very much, but she doesn't like driving to work.

2 You read about Harry and Sally Shepherd in Unit 2. They lived in Old Radford and then they moved to the Broxtowe Estate. Here are their opinions about Radford and Broxtowe.

Now write sentences like this about Radford and Broxtowe.

Old Radford was *such a* dirty place, but the neighbours were *so* helpful.

THE HOUSES HERE ARE VERY BIG.
THE STREETS IN RADFORD WERE DARK AND NARROW.
THE NEIGHBOURS WERE VERY HELPFUL
THE YOUNG PEOPLE AROUND HERE ARE BORED WITH THEIR LIVES.

RADFORD WAS A VERY DIRTY PLACE.
WE HAD GOOD NEIGHBOURS THERE.
WE WERE VERY HAPPY IN RADFORD.
PEOPLE HAD LARGE FAMILIES IN THOSE DAYS.

TRANSFER

1

STUDENT A

Find out about your partner's ideal holiday. Write down questions to ask. Ask about:
- places to go
- places to stay
- things to eat and drink
- things to do—during the day
  —in the evening
- people to go with
- length of holiday

Use the language of Likes and Dislikes on p. 60.

STUDENT B

Write notes about your ideal holiday. Write about:
- the places you like going to
- the places you like staying
- things you like doing
- people you like mixing with

Answer your partner's questions about holidays.

Express your likes and dislikes using verbs from the Language Focus on p. 60.

2 DISCUSSION

Now discuss with your partner what you like or dislike about these types of holidays. Which would you choose? Put five holidays in order, your favourite first.

CORK MOTORING TOUR FROM ONLY £32 HOLIDAY 1B7

Cork, second largest city in the Republic, is important commercially due to the ability of its harbour and city quays to accommodate the largest vessels. Historically, Cork goes back to the 6th century AD and there are many churches reflecting different architectural styles. 5 miles north of the city lies the village of Blarney with its famous "stone of eloquence".

Choose your hotel from the impressive **Imperial**, situated on fashionable South Mall, a superb establishment with all bedrooms recently renovated to international standards, or the **Metropole**, situated in the city centre with nightly entertainment and many other facilities free to residents.

A Cycling or Walking Holiday for You!!

See the North Norfolk countryside and coast from the saddle of a bike or on foot.
Routes selected for the stroller or the hiker. Bicycles available for hire, all 1981 models. Accommodation booked in advance.
Send for full details to:
North Norfolk Cycling/Walking Holidays, Folly Farm, Hindringham, Fakenham, Norfolk.
Telephone: Thursford 032877-599

Corfu

ASTIR PALACE – KOMENO BAY, CORFU
This luxurious hotel and its bungalows are in a superb position on a tranquil wooded headland fringed by sandy beaches at Komeno Bay, some seven miles from Corfu town. One of the island's leading hotels.
Amenities: Restaurant; taverna; bars and lounges; large swimming pool with snack bar; watersports; floodlit tennis courts; disco; shops; beauty salon; free hotel bus service.

The Fun Holiday for all the Family — surfing, water-skiing and much, much more

ROYAL LINKS HOLIDAY PARK
Overstrand Road CROMER
SELF CATERING

High quality SELF CATERING villas sleeping 4-8 persons on newly built luxury holiday park. Just 1 mile from centre of Cromer.
* ½ mile to sandy beach
* Spectacular cliff top walk to Cromer
* Superb sea views
* Golfing on doorstep
* Sportsfield/play area nearby
* Newly built villas
* Choice of 4 styles
* Furnished to high standard
* Free heated outdoor swimming pool
* Brand new clubhouse with bar
* Shop and laundrette

Coloured brochure from: **Blakes Holidays**
Wroxham, Norwich, NR12 8DH Tel: WROXHAM (06053) 2917
or contact Reception office, Royal Links Holiday Park Tel: CROMER (0263) 513833

3 PET HATES

Write a list of your pet hates about other people.

> I can't stand seeing men with earrings.
> I really hate getting phone calls late at night.
> I'm fed up with having smokers in my car.

Compare your list with your partner's list, and talk about your pet hates.

4

Find out what your partner likes and dislikes about where he/she lives. Ask for reasons.

'I thought she was too attractive!'

'My life was pretty boring,' confessed Tim. 'My two best friends moved away — one to Germany and the other to university — and I never really went out.

Tim Smith has always lived in Wells-Next-The-Sea in Norfolk. Wells being quite literally 'next the sea', it's maybe not surprising that 22 year old Tim is an in-shore fisherman. It's a job he enjoys, but it didn't do anything for his social life.

Tim sent off for the Dateline details but it took him a couple of months to pluck up the courage to actually join. But join he did and soon got his first list of four names. 'I met one girl from Norwich, but she wasn't really my type,' he said. Not daunted, he was preparing to send off for another computer run when a letter dropped through his letter box. An ordinary enough occurrence, but one which was to change his life, because the letter was from Suzanne Anderson, who had got his name and address from Dateline.

Suzanne, an attractive 19 year old assembly line worker from Kings Lynn, joined Dateline because she wanted to find one special boyfriend. 'I was a bit fed up. I had just finished some amateur dramatics and I had nothing else to do.' Unlike Tim, she didn't hesitate and joined Dateline as soon as she received the details. Tim was the first person she contacted. 'I sent him my phone number on the Friday and he phoned me two days later,' said Sue.

'We were both nervous,' remembered Tim, 'but she seemed friendly.' Fortunately Sue felt the same about Tim and the couple decided to meet outside the Conservative Club in Kings Lynn. Sue sent Tim a photograph of herself so he was able to recognise her when he arrived. He was very impressed with what he saw as he drove up. 'I thought she was too attractive to be a member of Dateline,' said Tim, laughing.

Sue and Tim went for a drink in the town centre and got on so well together that they went on for a steak together at the local 'Bernie', the Globe. Afterwards Tim took Sue home where they talked until one o'clock in the morning! 'It was as though we had known each other for years,' said Tim. Sue was delighted when Tim asked to see her again although 'I didn't expect him to, really,' she said, and the couple met two nights later. 'We went out virtually every night after that and it felt as though we had known each other for years.'

Nine days after they first met, Tim asked Sue to get engaged and she said yes. 'I was quite surprised,' she said. 'I didn't think he would ask me that quickly, although I was secretly hoping he would.'

The speed with which Sue and Tim found each other has surprised their friends and relatives — Suzanne was only on the Dateline computer for three weeks! 'Some people thought it was a little bit soon, but they're getting over the shock now,' said Sue. 'They all like Tim.'

And how does he feel about computer dating now?

'Before I joined Dateline I thought that the only people who used dating agencies were the real lonely-hearts types — that they were all ugly — but they're just normal people, very friendly.'

'Yes,' said Sue, 'I had a similar picture of Dateline. I was really surprised and I would definitely encourage people to join. They should have a go and see what happens.'

Just like Tim and Sue did...!

Does Dateline Work?

Yes, in many different ways! Some people simply have a wonderful time, meeting as many new people as possible, sharing new interests, going out, just enjoying themselves. Some are looking for the companionship, the love and romance of one or two relationships, and others are looking for a special love with marriage in mind.

Many thousands of couples have met and married through Dateline, as the Dateline questionnaire is designed to match couples through many facets of physical type, personality and life-style; not just matching those who want to meet people similar to themselves, but those who also want to meet someone different. With Dateline you meet the people you want to meet, who also want to meet you.

If you would like to be one of the many thousands of people nationwide who have been enjoying a new social life, and finding love and happiness through Dateline, complete the simple questionnaire below. We will send you confidentially and completely free, full details about Dateline and how it works, and details of just one of the Dateline members who are compatible with you. Send to:

Dateline Computer Dating, 23 Abingdon Rd., London W8. Tel: 01-938 1011.

1 READING

What have this story and the Dateline advertisement got to do with each other?
Read the story to find out.

Reading for information

		MAN	WOMAN
1	What are the names of the two people in the photograph?		
2	Where do they live?		
3	How old are they?		
4	What are their jobs?		
5	Their first date: • Where did they meet? • What did they do first? • Where did they eat? • What time did they leave each other?		

Finding reasons
1 Why was Tim's life boring? (there are two reasons)
2 Why did Suzanne decide to join Dateline?
3 Why were the couple's friends and relatives surprised?

Sequence of events

Put these events in Tim and Suzanne's lives into the right sequence.
- They met in Kings Lynn.
- They went out for nine days.
- They talked until one o'clock.
- Tim met his first Dateline girl.
- Tim joined Dateline.
- Tim got a letter from Suzanne.
- They got engaged.
- They went for a drink and a meal.
- Tim's friends moved away.

2 WORDS

Match these words and phrases from the text with their meanings.

social life	an event, a happening
to pluck up the courage	very happy
my type	a continuous row of machines in a factory
daunted	pleased, affected
assembly line	the right kind of person for me
impressed	put off, discouraged
delighted	time spent enjoying yourself with friends
virtually	to dare, become brave enough
an occurrence	almost

3

Ask your partner questions about him/herself, so that you can fill in this Dateline questionnaire about him/her.

4 DISCUSSION

What do you think about organisations like Dateline? Would you use one of these organisations? Give your reasons.

CONFIDENTIAL

FREE: Computer Test to Find Your Ideal Partner.

START HERE ➡

1 Do you consider yourself:
- Shy
- Extrovert
- Adventurous
- Family Type
- Clothes-conscious
- Generous
- Outdoor Type
- Creative
- Practical
- Intellectual

2 Indicate which activities and interests you enjoy by placing a '1' (one) in the appropriate box. If you dislike a particular activity, write a '0' (nought) in the box. If you have no preference, leave the column blank.

- Pop music
- Fashion
- Pubs
- Sport
- Pets
- Folk music
- Jazz
- Travelling
- Cinema
- Good food
- Politics
- Classical music
- Art/Literature
- 'Live' theatre
- Science or technology
- Creative writing/painting
- Poetry
- Philosophy/Psychology/Sociology
- History/Archaeology
- Conversation

☐ I am over seventeen and would like you to send me completely free and without obligation, a description of my ideal partner. Plus a free full colour brochure and lots more information about Dateline. I enclose two first class stamps.

3 Your sex ___ put M or F   Your Height ___ ft. ___ ins
Your Age ___ yrs.   Age you would like to meet Min. ___ Max. ___

Christian Name _____
Surname _____
Address _____
_____
Nationality _____ Religion _____
Occupation _____

Send today to:
Dateline, Dept ( )
23/25 Abingdon Rd.
London W.8.
01-938 1011

Dateline

UNIT 11 Eat better, feel better

PRESENTATION

1 It is becoming more and more important to eat the right food.
Experts say that the type of food you eat can damage your health. If you eat the right food, you will have a better chance of living a long and healthy life.
If you eat a lot of processed food, you will be more likely to have problems with your health. If people eat food with a lot of fat in it, they will have a greater risk of getting heart disease.
In some countries, people eat less fat in their diet. Scientists have shown that fewer people get heart disease in these countries. In Spain and Italy, for example, most people have less fat in their diets than people in England. And in England, the rate of heart disease is *double* the rate in Spain or Italy.
So if you eat less fatty food, you'll live longer. You'll feel better, feel fitter, and have more energy if you change to a simpler and healthier diet.

Check!
1 Why is it important what sort of food you eat?
2 What sort of food is bad for you?
3 What do scientists say about fatty food?
4 What sort of food should we eat more of?
5 What happens in countries where the diet is low in fat?
6 What will happen to you if you eat less fat?

VOCABULARY
processed food	food that is cooked or changed before you buy it
disease	illness, sickness
likely	possible, probable
scientists	experts; people who study how things work
diet	the things you eat
fatty	with a lot of fat

2

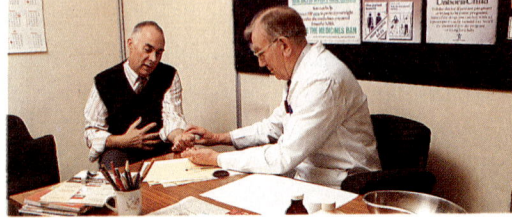

Doctor   Morning Mr Fells – now what's the trouble?
Patient I don't feel well, and I've had pains in my chest. I never have any energy, and I'm not sleeping well.
Doctor   You're a little overweight. You should eat less, and avoid eating fatty foods.
Patient What else should I do?
Doctor   You'd better cut out salt and sugar, and eat more fresh vegetables. I think you should take more exercise as well. Try to do a little swimming or cycling.

VOCABULARY
overweight	when your body is too heavy
to avoid	to find a way not to do something
to cut out	to stop doing something (eg smoking)

Check!
1 What's wrong with Mr Fells?
2 What does the doctor say he should do?
3 What does the doctor say he shouldn't do?

3

RED — stop and think
Sugar, sweets, chocolate, cakes, pies, sweet pastries, biscuits, heavy puddings, honey, syrup, treacle, jam, marmalade, fruit tinned in syrup, cream, butter, margarine, lard, cooking oil, fat on meat, salad dressing, salad cream or mayonnaise, chips, crisps, peanuts.

AMBER — go carefully
Fatty meats (like bacon or salami), sausages, liver paté, eggs, milk, oily fish (like herring, mackerel, sardines, tuna, salmon), cheese (except cottage cheese), thick creamy soups, nuts, bread (white or wholemeal), rice, pasta (like spaghetti and macaroni), savouries. Wines, beer and cider. Aperitifs, spirits and liqueurs. Most soft drinks and mixers.

GREEN — go right ahead
Fresh fruit, salads, green and root vegetables including potatoes (not fried), whitefish, seafood, poultry, game, lean meat, kidneys, cottage cheese, yoghurt (natural), skimmed milk, bran, wholegrain cereals, clear soups. Low-calorie soft drinks, coffee and tea (without sugar), water.

Check!
1 What sort of food should you be careful about?
2 What type of food should you avoid?
3 What kind of food is good for you?

Language Focus

Conditional 1:
> If you eat more vegetables, you'll be healthier.
> If he gives up smoking, he'll live longer.
> You'll live longer if you give up smoking.

> If you don't change your diet, you'll be very ill.
> You won't be healthy if you keep smoking.

ORAL EXERCISE   *example:* study hard/pass your exams
you: If you study hard, you'll pass your exams.

1   study hard/pass your exams
2   pass your exams/go to college
3   go to college/get a qualification
4   get a qualification/get a good job
5   get a good job/be able to buy a car
6   buy a car/be able to visit us

Giving advice:
> You should eat less processed food.
> You shouldn't eat late at night.

Giving stronger advice:
> You'd better stop drinking so much alcohol.
> You'd better not drink and drive.

Note: 'You'd better' is short for 'You had better'.

ORAL EXERCISE   *example:* work shorter hours/should
you: You should work shorter hours.

1   work shorter hours/should
2   go on a long holiday/should
3   try to relax more often/you'd better
4   start a new hobby/should
5   go out and meet new people/should
6   look after yourself more/you'd better

less (uncountable nouns) and **fewer** (countable nouns):
> You should eat **fewer** sweet things and fatty foods.
> You should eat **less** sugar and coffee.

ORAL EXERCISE   *example:* meat
you: You should eat less meat.

1   meat
2   vegetables
3   sugar
4   tomatoes
5   food
6   fatty foods

Verb + ing after prepositions:
> You will have a better chance of **living** a long life.
> There is a bigger risk of **getting** heart disease.

SMALL TALK

Asking permission
A   It's very warm in here. Do you mind if I open the window?
B   No, not at all.
A   I'm trying to work. Do you mind if I turn the radio off?
B   No, that's all right.

Ask permission:
- to borrow a pen
- to open the window
- to leave the room
- to close the door

Give your partner a reason.

UNIT 11

PRACTICE

1 Talk to your partner about ways to improve your health.

STUDENT A

bread   drinking alcohol   breakfast
cigarettes   coffee   using the car
exercise   eating sweet things   fat

Ask questions like this:

What should I do to improve my health?

What should I do about | smoking cigarettes?
                       | drinking alcohol?

What about sweet things?

STUDENT B

Do's
eat more bread
drink more fruit juice
exercise more
eat fewer sweet things
drink less alcohol

Don'ts
eat so much fat
drink a lot of coffee
go everywhere by car
miss breakfast
smoke cigarettes

Answer questions like this:

You'll be healthier if you | eat more bread.
                           | eat fewer sweet things.
                           | don't drink alcohol.

2 Ask and answer questions like this:
A What will happen to me in the future?
B If you stay in this job, you will become very rich.

a visit the USA/become a film star
b go to the casino/win a million dollars
c get married/have 6 children
d write a book/be a bestseller
e have a daughter/be an actress
f have a holiday in Greece/meet a beautiful stranger

3

Country	International licence	Green card	Take extra light bulbs?	First Aid Kit
Spain	yes	yes	yes	no
France	no	no	yes	no
Germany	no	no	no	yes
Italy	no	no	no	no
Morocco	good idea	yes	no	yes
Greece	no	yes	no	no
Sweden	no	no	no	no
Hungary	yes	no	no	yes
Yugoslavia	no	yes	yes	yes

A What do I need to remember if I drive in Spain?
B If you drive in Spain, you'll have to have an International Driving Licence.

Now talk about the other countries on the chart.

4

(Cartoon: Queen says "I can't pay my bills!" Advisor replies "You'd better get a second job.")

STUDENT A – *Problem:*
got no money
back hurts
always feel tired
can't get up in the morning
can't get a job

STUDENT B – *Advice:*
go to bed earlier
do a course at college
take some vitamins
get a second job
go to the doctor

5 A What should I do if the car doesn't start?
B In that case you should check the battery.

STUDENT A –
Problem:
doesn't start
the engine starts but the car won't move
the lights don't work
the brake won't work
it's very slow
the rain comes in the roof
there's a strange noise from the engine

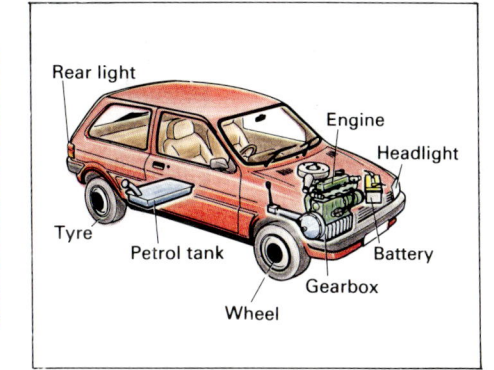

(Diagram of car with labels: Rear light, Engine, Headlight, Battery, Gearbox, Wheel, Petrol tank, Tyre)

STUDENT B –
Suggested action:
check the battery
check the gears
check the petrol
take it to the garage
get some new oil
buy a new car!
give it a service

TRANSFER

1 SURVEY

Give your own answers about eating and drinking in your country, and then talk to the other students in your group. Ask them about the diet in countries that they know.

	Your country	Britain	Country X	Country Y
EAT TOO MUCH:				
EAT TOO LITTLE:				
DRINK TOO MUCH:				
DRINK TOO LITTLE:				
GOOD POINTS:				
BAD POINTS:				
SUGGESTIONS FOR IMPROVEMENT:				

Fill in this chart about eating and drinking in 3 other countries. Talk about what people in these countries should do for their health.

UNIT 11

2 DISCUSSION

Do you want people to smoke in your office/cinema/theatre/school?

Discuss the arguments FOR and AGAINST smoking in these places, and then take a vote.

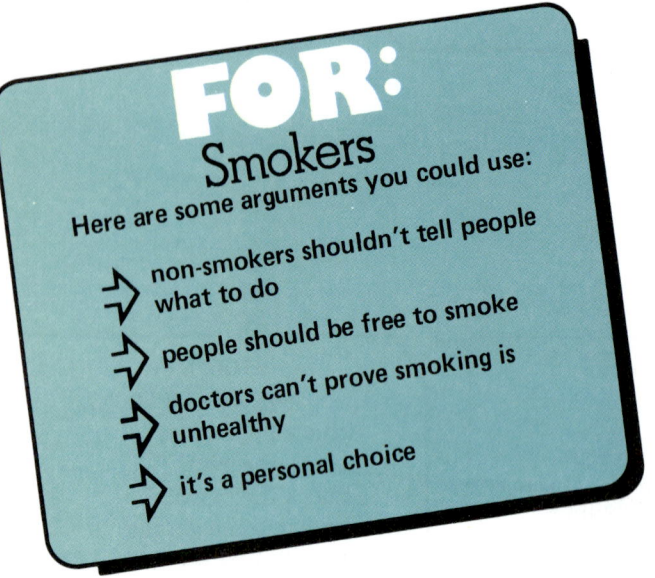

FOR: Smokers

Here are some arguments you could use:

- non-smokers shouldn't tell people what to do
- people should be free to smoke
- doctors can't prove smoking is unhealthy
- it's a personal choice

AGAINST: Non-smokers

Here are some arguments you could use:

- we should be able to breathe fresh air
- smokers make the air dirty for other people
- smoking is unhealthy for everybody
- people shouldn't smoke in cinemas, etc.
- smoking costs a lot of money

3

How should you advise people with these problems?

Talk to your partner, and give your advice like this: I think he/she should . . .

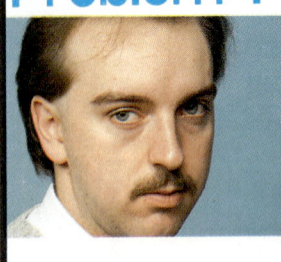

Problem 1
Paul Pringle has a large bank overdraft. He owes the bank £3000 and doesn't have a job. His boss sacked him last week for coming to work late.

Problem 2
Donna Davies can't get a job because she hasn't got any qualifications. She wants to be a nurse in a hospital.

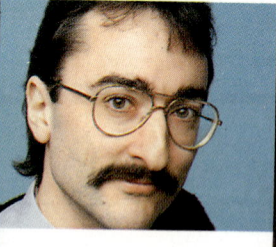

Problem 3
Sam Smith's wife has left him for a younger man. He has 2 children to look after, and a very busy job in a sales department. He doesn't know what to do with the children when he's at work.

Problem 4
Lorraine Lewis is a student. She has just failed her exams because she didn't work hard. She went out every night to the cinema or to a disco with her friends.

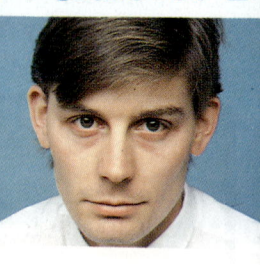

Problem 5
Harry Hogan has got a new job in Australia, but his wife doesn't want to go. She's going to have a baby, and wants to stay close to her family.

SKILLS

1 READING

This text (and a lot of the texts in Units 12–20) has a lot of new words. Don't try and learn them all! You don't need to understand **every** word. Just try to get an idea of the text, and answer the questions.

VOCABULARY

the key	the answer
to gain	to win
stained	dirty
to breathe	to take in air
infections	illnesses like colds, flu, viruses

Comprehension

1. What advantages will you have if you give up smoking?
2. What will you have **fewer** of?
3. How much money will you save if you stop smoking?
4. What will you be able to do more easily?

Words

Read the text again and find the words which have these meanings.

1. a problem
2. when you do something well
3. to get away from a problem
4. something you do every day, or very often

Writing

Make 5 sentences like this, using ideas from the text.

If I give up smoking, I'll . . .

SO YOU WANT TO STOP SMOKING

The big question is: do you *really* want to stop? Because this is the key to success. Make up your mind you are going to stop, and you will. Lots of people have been surprised how easy it was to stop once they had really made up their minds. To help you make your decision, think about what you gain by stopping.

RIGHT AWAY
- ☐ You will be free from an expensive and damaging habit.
- ☐ You'll have another £5-£10 a week to spend.
- ☐ You'll smell fresher. No more bad breath, stained fingers or teeth.
- ☐ You'll be healthier and breathe more easily – for example, when you climb stairs or run for a bus.
- ☐ And you'll be free of the worry that you may be killing yourself.

Think of the money you'll save.

FOR THE FUTURE
- ☐ You will lose your smoker's cough.
- ☐ You will suffer fewer colds and other infections.
- ☐ And you will avoid the dangers that smokers have to face.

---

2 WRITING

Look at this cartoon story about Harry Evans. You need to know these words:

a quick one	a quick drink with friends (usually after work)
I can't afford	I haven't got enough money
my round	my turn to buy the drinks

Write the story shown in the pictures

Use these sentences to start:

1. 'Harry was ready to go home after work, but his friends wanted to . . .'
2. 'Harry didn't want to go, but then he . . .'
3. 'In the pub, Harry and his friends had . . .'
4. 'Harry was very late. He didn't go home, but . . .'
5. 'Harry tried to leave, but . . .'
6. 'At 11 o'clock, Harry got into his car and . . .'
7. 'Harry's friend didn't know . . .'

What happened after these pictures? Discuss this with your partners, and then write the end of the story.

What is the writer of the story saying to us? Why did he or she write this little story?

UNIT 12 Conservation

PRESENTATION

1 The Earth is not as healthy as it was. The problems of dirty air, polluted rivers, acid rain, and nuclear waste make a lot of people worry about the future. They feel that it is important to do something quickly, before it is too late.

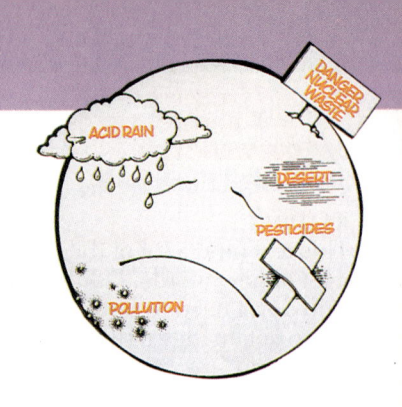

2 Acid rain is one of the biggest problems in Europe. Smoke from factories and power stations in European countries goes up into the atmosphere. This smoke contains sulphur and other chemicals. The wind blows the smoke across Europe, and it falls with the rain in Scandinavia, Germany and Britain. This is acid rain – it damages trees and kills the fish in lakes and rivers. In some Scandinavian lakes all the fish have died in the last few years. In Norway, 1711 of the 2840 lakes in the country are now 'dead' – they have no fish. Governments must now find a way to stop acid rain. Most of the European countries have agreed to reduce the amount of sulphur in the air. They want to reduce the amount by 30% by 1995, but the British government doesn't agree. British experts feel it's not enough to control industry. They are certain that the real problem is the smoke from the millions of cars in Europe.

VOCABULARY

acid	chemical that can burn through wood, metal or plastic
power station	place where electricity is made
lake	large area of water, not connected to the sea
amount	quantity
to reduce	to make smaller

Check!
1 What is acid rain?
2 Where does acid rain come from?
3 Which countries have acid rain?
4 What does acid rain damage and kill?
5 What do the European countries want to do in the next few years?

3 Listen to these two people talking about pollution:

Interviewer What do you think we should do about pollution?
First person I think acid rain is a real problem. I mean, killing fish and trees is wrong. I don't agree with the government, which wants to do nothing about it. I'm certain it's a British problem, actually, and I think we should control industry better. Power stations in other countries aren't allowed to produce all this sulphur, and we just can't go on killing things. It's not right.
Second person Everyone agrees that cleaning up the environment is important, but I'm sure the government is doing its best. I don't think we should stop industry and make a lot of people unemployed – just to save a few fish. It's impossible to make the air completely clean, isn't it? And it's not worth spending money on cleaning the rivers.

VOCABULARY

environment	the world we live in – nature, water, air, animals, trees
pollution	the man-made problems of dirty air, dirty water
it's not worth	it's not a good idea, it's not important

Check!
1 Do the two people agree with each other?
2 What does the second person think the government should do?
3 What does the first person think is wrong?

Language Focus

Verb + ing:
At the beginning of a sentence
> Killing fish is wrong.
> Understanding English is easier than speaking it.

After some prepositions
> I don't believe **in** controlling industry.
> There's a risk **of** killing other animals.

After some adjectives
> It's not worth building new roads.

To + verb:
After some adjectives

It's	not enough impossible important possible impossible good wrong	to	control industry. protect the environment. keep the air clean.

To express purpose

I'm going to England	to learn English.
I'm learning English	to get a better job.

After some nouns
> It's a good idea to control industry more.

ORAL EXERCISE   example: build new roads/it's not worth
                    you: It's not worth building new roads.

1 build more schools/it's worth
2 build more houses/it's a good idea
3 create more jobs/it's important
4 make people unemployed/I don't believe
5 find jobs for everybody/it's impossible
6 change the government/it's not worth

Giving opinions:

I'm certain I'm sure They feel	that	it's a British problem. the government is doing its best. it's important to do something.

Agreeing and disagreeing:

I think you're right I agree It's true	that	stopping pollution is important.

I don't agree I can't agree It's not true	that	acid rain kills all the fish.

> The government agrees with conservation.
> Most young people disagree with the use of nuclear power.

ORAL EXERCISE   example: in the future robots will do all our work
                    you: I don't agree that in the future robots will do all the work.

1 in the future robots will do all the work
2 most people need to work to be happy/We
3 people will stay at home more in the future/He
4 people will watch television all day/They
5 there will be no governments in the future/I
6 we should look forward to a new world/We

By:
Quantity
> They reduced the price **by** 30%, from £100 to £70.
> They increased the price **by** 50%, from £100 to £150.

Time
> Your car will be ready **by** 5 o'clock, sir.

UNIT 12

SMALL TALK

It's not allowed

A I'm afraid you're not allowed to smoke in here, sir.
B I'm sorry, I didn't see the sign.

A You can't go in there.
B Why not?
A Look at the sign. It says 'No Entry'.

Look at these signs and tell your partner what he/she is not allowed to do.

PRACTICE

1 Write sentences describing what these people are doing.
Then talk to your partner like this.

A Which is more difficult, riding a bike or riding a motorbike?
B Riding a motorbike is much more difficult.

difficult

easy

interesting

fun

tiring

dangerous

2 Finish the sentences with the VERB + -ING form or the TO + VERB form.

1 I don't think it's worth _____ government money on trees. (spend)
2 It's impossible _____ to Brian, he thinks he knows everything. (talk)
3 Do you enjoy _____ meat? (eat)
4 She doesn't believe in _____ alcohol. (drink)
5 I think it's a good idea _____ shops on a Sunday. (open)
6 _____ too much food will make you fat. (eat)
7 It's important _____ accidents on the roads. (reduce)
8 It's not enough _____ violence. We must stop it. (control)

3 A What does this sign mean?
   B It means you can't . . .
      It means you're not allowed to . . .
      It means it's forbidden to . . .

AVON FRIENDS OF THE EARTH
SAVE AND RECYCLE

RAGS
(No shoes please) Put in plastic bags & secure

SUMP OIL
– Leave in clean 5 litre cans

NEWSPAPERS
– Secure bundles with string

MAGAZINES
– Bundle & secure with string

KEEP RECYCLABLES SEPARATE

4 What do the Friends of the Earth think we should do?
For example:

- We should save old clothes and rags.
- We should re-use old oil.
- We should . . .
- We should . . .

Do you agree with these ideas?

UNIT 12

TRANSFER

Find out from your partner what the Friends of the Earth think about these issues. Does your partner agree or disagree with these opinions?

1 INFORMATION GAP

WHAT DOES FoE CAMPAIGN ON

STUDENT A

ENERGY
For: Conservation, more insulation in homes, alternative types of energy like windpower, water power, solar power, etc.
Against: ....
NUCLEAR WASTE
For: Keeping it at the power stations. More public discussion of the problem.
Against: ....
POLLUTION
For: Control of chemicals for farmers to use.
Against: ....
WILDLIFE AND COUNTRYSIDE
For: More money for the conservation of forests, rivers and animals.
Against: ....
TRANSPORT
For: More public bus and rail services, more special roads for bicycles.
Against: ....

STUDENT B

ENERGY
For: ....
Against: Nuclear power stations.
NUCLEAR WASTE
For: ....
Against: Transport of nuclear waste through cities, dumping waste in the sea.
POLLUTION
For: ....
Against: Acid rain, the use of too many chemicals in farming, industries discharging chemicals in rivers.
WILDLIFE AND COUNTRYSIDE
For: ....
Against: Very large farms, taking 'wild' land for farming, the killing of whales and seals.
TRANSPORT
For: ....
Against: Heavy lorries, too many cars in cities.

2 DISCUSSION

Work in groups. You want to discuss Jane's problem.

Jane Robinson is 32 and lives in Newcastle. She has two children, who are 3 and 6 years old. Her husband, Gordon, is an engineer with British Telecom. Jane was an office manager before she had children. Now she wants to go back to work again. Her company has said she can have her old job back, but Gordon is not happy about the idea. He wants Jane to stay at home with the children. What should she do?

Talk to your partners, and ask them about the reasons for and against Jane getting a job.

Make a list of the reasons like this:

For:
get more money
for the family
. . .
. . .

Against:
spend less time with
the children
. . .
. .

What do you think Jane should do?
Take a vote in your group.

SKILLS

1 LISTENING

Listen to John talking about the environment. He is explaining why he is a member of the Friends of the Earth.

1 Listen to the first part of the tape, and find out when he joined the Friends of the Earth.

2 Listen to the first part again, and find out what John was worried about when he joined the Friends of the Earth:
   a . . .
   b . . .

3 Listen to the second part, and answer the questions:
   a What does he agree with?
   b Which forms of alternative energy should we use more?
   c What does he disagree with?

4 Listen to the third part:
   a What should the government do?
   b What does John like about the Friends of the Earth?

5 Listen to the first part again, and read what John says. Find the missing words:
'There are several _____ why I think the Friends of the Earth are a good _____, mainly because of their work _____ pollution. I joined the organisation about 10 years _____, after university, because I was _____ about the development of nuclear energy, and the _____ of many wild animals.'
Write down the words.
   a _____ b _____ c _____
   d _____ e _____ f _____

75

2 READING

Worth seeing... worth saving... worth joining.

The National Trust looks after some of Britain's most famous places. Old houses, historic castles, beautiful gardens, open countryside and wild forests. It would take a lifetime to see them all. When you visit a National Trust property you can see where famous people lived, look at great pictures and wonderful art, or take a quiet walk in the peaceful countryside.

But it costs a lot of money to keep this for everyone to enjoy. There are roofs to repair, flowers to look after, paintings to clean, furniture to repair – a lot of work for a lot of people.

Last year, repairs and maintenance cost us £20 million. We get no money from the government, so we have to ask for your help. A year's membership of the National Trust costs £12.50 – no more than the cost of an evening out at the theatre. For that, you'll receive *free admission to all our properties, full information on a busy programme of special events, and a regular magazine.*

So if you enjoy discovering more about your heritage, please join us. It must be worth a few pounds a year to keep it in safe hands.

The National Trust

To: The National Trust, FREEPOST, BECKENHAM, Kent BR3 4UN. (no stamp needed)
Name _____ Address _____
Please tick form of membership required:
TWELVE MONTH MEMBERSHIP:
☐ Individual: £12.50. Each additional member of the household: £7.50.
☐ Family Group: £25. One card admits parents and their children under 18.
☐ Under 23: £7. Please give date of birth
LIFE MEMBERSHIP:
☐ Individual: £300. ☐ Pensioner (Men 65, Women 60): £200.
☐ Joint: £375 For husband and wife. ☐ Pensioner (Joint): £275.
I enclose cheque/PO for £ _____ or please debit my Access
No. _____
Signature _____
Or simply phone us on 01-658 8888 quoting your credit card account number.

Comprehension
1 What does the National Trust do?
2 What sort of places can you visit to see the work of the National Trust?
3 How much does it cost to join it?
4 What did they spend £20 million on last year?
5 What will you receive if you join the NT?
6 Why is it like an evening at the theatre?
7 What different types of membership are there? Which is the cheapest?

VOCABULARY
property — *a house or land that somebody owns*
maintenance — *work to keep something in good condition*
membership — *the cost of being a member (of the National Trust)*
to receive — *to get*
heritage — *history*

Writing
Write a letter to the National Trust, explaining that you would like to be a member. Give your reasons for wanting to be a member.

Who looks after old houses, historic places, and special parts of the countryside in your country? Explain this and write about some places you have

3 SOUNDS

🎧 Listen to the cassette and repeat this conversation:

A Shall we go to London tomorrow?
B Okay.

B agrees with A's suggestion, but is not very interested. Now listen again and repeat this conversation:

A Shall we go to London tomorrow?
B Okay.

This time B agrees with A's suggestion and sounds interested in the idea.
Now listen to some more conversations like these and decide whether B is interested or not in A's suggestions; mark the intonation on B's answer.

B's answer	Interested	Not interested
1 Yes		
2 Yes		
3 Okay		
4 Okay		
5 All right		
6 All right		

4 WRITING

Write a letter to a newspaper saying what the Government should do about these problems of the environment: ● the disappearance of some types of animals ● too many cars in the cities ● no fish in some rivers ● the death of trees from acid rain

76

Language Study 3

The '-ing' form of verbs The **-ing** form of a verb has many different uses, but it is never the only verb in a sentence.

As you already know, the **-ing** form is part of the present continuous:
- He's visiting his family at the weekend.

You can also use the **-ing** form after some verbs:
- I like living in the country.
- I don't mind living in the town.
- I can't stand driving to work.

Note The **-ing** form comes after most liking and disliking verbs.

. . . after some prepositions:
- There's a risk of catching flu.
- We have a good chance of going to Spain this year.
- I believe in protecting the environment.

and after **worth**:
- It's not worth building a third London Airport.

You can also use the **-ing** form, like a noun, as the subject or object of a sentence:
- Driving fast is dangerous.
- Speaking English is easier than writing it.
- I like swimming.

The Infinitive Like the -ing form you cannot use this part of a verb on its own.

Sometimes the word **to** comes before the infinitive:
- I'd like to see you at the weekend.
- I've got to work late tonight.
- I want to see the new Bond film.

Sometimes you do not need the word **to**:
- He can speak six languages.
- You must get to college by 9 o'clock.

You can use the infinitive after some adjectives:
- It's useful to have a bicycle.
- It's wrong to drink and drive.

and to express purpose:
- I'm going to Spain to learn Spanish.
- I'm learning Spanish to get a better job.

The Conditional This describes two-part sentences which say what will happen in the future under certain conditions. Notice that the verbs in the two parts of the sentence are different:

- If he gives up smoking, he'll be healthier.
- If he doesn't give up smoking, he won't live very long.
- He'll live longer if he gives up smoking.

Note The word **if** starts the Condition part of the sentence, and has the Present Simple. The other part has the Future with **will**.

So and Such a Use these words to qualify adjectives and noun phrases:
- I'm going to take my coat off. It's so hot in here. (**hot** is an adjective)
- I'm going for a swim. It's such a hot day. (**a hot day** is a noun phrase)

Less and Fewer Many English people use these words wrongly. They confuse them. But here is the rule:

Use **less** with uncountable nouns:
- You must drink less beer. It's bad for you.

Use **fewer** with countable nouns in the plural:
- There are fewer accidents on the roads these days.

Note **less** and **fewer** mean **not so much** and **not so many**; the opposite of them both is **mor**

Advising Advise people to do things like this:
- You should eat less chocolate.
- You'd better stop eating chocolate.

Advise people not to do things like this:
- You shouldn't work so hard.
- You'd better not telephone him this evening.

Agreeing and disagreeing Agree with people like this:
- I think you're right that sugar is bad for you.
- I agree that exercise is good for you.
- It's true that you need fresh air.

Disagree with people like this:
- I don't agree that you can work too hard.
- I can't agree that cats are friendly.
- It isn't true that English is a difficult language.

Permission Ask for permission like this:
- Do you mind if I open the window?

Answer this question and give permission like this:
- No, not at all.   or   • No, that's all right.

Saying something is not allowed:
- You're not allowed to smoke in here.
- You can't go in there.

EXERCISES

THE '-ING' FORM
- What do you like doing in the evenings?
- Make ten sentences starting like this:
  'Riding horses is . . .'
  'Climbing mountains is . . .'
  'Watching too much TV is . . .'

THE INFINITIVE
- What have you got to do this evening?
- What would you like to do at the weekend?
- Make sentences starting like this:
  'It's good to . . .'
  'It's wrong to . . .'
- Answer these **Why** questions with a purpose:
  'Why are you learning English?'
  'Why do people learn languages?'

THE CONDITIONAL
- What will you do if you can't find a job?
- What will you do if the fire alarm rings?

SO & SUCH A
- Add **so** or **such a** to these phrases: hot day; windy; good; large house; tired; fast car; heavy table; young.

LESS & FEWER
- Add **less** or **fewer** to these phrases: milk; oil; cars on the roads; apples; water; potatoes; money; bread; bicycles.

ADVISING
- Your friend is too fat. Advise him/her what to do.
- Your friend is feeling ill. Advise him/her what not to do.

AGREEING & DISAGREEING
- Agree and then disagree with these statements:
  'British people are very friendly.'
  'Summer holidays are too long.'
  'Eating meat is bad for you.'

PERMISSION
- Ask permission to: leave the room; go home early; make a telephone call.
- Tell someone what he/she is not allowed to do at work or at college.

UNIT 13 In the News

PRESENTATION

1

NEWS LINES

£2000 pub theft

Thieves stole £2000 in cash from a pub in Nottingham last night. They got into the Crown pub in Market Square through a downstairs window. The thieves took the money from the bar while the landlord was sleeping upstairs. "I noticed the theft when I was cleaning the bar in the morning" said Mr Barrett.

Butcher fined £650 for dirty shop

A butcher kept his shop in a 'very dirty condition' a Nottingham court heard today. Colin Gilman had to pay £650 after a health inspector went to his shop. "When I went into the shop, Mr Gilman was cleaning his knife with a dirty cloth" said the inspector. "He also lit a cigarette while he was cutting meat for a customer".

4 killed by train

Four men died last night while they were working on the railway line near Derby. The men were clearing snow from the line when the train hit them. British Rail is investigating the accident.

Notts woman moves to Japan

Leslie Stafford from Stapleford, near Nottingham, is going to go to Japan next week. She's leaving her home in England, and getting married to a Japanese student from Osaka. The couple met while they were studying computer science at Trent Polytechnic.

Check!
1 What does Colin Gilman do? Why did he pay £650?
2 Where did Leslie Stafford meet her husband?
3 What were the 4 men doing?
4 Where did the thieves find the money in the pub?

2

The Curry India is run by the Singh family, who came to England about 20 years ago. They have 2 sons, Rajiv and Surinder.
Jawinder Singh first came on his own from India, leaving the family behind until he had saved some money and found somewhere to live.

Jawinder I came over on my own in 1967, and stayed with some relatives I had in Leicester. At that time I lived with another man from my home town in one room in my uncle's house. We couldn't afford to get a flat, because both of us were saving money to bring our families over to England.
I got a job in a factory at first, and soon I was doing two jobs – I worked in a restaurant in the evenings. The owner was a friend of my uncle's, and he helped a lot. It was a difficult time for me, because I was living on my own, without my family, and I was trying to earn as much money as possible. It took me about a year to save enough for all of my family to come over, and to rent a small house.

Rajiv I don't remember a lot about living in India, because I was very young. I know we lived with my grandparents in a small village – some of us helped in the fields. We were waiting for him to send us the plane tickets. After a year, he had enough money, and we all came to England.

VOCABULARY
relatives	members of the family – cousins, uncles, sisters etc
to afford	to have enough money for something
owner	person who possesses something
on my own	alone; not with anyone
to earn	to get money for working
to rent	to pay someone money in order to live in a house

Check!
1 Who owns the Curry India restaurant?
2 How long did Jawinder live on his own?
3 Why was life difficult for him?
4 Who did he know when he came to England?
5 Where was his son before he came to live in England?

Language Focus

Past continuous:

I	was	saving money to bring my family to England.
I	was	trying to earn as much money as possible.
They	were	waiting for me to bring them over.

Past continuous & past simple:

While I was living on my own I worked at 2 jobs.
It was raining when I woke up this morning.
When I woke up this morning it was raining.

Questions & negatives:

What did you say? I wasn't listening.
What were you doing when I saw you yesterday?
Were you going to work?

ORAL EXERCISE   *example:* What were you doing at 7 o'clock yesterday?/wash the car
   you: I was washing the car.

1. What were you doing at 7 o'clock yesterday? wash the car
2. What were you doing at 8 o'clock yesterday? repair the TV
3. What were you doing at 9 o'clock yesterday? read the newspaper
4. What were you doing at 10 o'clock yesterday? paint the house
5. What were you doing at 11 o'clock yesterday? wash the clothes
6. What were you doing at 12 o'clock yesterday? have lunch

All/most/some/both of us

Before a noun:

All the family came to see us at Christmas.
Most people have a telephone these days.

Before 'of' + noun or pronoun:

All of them came to Britain.
Both of us were saving money.
Most of the cities in England have got Indian restaurants.
Some of us were in the fields.

all/both	= 100%
most	= 70–90%
a lot of	= 50–70%
some	= 30–50%
a few/ a little	= 10–20%

You **must** use 'of' before 'them', 'us', 'you' etc.
You **cannot** use 'of' before a noun on its own.

A few (+ countable things)

A few Indian restaurants sell English food as well.
A few of them sell English food as well.

A little (+ uncountable things):

He gave me a little money.
He gave me a little of the money.

ORAL EXERCISE   *example:* They like Italian food/both
   you: Both of them like Italian food.

1. They like Italian food/both
2. We are vegetarians/some
3. The family lives in London/all
4. The people watch TV every day/most
5. We prefer going to the cinema/both
6. They are on holiday at the moment/some

Must & can:

In the past tense, 'must' and 'have to' become 'had to':

I had to work very hard when I was at school.
He didn't have to go to hospital.

In the past tense 'can' becomes 'could':

I couldn't call you yesterday. I was busy.

ORAL EXERCISE   *example:* I must talk to Brian today.
   you: I had to talk to Brian yesterday.

1. I must talk to Brian today.
2. He doesn't have to work today.
3. She must come and see me.
4. We have to be there by 5 o'clock.
5. They don't have to buy a new car.
6. You have to call Sally today.

UNIT 13

Connectors: She came to see me. She wanted some help. She had a day off work. I was painting the house.

> She came to see me **because** she wanted some help.
> She came to see me **when** she had a day off work.
> She came to see me **while** I was painting the house.

SMALL TALK

At the restaurant

A Can you tell me something about these poppadums?
B They're large, round and made of flour, sir. They're a bit like potato crisps.

A What's this 'rogon josh' like?
B It's lamb in a hot sauce. It's made of small pieces of lamb, in a sauce with onions and tomatoes. It's got a lot of pepper and spices in it.

Ask your partner to describe these types of food to you.

| chips | chocolate | chilli |
| ice-cream | tea | hamburgers |

PRACTICE

1
A What were you doing when the lights went out?
B I was washing my hair.

Now ask your partner about the different people in the picture.
A What was the tall man in Flat 2 doing when the lights went out?
B He was . . .ing when the lights went out.

2
What's it made of?
It's made of brick and glass

Use words from this box.

brick	stone	concrete	wood
metal	glass	plastic	cloth
paper	cardboard	steel	foam
silver	gold	brass	diamond

3 Ask your partner about what people own.

A   How many people own their own homes in Switzerland?
B   In a report in 1978 it said that 30% owned their own homes.

Now talk about the other countries.

4 Now look at the chart again. With your partner, make sentences like this.
In Canada, most of the people own their own homes.
In West Germany, a few of the people own their own homes.

Make sentences with **most of / all of / some of / a few of**.

Who owns their own home worldwide

Country	Owner-Occupation Percentage	Year
Switzerland	30	1980
Norway	67	1980
West Germany	37	1978
USA	65	1981
France	47	1978
Netherlands	44	1981
Canada	62	1978
Australia	70	1981
Japan	60	1978
United Kingdom	63	1981
New Zealand	71	1978
Italy	59	1985
Spain	64	1981
Eire	74	1981
Brazil	60	1970
Hungary	76	1981
Colombia	54	1970
Philippines	89	1980
India	85	1973
Bangladesh	90	1970
		1971
		1981

5 **WHERE YOUR MONEY GOES**

The TV licence pays for all BBC services – two TV channels, four radio networks, local radio and regional programmes.

Regional Television 7%
Transmission of TV Programmes 2%
Capital expenditure Television 10%
Capital expenditure, Radio 5%
Transmission of Radio Programmes 1%
Radio 1 2%
Radio 2 4%
Radio 3 4%
Radio 4 5%
Local Radio 3%
Regional Radio 4%
BBC 2 18%
BBC 1 35%

TELEVISION
RADIO

In Britain you have to pay the government money every year for the BBC TV and radio service. This chart shows what happens to the money.
Talk to your partner like this.

A   Where does the money go?
B   Most of the money goes to BBC 1
    Some of the money . . .
    A little of the money . . .

TRANSFER

1 Ask your partner what he or she was doing when these things happened.

What were you doing when . . .?

July 1985
Becker wins Wimbledon

September 1985
US hostage plane seized

July 1984
Lewis grabs fourth Olympic gold

June 1986
World Cup fever hits Mexico City

December 24th
Merry Christmas to all our readers

Now write your own headlines – things that happened on a day you remember.
What were you doing on that day?

82

UNIT 13

2 Talk to your partner about these pictures. They show a bank robbery.
Tell your partner what happened. Use sentences like this.

The thieves took the money while the manager was calling . . .
When the police arrived, the thieves were driving . . .

3 Work in pairs. Ask your partner about the typical food he or she eats at home or in a restaurant. Ask and answer questions like this:

What's it like?
What's it made of?
What does it contain?

Write a menu for your partner's typical restaurant.

Ask several of your partners about which of these dishes they prefer to eat. Make a report on what they said:

Some of us said that . . .
Most of us said that . . .

MENU

Starters

Prices:

Main courses

Desserts

To drink

4 **DISCUSSION**
Work in groups. Talk about the problems of people who want to start life in a new country.
Some questions to talk about:

- What do immigrants find difficult in your country?
- What do people think about immigrants?
- What sort of jobs can immigrants get?
- What are the good things about living in a new country?
- What are the bad things?

Talk about these problems and the situation in your country.

SKILLS

1 READING

FAST FOOD THE £2.2 billion bonanza

MARKET VALUE £619m — of which takeaway is (82%) — FISH & CHIPS
£397m (37%) — HAMBURGERS
£273m (82%) — CHINESE
£171m (42%) — INDIAN
£154m (87%) — Chicken
£150m (24%) — PIZZA
£433m (67%) — SANDWICH BARS
£30m (66%) — OTHERS

KINGSIZE WIMPY — £1.50

Food	49p	Operating costs	12p
Wages	26p	Franchise fees	11p
VAT	20p	Rent	10p
Profit	17p	Rates	5p

Most people in Britain find the prices of good restaurants too expensive. Ordinary people can't afford to pay £30, £40 or £50 for a meal for two. They don't want to cook for themselves all the time, however, and it is nice to eat something different for a change. Many people are so busy that they don't have time to cook for themselves. Others live alone, and feel it's not worth cooking just for one person.

This has led to a massive increase in the 'fast food' business. The latest statistics show that Britons spend £2.2 billion each year on fast food, and this amount is increasing by 15% every year. Most of this is 'takeaway'. Many people prefer to eat in the comfort of their homes, instead of in a public restaurant, because they can relax in front of the television.

The traditional British takeaway food is fish and chips – and Britons spent over £619 million on fish and chips last year. That's £11.05 for every man, woman and child!

New types of food are taking over, however. Hamburger bars, Chinese restaurants, and Indian restaurants are becoming more and more popular. Macdonalds, the hamburger kings, have just increased the number of their restaurants in Britain from 133 to 166. They sold over £90 million worth of hamburgers last year, and the hamburger industry is worth a total of £397 million each year.

Chinese restaurants sold meals worth £273 million, and most of these meals were takeaways. Only 18% of the meals were 'normal' restaurant meals. Indian restaurants persuaded more people to sit and eat in the restaurant, but 42% of their meals were for taking home. Perhaps it will soon be possible to buy takeaway meals from the best French restaurants . . .

COMPREHENSION

1. What is 'takeaway' food?
2. Which is the most popular takeaway food?
3. How many of the pizzas sold in Britain are 'takeaway' pizzas?
4. How much Chinese food did people buy last year?
5. What types of food are becoming more popular?
6. What type of restaurant sold more 'restaurant' meals than 'takeaway' meals?

VOCABULARY

These words are from the text. Can you match them with their meanings?

increase	person who buys something
soon	very big
massive	not special
persuade	make something bigger
ordinary	make people believe you or do what you want them to
customer	in a short time, in the future

2 LISTENING

Paul & Luba are from Nottingham, but they now live in Canada. Listen to Luba talking about their move.

Listen to the first part and find out:

a When did they leave Nottingham?
b Why did they leave Nottingham?

Listen to the second part and answer these questions:

c What nationality were their families in England?
d What city in Canada do they live in?
e What is the best thing about living in that city?
f What do they want for their children?
g What job did Paul's father do?
h What language do their children speak at home?

Listen again and find the words Luba uses when she means:

a emigrated   b children   c grew up

UNIT 14 Life begins at forty

PRESENTATION

132

Brigitte didn't want to hear this terrible news. She was happy.

"But why?" she asked. "We were so happy together. You must be mad. You must think again."

"No," said Charles. "It's for the best." His voice was serious. She knew he meant what he said. He felt nothing as he looked at the tears which ran down her face.

"But why?" she asked again.

"I can't explain," said Charles. "You wouldn't understand. You're too young."

This was the end. Brigitte stood up and walked slowly towards the door, and then out into the hall. "Why?" she said to herself, "Why?" The front door opened and then closed. Charles poured himself a large whisky and smiled. He picked up the telephone and dialled a number. He waited. "It's me," he said after a few moments. "Yes, I told her." . . . "No, she didn't." . . . "Of course I did," . . . "No, I don't" . . . "Yes, she did" . . . "Look I'll be home tomorrow evening." . . . "Yes, I promise." . . . "How are the children?" . . . "Great!" . . . Mmm . . . "I love you too."

He put down the phone, and poured himself another drink. He smiled again.

169

All seven of them wore black diving suits. They moved quietly through the water — only their eyes and their teeth were visible in the pale moonlight. A mile away in the town, they could just hear the screaming sirens of the fire engines and bursts of machine-gun fire. But no ships were searching the sea. They were safe.

A few minutes later they reached the yacht — they climbed quietly up the rope ladder and staggered on to the deck. No one said a word until they were safely inside the captain's cabin. They peeled off their face masks and sat down. Pools of water formed at their feet.

"We did it, didn't we?" said Steve, out of breath, but smiling. "We did it."

"Yeah, you did it," said the captain, "but it's not over yet." "Take off your wet suits and get changed. The party's still in full swing. No-one's noticed anything. They're all talking about the bombing of course. Okay, go back in one by one — behave normally. If anyone says anything about the explosions, join in the conversation. Sound interested and excited like everyone else. That way no-one will suspect a thing. And smile. It's nearly over. You've all done a great job. The Doctor will be delighted. . . . Oh, I nearly forgot, the money will be in your Swiss bank accounts by tomorrow evening. Then you'll be free to go."

Richard Evans began a new life at the age of 40. He is now a full-time writer with 3 best-sellers to his name. Listen to this interview with him:

Interviewer Richard Evans, can you tell us how you became a writer?
Richard Evans Well actually writing always interested me. Even when I was a child, I used to spend a lot of my time writing stories.
Interviewer But you haven't always been a writer, have you?
Richard Evans No. My first job was in a bank – that was the worst time of my life. Then I spent 8 years as the manager of a shop – that was a dead-end job. After that . . .

VOCABULARY

a 'dead-end' job — a job with no future
to know something like the back of your hand — to know it very well

Check!

1 What jobs did Richard Evans do before he became a writer? (There were three.)
2 How do you know that he is richer now?
3 Why is he more relaxed now?
4 What does he miss about being a taxi driver?

Language Focus

Talking about past routines: 'used to'

What	did	you	use to	do?
Where		you		work?

I	used to	be	the manager of a shoe shop.
We		earn	about £200 a week.
		have	a holiday abroad every year.
			a big estate car.

She didn't use to work.
I never used to have a holiday.

ORAL EXERCISE

example: Where did he use to work?/shoe shop
you: He used to work in a shoe shop.

1 Where did she use to work?/bank
2 What did he use to be?/Maths teacher
3 What did you use to be?/footballer
4 How much did he use to earn?/£400 a week
5 What sort of car did they use to have?/a sports car

Some verbs can be followed by to + verb or verb + ing but their meanings are different:

stop:
She's	stopped	worrying.	= she used to worry, but not now.
I	stopped	to buy a paper.	= I stopped my car for the purpose of buying a paper.

like:
I	like	repairing cars.	= I enjoy this.
I	like	to watch car racing.	= I choose to do this.
I'd	like	to work with cars.	= I wish I could do this.

remember:
I remember	going	to the Job Centre.	= a past memory.
I remembered	to go	to the Job Centre.	= I didn't forget.

Question Tags: statements or real questions?

Statements:
You worked in a bank, didn't you?
There were lots of jobs, weren't there?

Real questions:
She works as a cleaner, doesn't she?
You have tried to find work, haven't you?

ORAL EXERCISES

example: He's got a job . . . (statement)
you: He's got a job, hasn't he?

1 You left school last year, . . .? (statement)
2 He's at the college now, . . .? (question)
3 His brothers have got jobs, . . .? (question)
4 He's found another job, . . .? (statement)
5 It's very depressing, . . .? (statement)
6 He earns twenty pounds a week, . . .? (question)

SMALL TALK

Moods and feelings

A How are you doing?
B Not so bad, thanks, but I'm feeling very tired – too much work probably.
A How do you feel about not getting the job?
B I'm very disappointed, and a bit angry, too. I think I was right for that job.

Ask your partner how he/she feels at the moment.

UNIT 14

PRACTICE

1 Look at these two pictures of the same town. Compare them and talk to your partner about how life has changed.

A There didn't use to be any cars in the streets.
B Now there are cars and buses.
A They didn't use to drive cars.

2 INTERVIEW

STUDENT A
You have applied for a new job as a travelling sales representative. Before your interview you wrote these notes about your last job:

Company: Offco Ltd.
Sales: Office equipment and stationery
Job: Sales representive for the North of England
Home: 51, Station Road Bradford
Car: Ford Sierra
Salary: £12,000 per annum

Answer the interviewer's questions, like this:
'I used to live in the North of England.'

STUDENT B
You are the personnel manager of Alders, a company which makes and sells typewriters. You are interviewing someone for the job of sales representative. Here is the form you have to fill in for each candidate:

Name: ....
Last address: ....
Previous job: ....
Job description: ....
Salary: ....
Name of company: ....
Type of sales: ....
Sales area: ....
Type of car: ....

Ask the candidate questions like this, and then fill in the form:
'Where did you use to live?'

87

3 Read this conversation with your partner. Two people are remembering their holiday in France last year. Add question tags where there are gaps. Make every statement sound like a statement.

A Do you remember the ferry from Dover to Calais?
B Yes, the sea was terribly rough, . . .?
A And everyone felt ill, . . .? Some of them couldn't stand up.
B And then we drove through France to the Mediterranean, . . .? We took about twelve hours, . . .?
A Yes. What was that town we stopped in for lunch?
B That was Lyons, . . .?
A That's right. It took ages to park, but the restaurant was fabulous, . . .?
B Yes, but the bill wasn't very nice.

TRANSFER

1 FIVE YEARS AGO

Find out how your partner has changed in the last five years. What was his/her life like 5 years ago?

For example: 'What sort of clothes did you use to wear?'

Ask about
- musical likes and dislikes
- interests and crazes
- friends
- sports
- worries and problems

I USED TO HAVE SHOULDER LENGTH HAIR

DID YOU? I USED TO BE INTO THE BEATLES AND ELVIS

2 READING

Read this text and answer yes or no to the ten questions for yourself.

Now ask your partner the questions and write down his/her answers.

Now with your partner talk about a third person you both know quite well – a friend, colleague, teacher, boss, parent etc. Answer the questions for him/her.

ARE YOU A WORKAHOLIC?

	YOU	YOUR PARTNER	PERSON 3
1 At parties, do you talk about your work most of the time?			
2 Do you work at home most evenings?			
3 On holiday, does it take you at least a week to relax?			
4 Do you often think about work problems at home?			
5 Do you *always* leave for work really early?			
6 Do you think you work harder than your colleagues and friends?			
7 Would you cancel a family outing if your teacher or boss asked you to do more work?			
8 Do you lie awake worrying about failing exams or about redundancy?			
9 Does your family complain that you spend too little time with them?			
10 Would you rather read a work report or a school book than a novel?			

HOW DID YOU SCORE

1–3 Yes answers	– You are serious about your job, but not too serious
4–7 Yes answers	– You are nearly a workaholic
8–10 Yes answers	– You are already a workaholic. Take it easy! You are probably a boring person!

UNIT 14

3 WRITING

What did life in your town or country use to be like? Write sentences like this.
- A lot of the people used to work as . . .
- They used to live in . . .

Think about these aspects of their lives.

work	spare time
money	clothes
food & drink	illnesses
families	children

4 DISCUSSION

If your partner is from the same town or country as you, compare the ideas you have written about. Do you agree or disagree?

If your partner is from a different town or country, ask questions like this:
- Did the people use to have any free time?
- What did they use to do?

SKILLS

1 LISTENING

Listen to the cassette. You will hear Colette talking about how she got her first job.

As you listen for the first time, find out:
- Where Colette went to college.
- What time of the year she first wrote to the hotel.

Now listen for words which mean the same as:
educational course, college teacher, spare job, a very long time

QUESTIONS

1 What sort of training did Colette do at college?
2 Why did she write to this particular hotel in Nottingham?
3 What month of the year did she first write to the hotel?
4 On which day of the week did she have her interview?
5 Why did it take her so long to find the hotel?
6 How did the hotel let Colette know that she had got the job?
7 When did she arrive in Nottingham to start work?

Listen again to the cassette.
Listen for and write down:
- 4 names of towns
- 2 jobs
- 3 days of the week
- 2 months of the year

Now look at these two letterheads.
Who wrote each letter?
Who was each letter to?
What question did each letter contain?

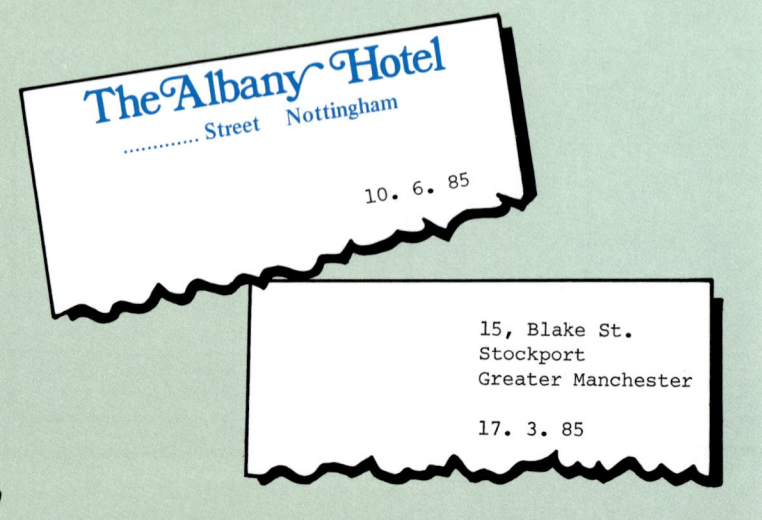

The Albany Hotel
.... Street Nottingham

10. 6. 85

15, Blake St.
Stockport
Greater Manchester

17. 3. 85

SOUNDS

Listen to the cassette and repeat this sentence:

You worked in a bank, didn't you?

The speaker is making a statement which he knows is correct, and he expects agreement
Now listen and repeat this sentence:

You worked in a bank, didn't you?

The speaker is asking a real question.

Now listen and repeat each sentence, mark the intonation on the question tag, and tick 'Statement' or 'Question'.

	Statement	Question
example: You worked in a bank, didn't you?		
1 There were lots of jobs, weren't there?		
2 You're a doctor, aren't you?		
3 She lives in Nottingham, doesn't she?		
4 You work in a supermarket, don't you?		
5 His brothers have got jobs, haven't they?		
6 He works very hard, doesn't he?		

2 WRITING

Colette wrote a letter to the hotel in Nottingham explaining that she would like a job and giving her qualifications. This is called a "spec" letter.
Read this example of a spec letter and the notes about it.

- Think carefully about what you want to say
- Do a rough copy first
- Show this to someone else. Can they suggest improvements?

> phone the company to find out the name of the personnel manager.
>
> PARAGRAPH 1
> show why you are writing
>
> PARAGRAPH 2
> describe your experience and qualifications
>
> PARAGRAPH 3
> write a few personal details
>
> PARAGRAPH 4
> say when you could come for interview and start work

Mrs M Brown,
Personnel Manager,
Waves Galore,
Dryer Street,
Ringsing
Blackshire X11 2XY

3 Roller Street,
Wigton,
Blackshire N2 3OZ
Tel: (0999) 78923

3 January 1984

Dear Mrs Brown,

I saw in today's Courier that you will shortly be opening a new branch in Wigton and would like to work for you.

I served a three year apprenticeship as a hairdresser with Supreme Styles Limited and during that time, through part-time studies, gained the City and Guilds 760 certificate in Ladies' and Men's Hairdressing. I then worked for Hair Beauty Limited for 4½ years until 30 November last year. These were both town centre salons and I gained a wide experience of cutting both men's and women's hair, also of bleaching, tinting, dyeing and perming in the latest styles.

I am 24 years of age, and I am available for full-time work and prepared to work Saturdays and late evenings, as required.

I am available for interview at any time and could start work immediately if required. I can provide good references from my two previous employers.

I look forward to hearing from you.

Yours sincerely
Alice Black

- give your full address, your telephone number
- give the date you wrote the letter

VOCABULARY

rough copy — first copy of a letter, not the one you send

experience — jobs or other things you have done in the past

WRITING

Write a spec letter, like the one above, to a famous international company you would like to work for, for example: The Ford Motor Company, CBS, the United Nations, etc.

CAMBRIDGE EVENING NEWS, Tuesday, July 16, 1985

Plea by boss with jobs to give away

By Chris Elliott

BAFFLED company boss Bill Griffiths is facing a dose of the dole-queue blues.

He is raring to expand his Cambridge-based firm, — but he cannot find the workers to do it!

Mr Griffiths, managing director of Henshall Bonded Assemblies at Milton, aims to open a new factory unit in Ditton Walk, Cambridge.

Advertised

To staff it he needs a number of experienced sheet-metal workers and glassfibre laminators.

But all his efforts to recruit the right people in Cambridge

'Only one person has responded'

have drawn a blank. Said Mr Griffiths: "It's incredible. I know Cambridge doesn't have a huge unemployment problem, but I would have thought there would be some suitable people in the area somewhere who would be keen to get a job.

"I have advertised widely, have had talks with the careers service, and have been to the jobcentre several times — all to no avail.

"There has only been one person respond so far — and he didn't turn up for the interview."

Mr Griffiths, whose firm makes interiors for the aircraft industry, has not put a figure on the number of people he needs.

He said: "It depends really on how many we can get. The work will be there, all we need is staff."

Benefit

He added he would now be advertising in other parts of the country in a bid to recruit the right workers.

"It's a shame, because being Cambridge-based, we wanted the local area to benefit from any jobs that were on offer," he said.

Anyone who wants an interview for one of the jobs should contact Mr Griffiths on Cambridge 62136.

3 READING

COMPREHENSION

1. Where is Bill Griffith's factory?
2. What is his company called?
3. Why is he unhappy and surprised?
4. What sort of workers is he looking for?
5. How has he tried to find people for his factory?
6. How can you contact Mr Griffiths?

UNIT 15 Music

PRESENTATION

2 The Young

When she was four years old Sade Adu and her family came from Nigeria to England. Sade grew up in a quiet English town and had a normal youth. Her first record *Your Love is King* was a big hit and made Sade a household name all over the world. Success has made her life easier: 'The funny thing is,' she says, 'this is just about the first time in my life when I can afford to have a good time.'

But fame has not changed her personality. She's clever enough to know that she has plenty of time to work at her musical career; 'I have doubts about my talent all the time. I know I'll never be as good as someone like Ella Fitzgerald, but I believe I have something. I'm only just starting out.'

Check!
1 Where did Sade come from?
2 Where did she grow up?
3 What was her first hit record?
4 How did this change her life?

1 The Old

Mick Jagger was born in London in 1943. He started singing with Alexis Korner, a blues musician. He was studying at the London School of Economics at the time, but in 1962 he gave it up and joined the Rolling Stones. At first the band played other people's songs, and their first hits came in 1964 with Chuck Berry's *Come On* and Buddy Holly's *Not Fade Away*.

The Rolling Stones became so famous, and so rich that they went to live in France, because the taxes in Britain were too high. Jagger made his first solo album in 1970 – songs from the film *Performance*; his next solo album appeared in 1983.

Meanwhile the group's success continued, with hits like *Miss You*, *Start it up* and *It's only Rock 'n' Roll*. Now that he is over 40 years old, Mick Jagger seems to be calmer and more serious than he used to be in the early days of the Rolling Stones. He lives with the international model Jerry Hall, he has four children, and spends most of his time at one of his four homes – in London, Texas, New York and France.

Check!
1 What happened to Mick Jagger in: 1983? 1970? 1962? 1943?
2 Who is: Jerry Hall? Alexis Korner? Buddy Holly?

4

Now listen to this conversation:

Anne Do you want me to buy you a weekend ticket for the Folk Festival, Mike?
Mike Who's on this year?
Anne It's a really good line-up. There's . . .

Check!
1 Look at the list of musicians at the Cambridge Folk Festival. Which three does Anne tell Mike about?
2 Why doesn't Mike want to stay at the festival all weekend?
3 What day did Mike decide to go to the Folk Festival?
What date was this? (Look at the poster.)

3 The Different

Billy Bragg is 27. He is thin, with ginger hair and a large nose. He comes from Barking, a poor area of East London. He left school at 16 and bought a guitar. He did several different jobs, including petrol-pump attendant, bank messenger and record shop assistant. He even joined the British Army, but he soon had enough of that and left after 90 days. He released two LPs and an EP, *Between the Wars*. For several years he had a small number of fans, but then in 1985 he appeared on television. Since then he has become a cult figure, because his music and his personality are unusual. Many of his songs are simple love songs, but some of his material is political. *Between the Wars*, for example, has four tracks about topics like unemployment, war and industrial strikes. He supports the British Labour Party and in 1984 he played free concerts for the striking coal miners. He sings about subjects that are close to the heart of the people, and he wants people to listen to his songs and think about the words. Unlike many pop stars, Billy hasn't got an image and he isn't interested in fashion. His music is honest and simple – he believes in what he does.

Check!
True or False (√ or X)
1 Billy Bragg comes from East London. ☐
2 He enjoyed being a soldier. ☐
3 *Between the Wars* was the name of one of his LPs. ☐
4 Billy Bragg is a socialist. ☐

TWENTY-FIRST CAMBRIDGE FOLK FESTIVAL

PROMOTED BY CAMBRIDGE CITY COUNCIL AMENITIES AND RECREATION COMMITTEE SPONSORED BY GREENE KING
WEEKEND OF 26-27-28 JULY 1985   CHERRY HINTON HALL GROUNDS

THE CLANCY BROTHERS & TOMMY MAKEM	JOHN MARTYN	THE CHIEFTAINS	LOUDON WAINWRIGHT III
TOM RUSH	PAUL BRADY	LONNIE DONEGAN	VIN GARBUTT
THE BATTLEFIELD BAND	THE POGUES	BILL KEITH	BLUES REUNION :
THE DOONAN FAMILY	DIZ DISLEY & BIRELI LAGRENE	JIM ROONEY	SPENCER DAVIS
SHEP WOOLLEY	PYEWACKETT	MARK O'CONNOR	BRIAN AUGER
THE KIPPER FAMILY	JON BENNS	BUSKIN & BATTEAU	PETE YORK
ADRIAN LEGG	JOHNNY SILVO	BRIAN COOKMAN	COLIN HODGKINSON
		THE CROFTERS	MIKE WHELLANS
			ROVER BOY COMBO

SUBJECT TO CONTRACT AND WORK PERMITS   ADDITIONAL COMPERES TERRY STOODLEY & KEITH DAY

Language Focus

Like/want:

Do	you	want	me to	buy	you a ticket?
Would		like		get	

He	wants				
He	'd like	her	to	go	to the festival.
She	doesn't want	him		buy	a weekend ticket.

ORAL EXERCISE   *example:* What does he want her to do?/buy him a ticket.
          you: He wants her to buy him a ticket.

1 What do you want me to do?/buy me a ticket.
2 What would she like him to do?/go on Sunday.
3 What do they want him to do?/come to their party.
4 What does he want people to do?/listen to his songs.
5 What do you want me to sing?/one of your new songs.
6 When would you like me to come?/at the weekend.

Agreeing with statements and opinions:

Statement/Opinion			Agreement		
I	like / liked	the Rolling Stones.	So	do / did	I.
I	don't like / didn't like	all the queuing.	Neither	do / did	I.

ORAL EXERCISE   *example:* I don't want to go to the cinema.
          you: Neither do I.

1 I like getting up early.
2 I hate going to bed late.
3 I didn't enjoy the weekend at all.
4 I spent an awful lot of money.
5 I saw Jenny yesterday.
6 I didn't speak to her.

Enough:

I	haven't got	enough	time.
There	aren't	enough	bars.

She's	clever / young	enough	to know / to be	she has plenty of time. / Mick Jagger's daughter.

ORAL EXERCISE   *example:* He goes to the cinema on his own./old
          you: He's old enough to go to the cinema on his own.

1 She's going to university./clever
2 I'm running in the marathon./fit
3 My car holds six people./big
4 He's buying a Rolls Royce./rich
5 She's my grandmother./old
6 He's my son./young

---

rather:

I'd rather	come / not come	on Sunday.

SMALL TALK

Complaining in a shop

A Good morning. Can I help you?
B I hope so. I bought this record here yesterday, and it sounds awful.
A I'm sorry, there's nothing I can do. We don't change records.
B But it's scratched. I'd like you to change it or give me my money back, please.

Complain about: new jeans with hole in pocket; new shoes which let in water; a new book with missing pages

PRACTICE

1 You and your partner both work for Mr Frederick. He is away this week, but he has left you a list of things he wants you to do during the week.

Talk to your partner about what you have to do this week.

A He wants me to organise Thursday's meeting on Monday.
B What does he want me to do?
A He wants you to visit a new client in London.
B What about Tuesday?
A . . .

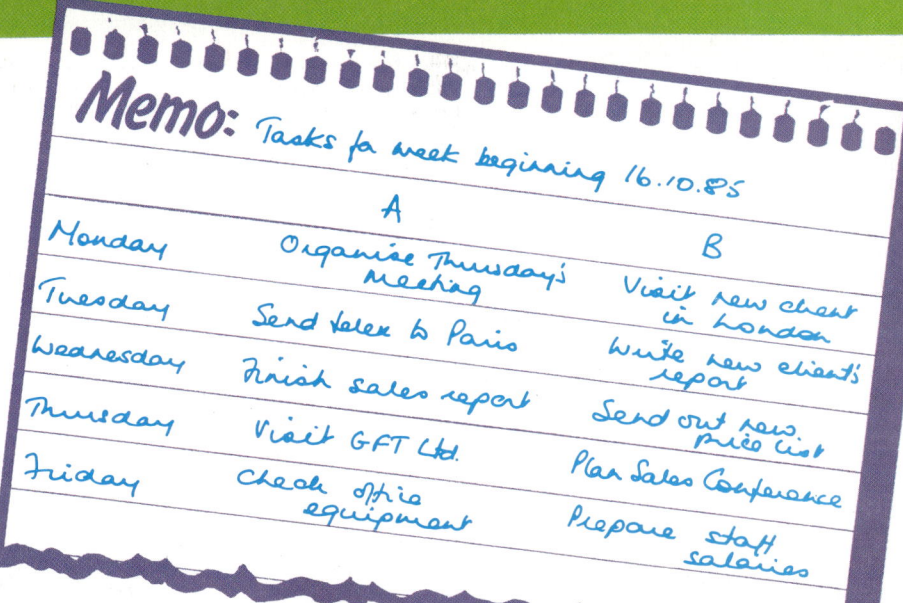

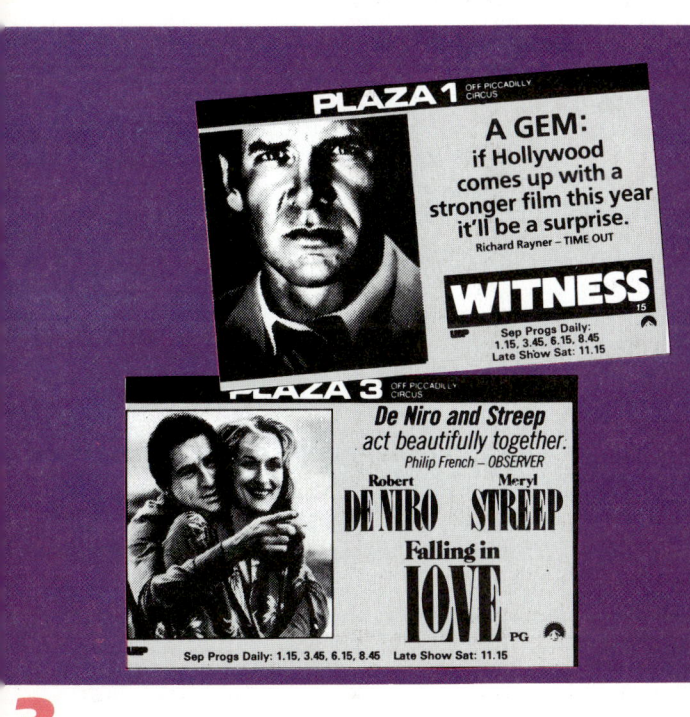

Memo: Tasks for week beginning 16.10.85

	A	B
Monday	Organise Thursday's Meeting	Visit new client in London
Tuesday	Send telex to Paris	Write new client's report
Wednesday	Finish sales report	Send out new price list
Thursday	Visit GFT Ltd.	Plan Sales Conference
Friday	Check office equipment	Prepare staff salaries

2 You are staying in London for a week. While you are there you want to see a film and go to a concert. Here are some of the choices.

Talk to your partner about your preferences. Decide which events to go to, the dates and the times. Use phrases like these.

I'd rather . . .
I'd rather not . . .
I prefer listening . . .
I'd prefer to . . .

3 Talk to your partner about the sorts of music you like or don't like. Tell your partner if you agree with his or her preferences, like this.

A I like pop music best.
B So do I. **or** I prefer jazz.
A I don't like classical music at all.
B Neither do I.
or Oh, I do.

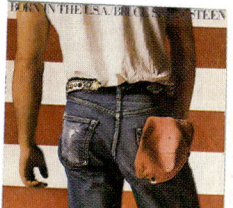

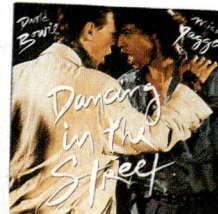

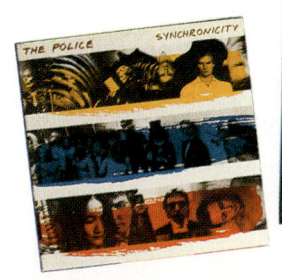

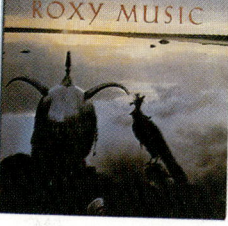

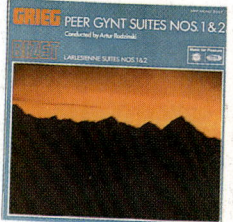

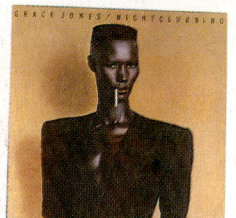

UNIT 15

PROJECT

FESTIVAL

Your class has decided to organise a weekend festival of music in your town to raise money for poor people in Africa.
Work in groups of 3 or 4

Stage One whole class together

Make decisions about:
- the type of music you want
- dates and times
- the audience you want to attract
- money – costs and profits

Use the *Festival Organisers' Checklist* to record your decisions.

Stage Two in groups

Now each group works on one part of the planning of the festival. Don't forget to use the Festival Checklist.

FESTIVAL ORGANISERS' CHECKLIST

Type of music

1. Pop ☐   Rock ☐   Reggae ☐
   Soul ☐   Heavy Metal ☐
2. Light music
3. Classical   Instrumental ☐   Operatic ☐
4. Jazz   Traditional ☐   Modern ☐
5. Folk   Traditional ☐   Contemporary ☐
6. Other kinds .... ☐ .... ☐
   .... ☐ .... ☐

Names of performers
....
....
....
....
....

Dates & Times

1. First choice of date ....../....../......
   Second choice of date ....../....../......
2. Times: Day 1 .... to ....   Day 2 .... to ....
   Day 3 .... to ....

Audience

Children ☐   Young people ☐   Middle-aged ☐   Elderly ☐

Cost: Your budget is £3000. You hope to make a profit of £10000
– for performers   ....% = £..............
– for publicity & promotion   ....% = £..............
– for T-shirts, souvenirs, etc.   ....% = £..............
– for venues   ....% = £..............

Make sure that all the organising groups have full details of these decisions before they start their final planning.

Group 1 — publicity

★ Share the jobs and consult other groups – 2 & 3

★ Design a poster, including details of dates, times, cost of tickets, star performers, main venues

★ Design a souvenir programme

★ Write a letter to possible advertisers in the town

Group 2 — programme of events

★ Share the jobs and consult other groups – 3 & 5

★ Plan a programme of events for the festival

★ Plan dates and times of concerts

★ Write a letter to the performers you want. Give them details of the festival and invite them to perform (free?)

FOR AFRICA

Group 3: venues

- Share jobs and consult other groups – 2
- Using a plan of your town, decide where to hold the festival events (e.g. Town Hall, park, college, etc.)
- Make a simple sketch plan of the school/college. Show on it where the festival venues are. This is for the souvenir programme
- Write a letter to the person in charge of the buildings, and ask to book the halls and rooms

Group 4: festival sales

- Share the jobs and consult other groups – 1 & 5
- Plan money-making festival spin-offs – e.g. badges, T-shirts, records, balloons, bags etc.
- Design these things, and plan where you are going to sell them. (Use a map of your town to think of good places.)
- Work out a price for each item
- Write a letter to local shops, asking them to sell some of these things for you

Group 5: promotion

- Share the jobs and consult other groups – 1, 2 & 3
- Write a preview of the festival for the local newspaper
- Write the script for a 30-second cassette for your local radio station
- !!Don't forget why you are organising the festival – for the poor people of Africa!!
- Write some small advertisements for local newspapers
- Plan a competition with free tickets for prizes

Stage Three whole class

Make a display of all the items you have designed and written.

All publicity material:
   logo, poster, programme, sketch map, badges, T-shirts, bags, balloons, adverts.

All written material:
   letters to advertisers, venues, local shopkeepers, performers etc.

UNIT 16 Radio Trent

PRESENTATION

1 🎧

Chris Hughes is the programme controller at Radio Trent, one of Nottingham's two local radio stations. Listen to what he says about the station.

Check! True or False (✓ or X)

1 Radio Trent is only for people who live in the city of Nottingham. ☐
2 Radio Trent has to make money. ☐
3 Most of Radio Trent's programmes are news programmes. ☐
4 Radio Trent never goes off the air. ☐

VOCABULARY

(to) reflect	to show, represent
surrounding	nearby, all around
profit	money from business/investment/interest on savings
shareholder	someone who puts money into a business to make more money
(to) broadcast	to send (programmes) by radio or TV

2 🎧

A recent survey asked people in the streets of Nottingham about Radio Trent. Listen to some typical answers.

Question 1 What do you like about Radio Trent?
Question 2 Have you any suggestions for improvements to Radio Trent's broadcasting?

3 Survey summary

Most people said they liked the local news programmes, but only about 50% said they liked the non-stop pop music. In fact several people said there should be other kinds of music. Nearly everyone said they listened to reports of local weather and traffic conditions, especially when they were driving around the city.

Perhaps most surprisingly, over 40% of the people said they never missed *Careline* – the daily phone-in programme about people's problems. In general most people said they liked programmes about local matters, and some suggested there ought to be more interviews with local personalities.

Check! Choose the right words from the list on the right to fill the gaps in these sentences.

1 Most people enjoyed listening to the _____ news programmes, and the weather and traffic _____ .
2 The _____ about people's problems is called _____ .
3 Some people wanted to hear more _____ music. They found pop music rather _____ .
4 A commercial radio station gets its money from _____ .

programme
local
classical
advertisements
reports
boring
Careline

Language Focus

Reporting what someone says:

Actual words:	'I like local news programmes.'
Reported:	He said he liked local news programmes.

Actual words:	'We never miss Careline.'
Reported:	They said they never missed Careline.

ORAL EXERCISE

example: 'I never listen to pop music.' (John)
you: John said he never listened to pop music.

1 'We often watch the late film on TV.'
2 'I listen to the news every morning.' (Sarah)
3 'I usually read the paper every morning.' (Dave)
4 'We always do our shopping on Friday evenings.'
5 'We never go to football matches these days.'
6 'I like listening to radio interviews.' (Sue)

Talking about obligations and responsibilities:

A local radio station	should	play classical music.
	ought to	make people feel important.

They	shouldn't	play too much pop music.
	ought not to	have advertisements so often.

ORAL EXERCISE

example: People drive too fast./(No)

you: People | shouldn't / ought not to | drive too fast.

1 People always wear seat belts in cars./(Yes)
2 Cyclists wear bright clothes at night./(Yes)
3 People drink and drive./(No)
4 People drive when they are tired./(No)
5 Pedestrians are very careful when there is a lot of traffic about./(Yes)
6 Children cross the road without looking./(No)

SMALL TALK

On the telephone

A Can I speak to Mr Lambert, please?
B Just a moment, please. I'll put you through to Mr Lambert.

A Can I speak to Jeremy, please?
B Jeremy? There's no one called Jeremy here. I'm afraid you've got the wrong number.
A Oh, I'm very sorry.

UNIT 16

PRACTICE

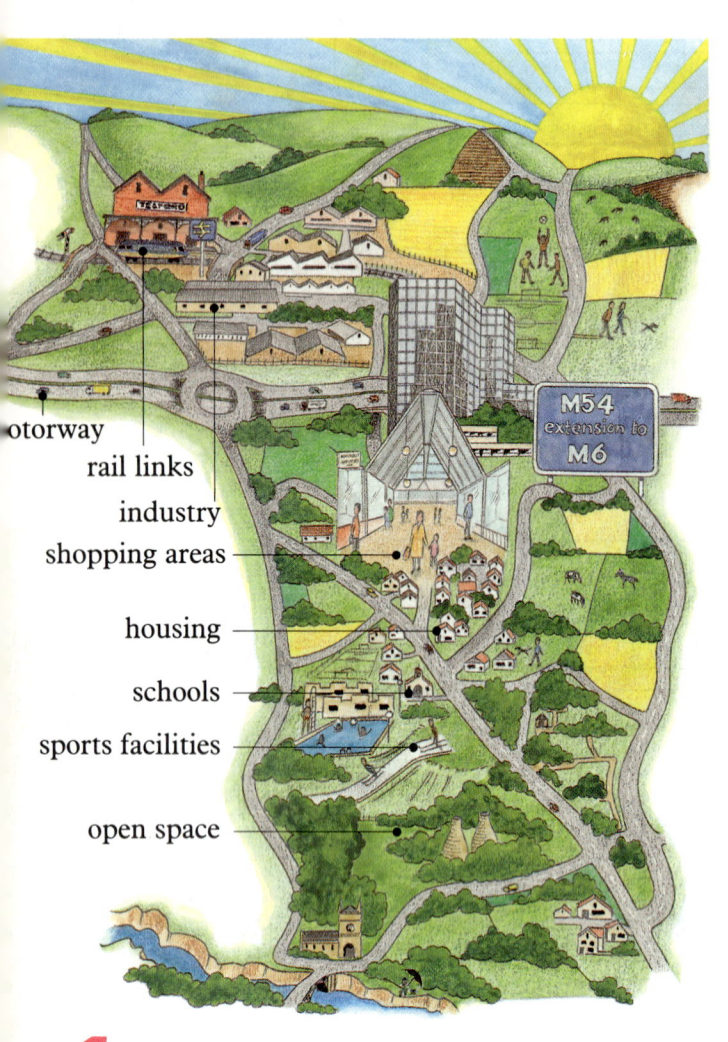

Map labels:
- motorway
- rail links
- industry
- shopping areas
- housing
- schools
- sports facilities
- open space

1 The ideal town: look at this picture and then make conversations with your partner, like this:

A What do you think shopping areas | should / ought to | be like?
B I think shopping areas should be free of traffic.
  or
  Cars should not drive through shopping areas.

IDEAS

Shopping areas –	no traffic/near bus station/few stairs/cafés
Factories –	not near housing or city centre/close to railways and motorways
Schools –	
Offices –	

2 You can also use **should** and **ought to** to give personal advice. Make conversations like this with your partner. (First match the problem with the place to go for help.)

A My tooth hurts.
B You | should / ought to | go to the dentist.

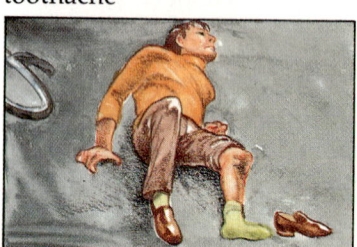

Problems:
- toothache
- broken leg
- stolen money
- burglary
- broken glasses
- sell house

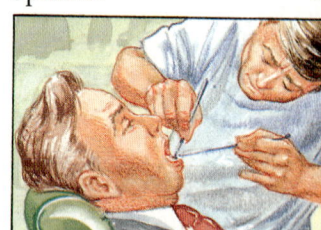

Places:
- police station
- optician
- dentist
- estate agent
- hospital
- policeman

99

3 Reporting a phone conversation. Work with a partner.

STUDENT A

You get this phone call from an old friend. He tells you all his news:

'Hi. It's Frank. . . . I'm back in England. I'm married now – my wife's name's Julie. We've got two children and we live on the outskirts of York. I teach in a large comprehensive school in the city. I really like being back in England again.'

Now answer your partner's questions about this phone conversation.

'He said his wife's name was Julie.'

STUDENT B

Your partner got a phone call from an old friend. You know Frank quite well and you are interested to hear all about him. Ask your partner questions about Frank.

- living – 'Where does he live now?'
- married?
- wife's name?
- children?
- work? – what kind?
  – where?
- feelings about being in England again?

TRANSFER

1 GROUPWORK
What do you expect from local and national newspapers? Discuss in groups of four.

- Write a list of essential features for a national or a local newspaper.
- Plan the contents of a 16-page newspaper for the town where you are a student.

100

UNIT 16

2

Living Debates are a regular feature in a popular British magazine. Readers give their opinions on important topical issues and these opinions are made into a survey. Here are the results of some recent debates:

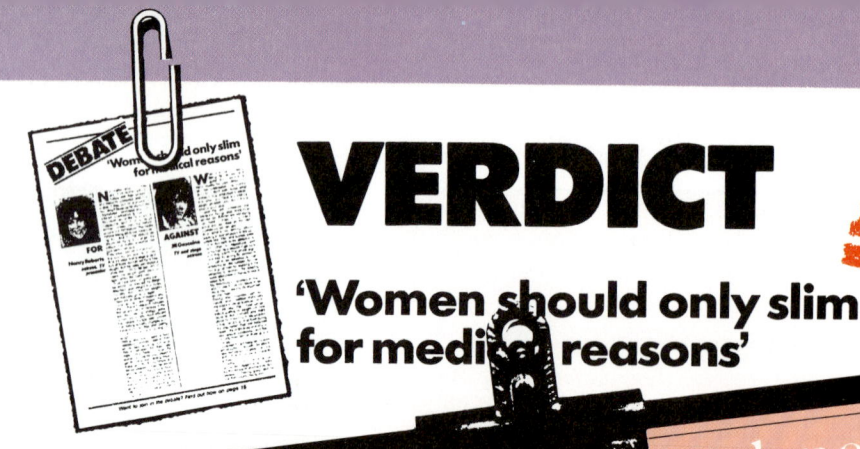

VERDICT NO

'Women should only slim for medical reasons'

Readers opinions

Issues	For	Against	Don't know
British pubs should stay open all day	65%	35%	—
Women should only slim for medical reasons	38%	58%	4%
Doctors should not let handicapped babies die	56%	42%	2%
Mothers of small children should not go to work	33%	59%	8%
Shops should not be open on Sundays	47%	56%	1%
Football hooligans should go to prison	76%	20%	4%
People should not smoke in buses or trains	59%	38%	3%

WRITING
Write sentences like this about people's attitudes.

33% of the readers said mothers of small children should not go out to work. Most people thought pubs ought to stay open all day.

DISCUSSION Work with a partner.
- Put the seven *Living Debates* issues in order of importance or seriousness.
- Discuss the rights and wrongs of the first two issues in your list.
- What do the figures tell you about British people's attitudes?

3 READING
Read this short text about *Careline*.

Careline celebrates first birthday

ONE year and nine thousand calls into its life and the **Radio Trent** Careline staff are still coming across new problems daily.

The Careline project was set up simply to help people. Whatever the problem, listeners to **Radio Trent** can ring the Careline on Nottingham 413121 and if the staff there can't help, they pass on the caller to someone who can.

It's not all serious business though. A church called in pleading for some top-soil in a hurry... the Careline got it thanks to one of their regular daily broadcasts on **Radio Trent**.

Another caller wanted to know how to blow up a million balloons... the Careline borrowed the necessary equipment.

One caller simply wanted to get rid of a two thousand pound organ to a good home. The Careline found one... the Nottingham Hospice. The Careline found a home for 36 unloved chickens, some fertile duck eggs for a broody duck and some sheep's milk for a baby suffering an allergy to cow's and goat's milk. And while the staff take the light-hearted calls in their stride, they are equally confident with queries about unemployment benefits, education courses and welfare rights.

Radio Trent's programme controller Chris Hughes, who dreamt up the Careline, said: "We felt there was a need for the kind of service the project offers. Quite frankly, we've been amazed at just how successful the Careline has been. The number of calls grows steadily, and we like to think it's just part of **Radio Trent's** job to help the community. With the Careline we can do just that."

Careline broadcasts at 10.30, 12.30, 15.30 and 23.30 each weekday.

Facts about *Careline*. Answer these questions.

1. When did *Careline* start?
2. Whose idea was it?
3. How many phone calls has the programme received?
4. What is the *Careline* telephone number?
5. When is *Careline* broadcast on Radio Trent?

Problems

1. What sorts of problems do *Careline* callers ask for help with?
2. Give some examples of one sort of problem.

Words Here are dictionary definitions of some words from the *Careline* text. Find the words.

1. a group of people working for one organisation (n.)
2. someone who makes telephone calls (n.)
3. (to) ask urgently (for something) (vi.)
4. not serious (adj.)
5. questions/enquiries (n.pl.)
6. all the people living in one place (n.)

SKILLS

🎧 LISTENING

Radio Trent is a commercial radio station. That means that its money comes from advertising. Listen to these radio advertisements and answer the questions.

1 Radio Trent

Which of these reasons do people give for liking Radio Trent?
- It's in stereo. ☐
- The travel news is useful. ☐
- It's easy to listen to. ☐
- It's local. ☐
- They play your records. ☐
- The presenters are friendly. ☐
- The music is good. ☐
- The news is interesting. ☐

Radio Trent broadcasts on these two wavelengths: _____ and _____ .

2 Music Concerts

a Who is presenting this series of concerts with Radio Trent?
b Fill in this concert ticket:

The Harry Beckett Quintet
presents an evening of modern jazz at
The Nightingale Hall University of Nottingham
Date .... Time .... Cost ....

3 Barry Austin clothes sale

a Where do you think this conversation takes place? on a bus ☐ in a pub ☐ in an office ☐
b Which of these clothes does Chris mention?
shirts ☐ trousers ☐ jeans ☐ pullovers ☐ shoes ☐ jackets ☐ suits ☐ raincoats ☐

4 David Sale, Estate Agent

a Make a list of the attractions of the house in Harrow Road, Woolaton.
b This house costs £ _____ .
c David Sale's telephone number is Nottingham _____ .

5 Fill in these advertisements.

NEW SERVICE
DAILY FROM EAST MIDLANDS AIRPORT
to ....
For further information
Telephone Derby ....

THIS WEEKS BARGAIN
Save £ .... on a new
LEC T241 Freezer
★ ★ ★
Now only £ ....
Delivery ....

mavericks
Open for Breakfast — every day
from .... to .... am
You can have:
....
Maverick's special ....
Hash brown
You can drink:
....
....
Where to find us
.... of Exchange Walk and
Wheelergate

6 SOUNDS

🎧 Listen to the cassette and repeat B's response to what A says:

- A The woman we saw at the theatre was Jane's mother.
- B I thóught she was.

B is pleased because he was right. Now listen and repeat B's response to what A says:

- A The woman we saw at the theatre wasn't Jane's mother.
- B I thought she wás.

This time B is disappointed because he was wrong.

Now listen to some more conversations. Put the stress on B's responses, and tick 'Pleased' or 'Disappointed'.

B's response	Pleased	Disappointed
1 I knew it was.		
2 I knew they didn't.		
3 I thought she did.		
4 I thought she did.		
5 I thought they were.		
6 I thought he was.		

Language Study 4

Talking about the past — Use the Past Continuous to talk about things happening in the past and continuing for some time:
- What were you doing at 3 o'clock yesterday?
- At 3 o'clock I was working in my office.

You can often use the Past Continuous and the Past Simple together in the same sentence:
- What were you doing when the telephone rang?
- When the phone rang, I was having a bath.

Use **used to** to talk about past routines – actions which often happened in the past, or were often true – when these actions no longer happen or are no longer true.
- Where did you use to live?
- We used to live in Bristol. I didn't use to earn much money.

Modal verbs — The Simple Past of the verbs **must** and **have to** is **had to**:
- Yesterday I had to work late.

The Simple Past of **can** is **could**:
- Last year I couldn't speak English.

Note The Simple Past of **be able to** is **was able to**.

Use **should** or **ought to** to talk about obligations or to give advice. They are very similar in meaning; **should** is usually for personal opinions:
- I think you should write to your brother.

ought to is sometimes for laws and rules; and for stronger opinions:
- That car ought to have its lights on.

Note Use **should not** as the negative of **ought** and **should**, it is more common than **ought not to**.

The '-ing' form and the Infinitive — Before you read this, check Language Study, Units 9–12, p. 77. Remember, you have to use the **-ing** form after some verbs:
- He misses living in London.
- Do you like living here?

And you have to use the Infinitive form after other verbs:
- I wanted to see you yesterday.
- She decided to buy a luxury flat.

But you can use the **-ing** form or the Infinitive form after some verbs; the meaning depends which of the two you use:
- I remember going to the bank. (*Meaning*: This event – my going to the bank – is still in my memory.)
- I remembered to go to the bank. (*Meaning*: I didn't forget the bank, and I went there.)

Note Other verbs which have two meanings like this: stop, remember, forget, try, prefer.

Want — Remember that the Infinitive form comes after want:
- I want to buy a ticket. (for myself)

If you want somebody else to do something for you:
- I want him to buy me a ticket.

Would like is the same:
- She'd like us to buy her a ticket.

Reporting somebody's words — When people speak, the actual words they use are called **direct speech**:
- 'I play in an orchestra.'

When somebody else reports a person's actual words, this is called **indirect** or **reported speech**:
- He said he played in an orchestra.

Note Notice how **play** changes to **played** in reported speech; this is because the reporting verb – **said** – is in the past.

Question Tags Use a negative question tag after a positive statement:
- It was a great party, wasn't it?
- You're learning English, aren't you?

Note The form of the question tag depends on the main verb:
- You smoke, don't you?
- He drove here, didn't he?

Some question tags ask real questions, which need an answer:
- You've got a new job, haven't you?
  - Yes, I have.
  - No, unfortunately not.

Some follow a statement and simply ask someone else to agree:
- He's got a new job, hasn't he?
  - Yes, he has.
  - No, he hasn't actually.

EXERCISES

THE PAST CONTINUOUS
- What were you doing last night at these times: 6 pm; 7 pm; 9 pm; 11 pm?
- Ask your partner what he/she was doing yesterday morning at: 6 am; 8 am; 11 am.
- What were you doing today when the teacher arrived?

USED TO
- Write three sentences about your life 5 years ago; start like this: 'Five years ago, I used to . . .'
- Write three more sentences in the negative: 'Five years ago, I didn't use to . . .'

MODAL VERBS

must/had to
- What did you have to do at school/home yesterday?

can/could
- Write six sentences about the things you 'could' or 'couldn't' do when you were 4 years old: eg 'I could walk, but I couldn't ride a bicycle.'

should/ought to
- What should people do to make your town a better place to live in? Start like this: 'They should . . .' or 'They ought to . . .'

-ING FORM & INFINITIVE

miss
- What do you miss about no longer being a child? (Write 4 sentences.)
- Now ask your partner.

decide
- Write a list of some of the things you have decided to do in the future.

remember
- Your earliest memories: write about some of the things you first remember doing as a child.
- Now ask your partner: 'Do you remember going to school for the first time?'
- You and your partner are going away for the weekend. Check that he/she has done everything. Ask like this: 'Have you remembered to lock the doors?'

WANT
- What do/did your parents want you to do when you leave/left school?
- Ask your partner what his/her parents want/wanted him/her to do.

REPORTED SPEECH
- Put this conversation into reported speech:
  A I hate waiting for buses.
  B Yes, I usually go to work by car.
  A I can't drive, so I have to get the bus.

QUESTION TAGS
- Add question tags to these sentences:
  'You've got a video, _____?'
  'He's very friendly, _____?'
  'They went out last night, _____?'
  'You've been to England, _____?'
- Now say these 4 sentences to yourself, as real questions, and then as statements.

104

UNIT 17 Arts and Entertainment

PRESENTATION

1 Nottingham is one of the few English cities which has spent its money on new facilities for the arts instead of office blocks. It has rebuilt the old theatre instead of closing it down. The Theatre Royal, which first opened in 1865, closed in 1969. Nottingham City Council bought it, and spent £5 million on rebuilding and enlarging it. It now seats 1,100 people.

Today it is part of the £17 million Royal Centre complex which includes a concert hall, a conference centre, a restaurant and several bars, in addition to the theatre. It is in the centre of the city, next to a car park – very convenient for the people who come by car from the towns and villages around Nottingham.

'This is a great city for the arts,' says the manager of the Theatre Royal, Charles O'Neill. 'We've been able to fill the theatre almost every night since we re-opened. A lot of the people who come to our shows travel from larger cities like Sheffield and Derby. They seem to like our varied programme.'

VOCABULARY
- facilities *public services (eg theatres, sports centres, transport, shopping centres, libraries)*
- to seat *have enough places or seats for*
- convenient *easy to get to, easy to use*

Check!

1. How is Nottingham different from many English cities?
2. How did the City Council improve the Old Theatre Royal?
3. What facilities are there in the Royal Centre?
4. Why is it surprising that people come from Sheffield and Derby to go to the Theatre Royal?

2

a) The Colchester Arts Centre is in St Mary's, which used to be a church, before it became a base for arts and entertainment in Colchester. The man who started the centre, director Michael Prochak, explains what goes on there.

b) Although a lot of people use the Arts Centre, it doesn't make a profit because it doesn't charge high prices for its events. It gets money from the government and from the local council, but this is not enough. It is likely that during the next few years arts centres all over the country will have serious financial problems. As Michael Prochak says, 'Unless we get more money, we won't be able to continue. If the government doesn't pay up, the centre will have to close.'

VOCABULARY
- community affairs *entertainment for the people who live in the town and the area (for example, a play about housing problems in Colchester).*
- resident *regular events which have their 'home' at the arts centre are resident.*

Check!

1. What did the Colchester Arts Centre building use to be?
2. What events are resident at the Arts Centre?
3. How often do these events take place?
   - The Alternative Cabaret
   - The Folk Club
   - The Jazz Club
4. Which of these types of music do not take place at the Arts Centre?
   classical, jazz, rock and roll, folk, ethnic, reggae

Language Summary

Relative pronouns: who, which

Specifying

Charles O'Neill is the man	who	organises the programme.
Nottingham is one of the cities	which	has spent money on the arts.

A lot of people	who	come to the theatre	travel from Sheffield.
The theatre	which	is in the High Street	opened in 1983.

ORAL EXERCISE example: There's the doctor. He works with children.
          you: There's the doctor who works with children.

1. There's the pilot. He flies Concorde to New York.
2. There's the Jazz Club. It opens next month.
3. We parked in the car park. It is near the Royal Centre.
4. We saw the actor. He is the star of the James Bond film.
5. There's the new theatre. It opened in 1969.
6. She has a lot of friends. They are unemployed.

Giving more information

Charles O'Neill,	who is 45,	manages the theatre.
The theatre,	which opened in 1865,	had to close in 1967.

ORAL EXERCISE example: His mother came to see us yesterday. She lives in London.
          you: His mother, who lives in London, came to see us yesterday.

1. His brother is coming at the weekend. He lives in Paris.
2. Sarah's friend won a fashion competition. She works in a museum.
3. The Arts Centre opened 2 years ago. It's in an old church.
4. My father sent me a postcard. He's on a business trip in Greece.
5. The car park holds 1,000 cars. It's just behind the theatre.
6. The tickets are on sale from Saturday. They cost £5 each.

Warnings and threats: unless/if . . . not

Unless	we get more money	we won't be able to continue.
	the government pays up	
If	we don't get more money,	we'll have to close.
	the government doesn't pay up,	

ORAL EXERCISE example: If you don't invite me, I won't come.
          you: Unless you invite me, I won't come.

1. If you don't work hard, you'll fail your exams.
2. If you don't go to bed early, you'll be tired in the morning.
3. If you don't apply for jobs, you won't find work.
4. If I don't pay them £2,000, I won't get my daughter back.
5. If she doesn't practise, she'll never learn to play the piano.
6. If he doesn't work hard, he'll lose his job.

Modals: Must and Can

Future with 'will'

The centre	will / won't	have to close down.	(must)
	will / won't	be able to continue	(can)

Present Perfect

We	have had to	enlarge the theatre.	(must)
	have been able to	fill all our seats.	(can)

ORAL EXERCISE example: We must be careful with our money. (Future)
          you: We'll have to be careful with our money.

1. We can't go on holiday this year. (Future)
2. He must work a lot harder. (Perfect)
3. She can't earn any more money. (Perfect)
4. They must send us a letter. (Future)
5. I can't buy any new records this month. (Future)
6. I must phone my parents (Perfect)

UNIT 17

SMALL TALK

Suggestions

A Shall we go to the theatre tonight?
B I think I'd rather go to a concert really.

A What about going to the Jazz Club tonight?
B That's funny, I was going to suggest that.

Talk to your partner about places to go to this evening.

PRACTICE

1
A What does an actor do?
B He's someone who works in the theatre.

Now talk about the other people and their jobs.

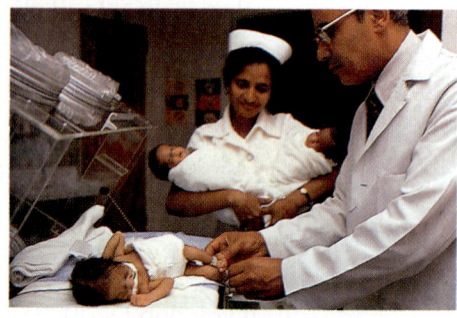

2 Read these short newspaper reports and then rewrite them in one sentence, like this:
example:

SIX FOR HUTCHINGS
Yesterday Martin Hutchings became the first man to score 6 goals in an English football match. Hutchings plays for Oxford City.

SIX FOR HUTCHINGS
Yesterday Martin Hutchings, who plays for Oxford City, became the first man to score 6 goals in an English football match.

100 miles an hour on M4
Mr P Jones was driving his blue Rolls Royce at over 100 miles an hour on the M4 motorway, when the police stopped him. Mr Jones is 38.

RICH AT 23
23-year-old Mrs Anne King has won this weeks star prize of £50,000. Mrs King lives in Broad Street, Nottingham.

Fog hits 707
A Boeing 707 had to make an emergency landing at Heathrow Airport this evening because of thick fog. The plane was on its way from Brussels to Dublin.

Bomb injures three
Three people are in hospital tonight after a bomb explosion in central London. They were all standing near the entrance to the station.

Thieves get away with Diamond
A gang of thieves broke into the Castle Museum in Queens Street late last night and stole the Windsor Diamond, and several valuable rings. The diamond is worth at least half a million pounds.

3 WARNINGS

Look at this picture. In each bubble someone is warning someone else. Turn these warnings into **unless** sentences and **if . . . not** sentences.

Speech bubbles:
- TIDY YOUR ROOM, OR YOU'LL LOSE YOUR POCKET MONEY!
- GET UP, OR YOU'LL GET NO BREAKFAST!
- TURN THAT MUSIC DOWN, OR I'LL CALL THE POLICE!
- STOP SEEING THAT WOMAN, OR I'LL LEAVE YOU!
- MOVE YOUR CAR, OR I'LL PHONE THE POLICE!
- PUT YOUR SEAT BELT ON, OR I'LL STOP THE CAR!

4 GIVING ADVICE

Work in pairs.

example: Paul I haven't got any money left.
You You'll have to go to the bank.

	PROBLEM	ADVICE
1 JANE	I FEEL TERRIBLE	DOCTOR
2 PETER	WE'VE GOT NO FOOD LEFT IN THE HOUSE.	SUPERMARKET
3 ROSEMARY	I'M WORKING TOO HARD. I'M TERRIBLY TIRED.	BED EARLY
4 JOHN	MY CAR'S BROKEN DOWN.	GARAGE
5 SUE	I'VE HAD AN ACCIDENT, I'VE CRASHED THE CAR	POLICE

5 LATER THAT DAY . . .

. . . somebody is asking about Jane, Peter, Rosemary, John and Sue. Answer their questions like this.

A Have you seen Paul?
B Yes, he's had to go to the bank.

Now say and write the answers to similar questions about the others.

6

Match these halves of conversations.

- Paul   I haven't got any money.
- Jane   I feel terrible.
- Helen My typewriter's broken.
- John   My car won't start.
- Peter We've got no food left in the house.

• You won't be able to drive to work, then.
• You won't be able to finish your letter, then.
• You won't be able to have any lunch then.
• You won't be able to buy anything, then.
• You won't be able to come to the party, then.

Now write sentences like this: Paul hasn't got any money, so he hasn't been able to buy anything.

108

UNIT 17

TRANSFER

1 Write as many facts as you can about these people. Now check these facts with your partner. Ask questions like this:

  Isn't Martina Navratilova the tennis player who won Wimbledon in 1984?

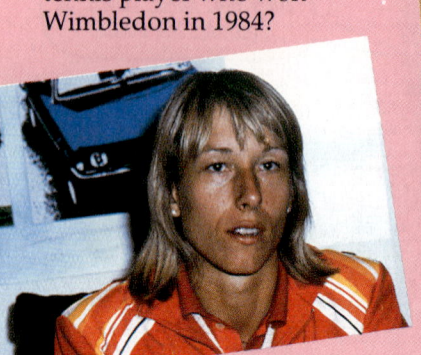

A FISTFUL OF DOLLARS

Rambo

CASABLANCA

E.T.

The Empire Strikes Back/Star Wars

THE GODFATHER

Butch Cassidy and the Sundance kid

2 Discuss these films with your partner. Ask each other questions like this:

  Isn't Casablanca one of the films which starred Ronald Reagan?

When you have agreed on several facts about each film write a list of 'Agreed Facts'.

3 Imagine yourself in the position of one of these people.
- the non-smoker in the train
- the cinema-goer who can't <u>see</u> or hear the film
- the driver who can't get his car out

Make up
- a polite request   (*Please will you . . .*)
- a command   (*Stop . . .*)
- a threat   (*Unless you . . .*)

Now have a conversation with your partner who is one of these people.
- the smoker in the train
- the cinema talker
- the driver of the parked car

SKILLS

1 READING
Questions
Is this text about:
sports / science / music & drama / universities?
Is it from: a newspaper / a poster / a tourist leaflet / a book?

Look quickly at this text but do not read all of it.

Skimming
Now read the text through quickly without using a dictionary, and find out:
- What sort of event the text is describing.
- Where King's Lynn is.

VOCABULARY
Match these words from the text with their meanings.

unique	historic, from the years 1100–1500
region	refreshing
medieval	there is only one like this, very special
steeped in history	full of things from the past
echoing	seem to get bigger as the music fills them
bracing	reminding you about
swell with the music	a part of the country, an area

DICTIONARY
Use your dictionary to check the meaning of these words:
countryside   puppet
seascape   contemporary
major

Comprehension
1. Where do the three most important East Anglian festivals take place?
2. What is special and attractive about East Anglian towns?
3. When do the festivals take place?
4. What sorts of music can you hear?
5. Do you think there are any foreign events?

Make a list of all the artistic events you can see or hear at these festivals.
Which of these activities do the three photographs relate to?

Writing
Describe arts festivals, or city festivals in your own town or region.
- What sort of festivals are there?
- When do they take place?
- Where are they?
- Who goes to them?
- What do people see at these festivals?
- Is there anything unique about them?

The Arts Festivals of East Anglia

During the summer months, visiting East Anglia is a unique experience. A region of medieval towns steeped in history, attractive small villages echoing a time long gone, beautiful open and rolling countryside, bracing and delightful seascapes. In June and July it bursts into activity during its three major arts festivals — Aldeburgh in Suffolk, Cambridge, and King's Lynn in Norfolk.

Cambridge Folk Festival
Aldeburgh Foundation at Otley Hall, Suffolk

The halls swell to the music, the streets come alive with folk music, dance and theatre; often a carnival atmosphere presides.

The choice is yours — music, theatre, dance, visual arts. From orchestral performance to folk singers, high drama to street theatre, Morris dancers to puppet shows, traditional to contemporary. Not everything is British, but it is all played with enthusiasm and style.

Front cover: Aldeburgh Festival performance at Framlingham Castle, Suffolk
Louis Clark, conductor of the Royal Philharmonic Orchestra

2 LISTENING
Michael Harris (called Harry by his friends) plays in a rock band. Listen to the first part of the tape once and try to find out:

a the name of the band he plays in.
b the name of the town where they play together.

Now listen to the second part and answer these questions.

c Has the band made a record?
d Do they have other jobs?
e How much money do they charge when they play?
f What would Harry like to do?
g How much does it cost to record a single?

Listen again to the second part of the tape and find the missing words in the conversation.

'We've all got . . . . . . jobs, which again poses a . . . . . . because we can't do . . . . . . too big, as we're all working . . . . . . Ideally what we'd . . . . . . to do is to get good . . . . . . to get rid of our daytime jobs, maybe . . . . . . get some money behind us for a . . . . . . perhaps, who knows?'

110

UNIT 18 Living in the city

PRESENTATION

1

SHELTON HOTEL OPENS CONFERENCE CENTRE

The Shelton Hotel will open its new conference centre next month. 'We've been working very hard on the new centre', says manager Neil Sinclair. 'We've been building an extension to the hotel, with a new restaurant and bigger meeting rooms. We are looking forward to the opening at the end of next month'.
The Shelton Hotel has been holding conferences in Nottingham for more than 20 years. Many companies now come to Nottingham for conferences that they used to hold in London.

Check!
1 What is new about the conference centre?
2 When will it open?

2

Reporter This is Mr & Mrs Leigh, who have been staying in this hotel for the last 6 months. Can you tell me why you've been living here for so long?
Couple We're homeless. We had to leave the flat that we were living in, because the landlord wanted to sell it. We've been looking for a flat or a council house for 6 months now.
Reporter And the council haven't found a house for you, have they?
Couple Well, they've been promising to find something for us, but nothing's happened. The council has been paying for this hotel, but it's not as good as a house of our own.

Check!
1 Why are Mr & Mrs Leigh living in a hotel?
2 Who is paying for the hotel?
3 What do Mr & Mrs Leigh want to do?
4 How long have they been homeless?

3

Mother Stuart always used to be such a good boy, but recently he's been behaving strangely. He's been drinking heavily, and coming home very late at night.
Father He's been fighting with his brothers and sisters, and he hasn't been going to school. He's been acting very aggressively.
Mother We haven't been strict enough with him, have we? We've always let him do what he wanted.
Father I think he's been taking drugs or something . . .

Check!
1 What is the problem with Stuart?
2 What has he NOT been doing?

4

Interviewer How long have you been studying here?
Sue Nearly 2 years – I'm in my second year now. I'm studying sociology, which is really interesting. I've been learning about how people live in other countries.
Interviewer What else have you been doing here, besides studying?
Sue I've joined a lot of student groups. I mean, you can't study all the time, can you? I wanted to get involved in something that was creative so I've been working with the University Theatre Group.
Interviewer Do you live on the campus?
Sue Most students live outside the university, and I used to have a flat in the town. Since the beginning of this year, though, I've been living in the university. It helps me a lot, because I can work in the theatre until late at night.

Check!
1 How long has Sue been studying at the university?
2 What is she studying?
3 Where did she used to live?
4 What does she do when she's not studying?

Language Focus

Present Perfect Continuous:

| What | have you been | doing here? |
| How long | | studying here? |

| We've | been | building | an extension to the hotel. |
| I've | | working | with the university theatre group. |

She's		studying		for nearly 2 years.
I've	been	living in the university	since	the beginning of the year.
The hotel has		holding conferences		about 1965.

| He hasn't | been | going to school. |
| We haven't | | wasting our time. |

ORAL EXERCISE   example: learn Spanish   2 years
                you: I've been learning Spanish for two years.

1 learn English/3 months   2 learn French/1984
3 play golf/1970   4 live in Canada/last 6 months
5 live in California/7 years   6 play football/1965

Relative pronouns: that:

| I like people | that | know how to tell stories. |
| The car | | won't start   is John's. |

You can leave out **'that'** *in sentences like these:*

| Companies come for conferences | (that) | they used to hold in London. |
| Most people | | I know love university life. |

ORAL EXERCISE   example: Look, there's the clock. You bought it.
                you: Look, there's the clock (that) you bought.

1 I've had a ride in the car. Mary just bought it.
2 I've just seen the man. You met him last weekend.
3 We really enjoyed the meal. Peter cooked it.
4 The photos are wonderful. You took them on holiday.
5 All the children are very intelligent. I teach them.
6 The letter arrived this morning. You wrote it on Friday.

Relative pronouns: when, where, why, whose:

We travel at night	when	there's not much traffic.
She showed me the street	where	her father lived.
I don't know the reason	why	we came to Nottingham.
That's the man	whose	house burned down last week.

Positive question tags:

You **can't** study all the time,	**can** you?
You **won't** forget to do that,	**will** you?
They **haven't** found you a house,	**have** they?
You **haven't** seen my pen,	**have** you?

ORAL EXERCISE   example: You won't forget her birthday.
                you: You **won't** forget her birthday, **will** you?

1 You shouldn't smoke.
2 They aren't coming to the wedding.
3 She can't swim.
4 We haven't got enough money.
5 Today isn't Sunday.
6 The film wasn't very good.

while/during:

| She worked very hard while she was at university. |
| He was a soldier during the war. |
| During the war he was a soldier. |

112

UNIT 18

SMALL TALK

Money

A I like your sweater – how much did it cost?
B It was quite cheap. I think it was around £10.

A How much would I need to get a car like yours?
B Oh, it would be about £4000, I imagine.

Ask your partner about things you want to buy.

PRACTICE

1 What have they been doing?

A What do you think he's been doing?
B I think he's been taking photographs.

"I STARTED WORK AT THE FACTORY WHEN I WAS 16. THAT WAS IN 1947."

"WE MOVED HERE IN 1976. THAT'S MORE THAN 10 YEARS AGO."

"I TOOK UP GOLF AT THE AGE OF 17, WHEN I LEFT SCHOOL."

2 Point to one of these people and talk to your partner, like this.

A How long has he been working at the factory?
B He's been working there | since he was 16.
                           | for about 40 years

Now write sentences about these people.

"I LEARNT TO DRIVE IN 1940."

"I GOT THIS JOB 6 YEARS AGO."

"I STARTED WORKING IN THE GARDEN AT 10 O'CLOCK THIS MORNING."

113

3
Finish these sentences using the right words

since   for   while   during

1. Her son disappeared _____ he was on a trip to Scotland.
2. I haven't seen him _____ February.
3. She has worked for us _____ 3 years.
4. _____ the day she looks after the children.
5. _____ the beginning of the year she's been living in London.
6. I prefer to read _____ the rest of the family watches TV.
7. _____ 3 years now we've been involved in the University Theatre Group.
8. They'll fix the roof _____ the summer months.

4
Fill in the gaps in the text, using the right word.

that   who   which

The man _____ lives next door told me an interesting story _____ he heard from his father. His father, _____ was a policeman, stopped a car _____ was driving too fast. He walked over to the righthand side of the car, to speak to the driver. He put his head through the window, _____ was open, and spoke to the man _____ was sitting there. He noticed that the man was drunk, and he asked him to get out of the car. He gave the man a breath test, _____ showed he was very drunk. 'You can't drive any more' said the policeman. 'But I'm not driving' said the man, _____ was now laughing at the situation. The policeman looked at the car, _____ was very new, and saw that the steering wheel was on the left, not the right. It was a foreign car _____ was on a trip to England, and the real driver was sitting quietly behind the steering wheel on the other side of the car.

5
REMINDERS
You are planning a shopping trip with your partner.
You want to make sure he/she doesn't forget the important things:

You haven't bought the milk,   have you?
You won't forget the milk,   will you?

Student A
- milk
- eggs
- butter
- potatoes
- sugar
- coke
- tissues
- bread
- bacon
- vegetables

Student B
- chilli beans
- beef
- onions
- green peppers
- tomatoes
- red wine
- spaghetti
- garlic
- rice
- chocolates

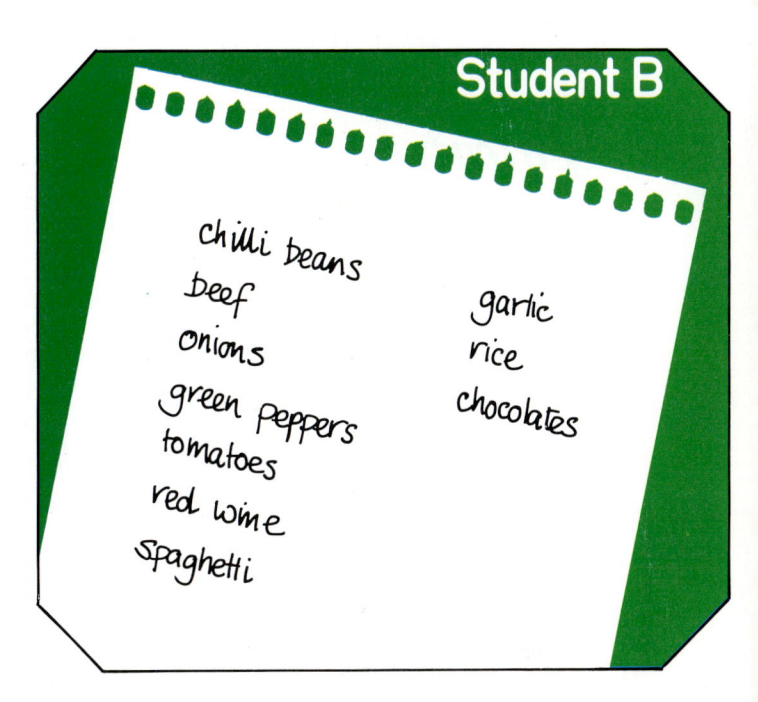

UNIT 18

TRANSFER

1 WHAT HAVE YOU BEEN DOING?

Imagine you have not seen your partner for 5 years. Find out what he/she has been doing since you last met. Ask about:

- where he/she lives
- his/her family (e.g. parents, brothers and sisters)
- life at school, college or work
- current interests (sports etc.)
- friends

2 WRITING

Now write about what your partner has been doing since your last meeting.

3 ROLE PLAY

STUDENT A
The person you share a flat with has gone away for a week's holiday. While he/she is away you have decided to make some changes and improvements to your flat.
Write notes about what you have been doing.
Example: *Redecorating the kitchen*
....

STUDENT B
You are away on holiday for a week. On the day before you return, you decide to telephone your flat-mate to find out what he/she has been doing while you've been away.
Ask questions like this:
Example: *What have you been doing? - mornings, afternoons, evenings*
....

Now make another conversation between one of these pairs of people.

Office manager
You have been looking after the office you work in, while your boss has been away on an overseas trip.
Tell him/her what has been happening and find out what he/she has been doing.

Managing director
You have just come back from a week's business trip abroad - to England. Now you are back, you want to know what has been going on at the office.
Find out from your office manager, and also report to him/her what you have been doing in England.

Parent
Your son/daughter has been away at college or university for 3 months. This weekend he/she has come home for a visit. Find out what he/she has been doing, and tell him/her all your news.

Student (son/daughter)
You have been away at college or university for 3 months. You go home for a weekend and want to find out what has been going on in your family. They are also interested, of course, to find out what you have been doing.

Student
You have been away from school or college for the last 3 weeks, with a mystery illness. You had to stay in bed for the first week. When you get back you meet your best friend. Find out what everyone's been doing during the last three weeks - and tell him/her how you have been spending your time.

Student
Your best friend has been away from school/college for the last 3 weeks. He/she has been ill. Find out what he/she has been doing at home, and tell him/her what has been happening while he/she has been away.

SKILLS

1 LISTENING

Kim is talking about her life in Nottingham, studying at Nottingham University. Listen to the first part of the tape, and find out:

a What she studied at the university.
b How many halls of residence the university has.

University Park

University Park is situated 2½ miles west of the City Centre, adjacent to the University Campus, and was provided in 1932 by the first Lord Trent, better known as Sir Jesse Boot.

The Park lies on both sides of University Boulevard. Included on the University site is a lake of 14 acres open for public boating during the summer months. The land to the south of University Boulevard provides playing fields for the University and the City. The park now affords attractive woodland and lakeside walks together with an impressive rhoddendron border and extensive floral displays. There is also a semi-adventure play area.

Listen to the first part again, and answer the questions.
1 What do the buildings look like?
2 Where can you go in boats?
3 What is the name for the buildings and land of the university?
4 What can you do in the evenings? Give two examples.
5 Where can you go for lovely walks?

Listen to the second part, and list all the *good* things Kim says you can find in Nottingham.

1 _____
2 _____
3 _____
4 _____
5 _____
6 _____
7 _____

Listen to the third part, and read what Kim is saying. Find the missing words, from the tape.

> You can't go to the _____ at 11 o'clock at night. I think – there are more _____ than disadvantages, because it's _____ a lot cheaper to live in Nottingham than London. The people in the _____, I still think, are friendlier, much more _____ than people in London. And I like the atmosphere of a Northern _____ Near to the Peak District of _____, near to Derbyshire, near to beautiful countryside.

Write down the missing words.

3 WRITING

a What have you been doing in the last 5 years? Describe your life.
b How long have you been learning English? Have you found it easy? What have you been learning to do?

2 SOUNDS

Listen to the cassette and repeat this sentence:

   He doesn't study all the time, does he?

The question tag doesn't ask a real question. The speaker is making a statement and expects agreement. Listen again and repeat this sentence:

   He doesn't study all the time, does he?

Here the question tag asks a real question. Listen and repeat these sentences and provide the right question tag, as a question (╱) and as a statement (╲).

1 They haven't found you a house, _____?
2 You haven't forgotten to post the letter, _____?
3 You don't drink very much, _____?
4 Jeff didn't miss the train, _____?
5 You aren't angry, _____?
6 Your parents haven't gone on holiday, _____?

116

UNIT 19 Britain and the USA

PRESENTATION

There are over 300,000 British immigrants in southern California. Not all of them are film stars like Joan Collins or rock stars like Rod Stewart.

Bill Parkinson

Bill Parkinson's life story is typical of the British in California. He left school at 15, with no qualifications. He was a cook in the Army, worked as a salesman and then as a waiter. 'I was a waiter in London. I woke up one morning, when it was raining and windy and cold, and I decided I'd rather be poor in warm weather. So I came to California and got a job in a bar in Los Angeles. A lot of the customers I got to know were English themselves. They all used to say that they missed English pubs. So I decided to open one'.

He opened the Charles Dickens in 1974 and has never lost money. He started with a small bar and then expanded into the empty shops next door.

'I've had the place extended several times, and we're going to get a new restaurant built next year, so we can have more people. There are more possibilities here. In England, you had to pay a lot more of your money to the government. At the end of the day, you had nothing left for yourself. Things don't seem so difficult here'.

Phyllis Barrow

Not all of the British in America have come from poor backgrounds. Phyllis Barrow has a more middle-class accent and would be perfectly at home in the richer suburbs of London. In Los Angeles, she organises a social club for the British away from home. They have bridge evenings, pub nights, and picnics on the Queen's birthday. She enjoys living in America, but it is clear that she still feels very English.

'Most of our friends are English – we usually keep to ourselves. I do things the way I always did them at home. We've not really become Americanised yet, although we feel different when we go back to England. But when I'm going to England, I say I'm going home. In England, I say I'm going back to the States. I still feel English, I suppose'.

Don Wallace

Don Wallace left school at the age of 13 and worked as a plumber. His wife, who comes from the same part of London as Don, used to be a shop assistant in Woolworth's. After 10 years working in London, and studying engineering in the evenings, Don moved to America. Now Don is Vice-President of a Californian computer company, and they live in a luxury house in Los Angeles. He works much harder than in England, and is at his desk by 6.30. 'At my last job, which was quite well-paid by British standards, I earned about £120 a week. Here, I earn over $100,000 a year. Of course, the cost of living is higher, but we can live a much better life.'

VOCABULARY
qualification	examination certificate, to help you get a job
to expand	to make something bigger (eg a business)
to extend	to make something bigger (eg a building)
background	a person's past, education, home and parents
bridge	a card game
plumber	person who repairs water systems, mends pipes and heating systems
standards	levels; ways of measuring something

Check!
1 What did Bill do before he came to the USA?
2 What was Don's first job?
3 Why did Bill open the Charles Dickens pub?
4 What does Phyllis think about England?
5 How does she help her British friends?

Language Focus

Getting things done:

I've / He's	had the place extended. / had the horses sent from England.
We're going to / In America you can	get a new restaurant built. / get pizzas delivered to your house.

ORAL EXERCISE *example:* Someone painted the house/have
  you: I had the house painted.

1 Someone painted the house/have
2 Someone repaired my car/get
3 A builder fixed my roof/have
4 A friend cut my hair/get
5 A shop sent me some English sausages/have
6 Someone changed my telephone number/get

Reported speech – instructions:

My friends told me / I'll tell him	to	forget the idea. / write to you this evening.

ORAL EXERCISE *example:* She said 'Please take the car to the garage.'
  you: She told me to take the car to the garage.

1 He said 'Please book me a seat on the flight to Rome.'
2 They'll say 'Get us two tickets for the opera.'
3 We said to them 'Find us a new flat.'
4 You said to us 'Phone me at 9.30.'
5 She said 'Collect the car at 5 o'clock.'

Reported speech – information:

She said to me	that	she didn't like my brother.
They told him	(that)	they really liked English beer.

ORAL EXERCISE *example:* She said 'I really like your sister.'
  you: She told me she really liked my sister.

1 He said 'I went to London at the weekend.'
2 They said 'We enjoy living in New York.'
3 I said to him 'I work for IBM.'
4 He said to her 'I'm bored with my job.'
5 We said to them 'The shops close at 5.30.'

Reported speech – requests:

They / He	asked	me / her	to	open an English pub. / marry him.

ORAL EXERCISE *example:* 'Will you marry me?' he asked her.
  you: He asked her to marry him.

1 'Could you lend me five pounds?' (she asked me)
2 'Will you turn the television on?' (he asked his father)
3 'Would you post a letter for me?' (I asked my friend)
4 'Can you find the newspaper?' (you asked me)
5 'Would you like to come to my party?' (I asked her)

Still & yet:

We're not Americanised yet. = We're still not Americanised.
I still feel English. = I don't feel American yet.

SMALL TALK

Asking for help with words.

A What's the British word for fender?
B I think it's bumper, but you'll have to check it.

A How do you say 'escuela' in English?
B It's 'school', isn't it?

Ask your partner to help you with some words in your own language – ask what the English word is.

American spelling

UK	USA
labour	labor
colour	color
centre	center
theatre	theater
programme	program
travelled	traveled
travelling	traveling
night	nite (not in correct writing)
through	thru (not in correct writing)

118

UNIT 19

PRACTICE

1 You are preparing for a long trip. You are taking your car to the garage for a service. These are things you must get done before you go. Talk to your partner like this.

A What are you going to have done?
B I'm going to get the car washed.

☆ **Check**
1 tyres
2 battery
3 brakes
4 steering

☆ **Fit**
5 new light bulbs
6 rear seat belts
7 wing mirrors

☆ **Change**
8 oil
9 water

☆ **Repair**
10 exhaust pipe
11 radio
12 speedometer

2 Vocabulary

These lists of British and American words are incomplete. Use a dictionary to find the missing words.

UK	USA
holiday	....
....	store
toilet	....
....	parking lot
aubergine	....
....	check (in a restaurant)

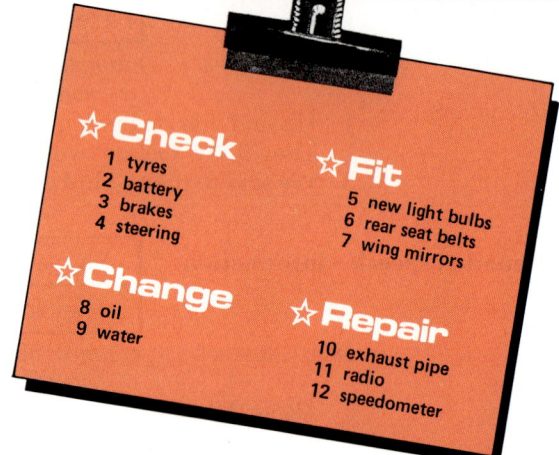

3 The new manager of this company decides to modernise his office.

Talk to your partner about the changes.

A Look at the desks!
B Yes, he's had the old desks replaced with new ones.

Here are some useful verbs:

repaint
redecorate
repair
mend
clean
tidy
knock down
fit
change
replace
take out
put in

4 Imagine your partner was the person who did all the work of modernising this office.

- A What did Mr Steel tell you to do about the desks?
- B He told me to replace them with new ones.

Now talk about the other office changes.

5 You started work in this office yesterday. Things are very busy. One evening 10 minutes before you are due to go home, everyone asks you something at the same time. What did they ask you to do?
Say and then write sentences like this:

'Someone asked me to phone the bank.'
'Then someone else asked . . .'

TRANSFER

1 Look at this photograph of a run-down part of an old industrial city. Discuss with your partners what the city council should do to improve this environment for the people who live there.

   They should have the houses repaired.

Write a list of the 10 most important changes you have discussed.

120

UNIT 19

Report on conditions of school/college

We want to have the walls repainted.
We want to have the central heating repaired.

2 WRITING

Write a report suggesting what you want to have done to modernise or improve your school or college.
Write from the point of view of a representative of your class or group. Start your report like the one here.

Think about classroom, sporting and leisure facilities; the timetable, school subjects.

3 SOUNDS

Listen to the cassette and repeat this sentence:

The man who manages the theatre is retiring next month.

This tells us 'which' man we are discussing.
Listen again and repeat this sentence:

Mr James, who manages the theatre, is retiring next month.

This doesn't tell us 'which man' (we already know). It simply tells us something extra about Mr James.
Now listen to the cassette and repeat these sentences.
Add commas if they are necessary.

1 Nottingham which is in the Midlands is a large city.
2 The people who live there think it's a wonderful place.
3 Many of the tourists who visit the city are from abroad.
4 Judy Kingston who works in the library came to Nottingham in 1979.
5 Radio Trent which is a local radio station broadcasts from Nottingham.
6 One of the men who runs Radio Trent is called Chris Hughes.

SKILLS

1 LISTENING

Anita is talking about life in America. She is describing what people do on national holidays.

Listen to the first part of the cassette.
1 Which special day is she talking about?
2 What year did this celebration start?

Listen again, and answer the questions.
3 Which people always have the day off work?
4 When do the children finish school?

Listen to the second part.
5 What do people eat on July 4th?
6 Where do they eat?
7 What do they go and see in the evening?

Listen to the third part of the cassette, about Thanksgiving Day.
8 When is Thanksgiving?
9 What do people do on this day?
10 List three things that they eat on this day.

Listen to the third part again, and try to find the missing words.

'Thanksgiving is celebrated in _____. It's always on the _____ Thursday of the month. This day we celebrate the _____ of the harvest season. It started when the first _____ came from Europe to live in America, and _____ their first harvest they got _____ with the American Indians, who _____ them with their harvest, and had a big _____ together.'

2 READING

Americans are good at many things, but making beer is not one of them. American beer is fizzy, weak and doesn't have much taste. But finally the British are helping out. For the past twelve months, Richard Wrigley, an English businessman, has been producing 'real ale' in the heart of New York. The New Yorkers love it and have been filling Richard Wrigley's bar ever since it opened.

The beer is made by a British brewer, using British ingredients and British brewing equipment – only the water is American. Mark Witty, who comes from Yorkshire, studied brewing in Scotland and now produces 1500 gallons of real ale every week.

The beer from the Manhattan Brewery doesn't have to travel very far. Customers at the bar downstairs in the Brewery drink all the beer produced.

Wrigley borrowed $2 million to start the Brewery, which is an old power station in the middle of Manhattan. He has created an international atmosphere, a mixture of the old English pub – with English food, American drinking hours, and the feeling of a German bier-keller. Now he wants to expand. He is planning to produce more beer and sell it to other bars in New York and in the area.

QUESTION
In what way is the bar of the Manhattan Brewery 'international'?

Questions   Answer with a number
1   How long has Richard Wrigley been making beer in Manhattan?
2   How many gallons does he produce per week?
3   How much money did Wrigley borrow to start the brewery?

Check!
True or false? (√ or X)
1   Richard Wrigley is English.
2   Mark Witty is Scottish.
3   The bar of the Brewery serves American food.

VOCABULARY
fizzy   *with gas, sparkling like lemonade or champagne*
real ale   *old-fashioned, traditional British beer*
gallon   *British measurement (1 gallon is about 4½ litres)*

Words
1   Here are the definitions of some words from the text. Find the words.
a)   all the things that go into the making of something – usually food and drink
b)   watery, not strong
c)   someone who makes beer
d)   the place where they make beer
e)   people who buy things in shops, restaurants or bars.

Pronouns   What do these pronouns from the text refer to?
example: 'making beer isn't one of *them*'
them = the things that the Americans are good at.
a)   New Yorkers love *it*
b)   . . . ever since *it* opened
c)   . . . *which* is an old power station
d)   Mark Witty, *who* comes from . . .
e)   . . . beer and sell *it* in other bars

3

Rewrite these sentences and phrases. Put them into your own words to show you understand the meaning.
a)   The British are helping out.
b)   British brewing equipment.
c)   The beer . . . doesn't have to travel very far.
d)   He has created an international atmosphere.
e)   Now he wants to expand.

UNIT 20 Magazines

PRESENTATION

1

In Britain there are thousands of different magazines on sale – some weekly, some monthly. Last year, people in Britain bought several hundred million magazines, from shops and street stalls. Many people have them delivered to their door by the local newsagent. In addition to the many general magazines, there are also the specialist magazines about computers, babies, hairstyles, weddings, the home, motorcycles, music and so on; the list is endless. And magazine readers are just as varied, ranging from children buying comics, to adults buying magazines which tell them how to improve their homes; and from grandmothers buying knitting magazines, to teenagers reading the pop music papers. Although a lot of people are short of money these days, magazine publishing is a growing business. A recent report by market researchers said that people were spending more money on leisure and entertainment, because they had more free time than ever before.

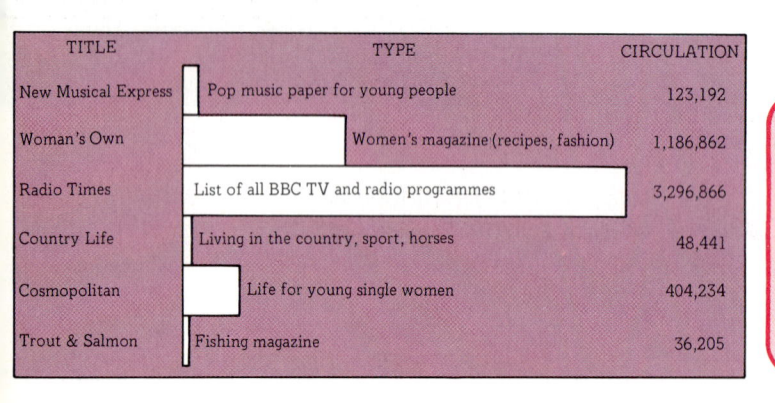

VOCABULARY

to deliver	to bring (usually to a house)
in addition	also, what is more
general	about many different subjects
specialist	about one subject
varied	different (interesting)
leisure	free (spare) time / non-working time
circulation	the number of copies of a magazine sold each week
trout / salmon	two kinds of river fish

TITLE	TYPE	CIRCULATION
New Musical Express	Pop music paper for young people	123,192
Woman's Own	Women's magazine (recipes, fashion)	1,186,862
Radio Times	List of all BBC TV and radio programmes	3,296,866
Country Life	Living in the country, sport, horses	48,441
Cosmopolitan	Life for young single women	404,234
Trout & Salmon	Fishing magazine	36,205

Check!

1. Why is it surprising that magazine sales are going up?
2. What is the circulation of Woman's Own?
3. What sort of people read Cosmopolitan?
4. How many magazines did people buy in Britain last year?

2 A day in the life of a magazine journalist

Joanna Denham is the editor of a weekly magazine for young women: LIFESTYLE. It started only a few years ago, but already it is one of the biggest-selling magazines for the 17–25 year-old age group. Ms Denham is a dynamic, energetic woman who takes her work very seriously. Although her job leaves her very little free time, she was able to spare a few minutes to tell us about her busy life as the editor of Lifestyle:

'My alarm usually goes off early, at about 6.30, although I'm not a morning person. I actually prefer to stay up late at night, but not when I'm working the next day. Yesterday was fairly typical.'

VOCABULARY

age group	group of people of about the same age
dynamic	full of energy and new ideas
to make contact	to meet, get to know
media	newspapers, television, radio

Check!

1. What is Joanna's favourite time of day?
2. Why does she like to start work early?
3. What did she do yesterday between 9 and 10.30?
4. How long did the editor's meeting last?

Language Focus

Word Order: Always, usually, sometimes, never:

My alarm		goes off early.
I	never	get up later than 7 o'clock.
I don't	usually	get up before 6 o'clock.

Time phrases:

| Last year | people bought hundreds of millions of magazines. |
| In the afternoon | I read several new articles. |

| People bought hundreds of millions of magazines | last year. |
| My secretary came in | at nine o'clock. |

ORAL EXERCISE   *example:* She works on Sundays/often
           you: She often works on Sundays.

1 She works on Sundays/often
2 I started work at the factory/2 years ago
3 The London train leaves/at 10 o'clock
4 Most people leave their houses unlocked/never
5 I bought three magazines/at the weekend
6 The film we saw started at 8/yesterday

Although:

| Although | a lot of people are poor, magazine publishing is a growing business. |
| | her job leaves her no free time, she talked to us about her work. |

| My day started at 8 o'clock | although | the office doesn't open until 9 o'clock |
| I enjoy writing | | my teachers used to say I was terrible at English |

ORAL EXERCISE   *example:* She gets up early. She's not a morning person.
           you: She gets up early although she's not a morning person.
           or: Although she's not a morning person, she gets up early.

1 People buy a lot of magazines. They haven't got much money.
2 I get to work at 8 o'clock. The office doesn't open until 9.
3 She enjoys her job. She has to work very hard.
4 'LIFESTYLE' has a large circulation. It started only 2 years ago.
5 He's very rich. He's only 21.
6 I usually go to work by bus. I actually prefer to walk.

Reporting what people say:

Actual Words	Reported Speech
'You're terrible at English'.	My teachers said **I was** terrible at English.
'People **are spending** more money on magazines'.	A report said that people **were spending** more money on magazines.

ORAL EXERCISE   *example:* People have more free time now/they
           you: They said that people had more free time now.

1 It's raining outside/she
2 He has got a new job in London/they
3 I have just bought a new car/Alan
4 They are having a party tonight/she
5 I don't like red wine/Susan
6 We are getting married next week/we

SMALL TALK

Hobbies & Interests

A Do you have any hobbies?
B Well, I'm quite keen on gardening.

A What sort of thing do you do in your spare time?
B I go to jazz concerts. I'm particularly interested in modern jazz.

Talk to your partners – find out what their hobbies are. Explain your own. Say what you're interested in – eg jazz/squash/French cooking/Cubism.

UNIT 20

PRACTICE

1 Talk to your partner like this.
   A Last October Alan Baxter visited Spain.
   B What did he do there?
   A He talked to top bullfighters.

Now write about where Alan Baxter went and what he did there.

October
Arena of death
Our International Reporter, Alan Baxter, visits Spain and meets the top Bullfighters.

To some people, it is the ancient duel of man against beast, to others it is a cruel and useless torture. Nothing excites the emotions more than bullfighting. I went to Madrid, to the famous Plaza de Toros, the bullring, and spoke to the men who risk their

November
New voice in the Kremlin
Alan Baxter flies to Moscow to interview the new Soviet leader.

On an icy morning in Moscow we drove along the broad streets towards Red Square. The people out shopping were dressed as usual in heavy, black overcoats to keep out the cold. But as I discovered when I met the Russian leader there is a new

December
Aussie Xmas
International Reporter, Alan Baxter, flew to Sydney to spend Christmas in Australia.

It's Christmas Day but I'm not sitting in front of a blazing fire. It isn't snowing. I'm sitting on the beach, the temperature is 30°, the sun is shining. People are swimming and surfing. It doesn't feel like Christmas Day, but pe-

January
Going north of the border
Alan Baxter travels to Texas and meets the families who leave Mexico looking for a new life in the USA.

Every day families arrive at the border between Mexico and the United States. They bring their cars, their furniture and the money they have saved. They want to live in America. I talked to

February
Good Morning Mr President
The American President gives an exclusive interview to our reporter, Alan Baxter.

The President is one of the most powerful men in the world. He makes decisions that affect all our lives. But what is he really like? Today I went to the White House and talked to the leader

March
Life at the South Pole
Our international Reporter, Alan Baxter, travels to Antarctica to meet the men who live and work at the South Pole.

Over 75 years ago, men first reached the South Pole. Now a group of scientists live there all year, working in temperatures of −40°. I spent a week in their

2 Here are notes from the first drafts of Alan Baxter's six international reports. Use these notes to write his first sentences.

example: I really enjoy travelling all over the world. I get very tired.
first sentence: Although I get very tired, I really enjoy travelling all over the world.

- I can't say I agree with bullfighting. The bullfighters I spoke to were fascinating people.
- I was quite nervous when I walked into the Kremlin. I've been interviewing the world's leaders for 10 years.
- I couldn't imagine what Christmas in Australia would be like. I've heard stories about people eating Christmas dinner on the beach.
- I've never understood the problems of immigrants in the USA. I've seen several programmes about immigration on TV.
- I've never been inside the White House before. I've interviewed three American Presidents.
- There are a lot of experiments to do at the Pole. I often get bored.

3 Which of the people Baxter spoke to in his October–March reports said these things:

"We can't get jobs, so we're moving to New York."

"Last year I killed thirty bulls."

"It's very dangerous living here because of the extreme cold."

"My wife's making the White House into a real home."

"We open our presents and then we go for a swim."

"We're modernising Russia as quickly as we can."

Baxter includes these quotations in his articles, but in Reported Speech, like this.

The Mexican immigrants said they couldn't get jobs, so they were moving to New York.

Now write the other quotations in reported speech.

PROJECT

Introduction
Your class/group is starting a new magazine for people in your school/college/office/workplace. The title of the magazine at the moment is *CHOICES*, but you can change this if you like. You must decide what sort of publication this will be, design publicity material and then write the 'preview' issue.

PROJECT TASK 1

Make basic decisions about:
- the contents of the magazine.
- the type of readers you want.
- the image of the magazine.

Use this Planning Checklist to record your decisions. Some decisions have already been made.

Discuss your ideas. Before you go on to Task 2, make sure everyone knows about the basic decisions.
Question
Are you happy with the name *CHOICES*?

MAGAZINE CHECKLIST

Contents:
1 News ✓
  - 1.1 School/college/workplace
  - 1.2 Town/Region
  - 1.3 National
  - 1.4 International
2 Opinions ✓
  - 2.1 Your own
  - 2.2 Readers'
  - 2.3 Famous people's
3 Public Information
4 Advertising ✓
5 Readers' Letters

Subjects of News and Opinions:
6 Current affairs (politics etc.)
7 People in the news
8 Fashion ✓
9 Arts and entertainment ✓
10 Sport ✓
11 Education
12 Health
13 Subjects NOT to write about ....

Readers:
14 Men   15 Women   16 Everyone
17 Age group: 14–16   17–20   21–30   30+

Image:
18 Expensive (colour)   19 Cheap (Black & White)
20 Tone: Serious   Fun   Mixture of serious & fun

PROJECT TASK 2 PUBLICITY

Now it is time to produce publicity material to let people know what *CHOICES* is all about. Tell them about its contents, why it is different and who it is for.

Group Tasks

- **Group 1** • Write a simple handout for your school/college/workplace.
- **Group 2** • Write a short report for the local newspaper.
- **Group 3** • Write some short advertisements to go into local newspapers and magazines.
- **Group 4** • Design and produce an idea for a poster to show the image of *CHOICES*.
- **Group 5** • Write the script for a 20-second advertisement on your local commercial radio station.
- **Group 6** • Write short profiles of some of the people who will write articles in *CHOICES*.

UNIT 20

PROJECT TASK 3 WRITING THE PREVIEW ISSUE

Each group should choose one of the departments: News, Fashion, Arts and Entertainment, Sport, Advertising. Other groups can write about extra subjects. (Look back to your decisions from **TASK 1**.)

GROUP A NEWSDESK

Many magazines avoid writing about news and current affairs. The news page is one of the things that makes *CHOICES* different.

- Decide which news stories to write about. Talk about local, national and international news. Look at today's newspapers.
- Decide how important each story is. The more important the story, the longer it should be.
- Each group member writes ONE story. Share out the stories.
  Remember – Write an interesting headline.
  – Give people's names and ages in the stories.
  – Use 'actual words' or 'reported speech'.
  – Write the story in short sentences.

*Don't forget who your readers are. Write what will interest them.

GROUP B FASHION DEPARTMENT

CHOICES wants to keep readers up-to-date with latest fashion trends.

- Decide what kinds of fashion to write about (for example: hairstyles, clothes and shoes, jewellery). For famous people? For men? For women? Fashions from other countries? Think about fashions for different occasions (eg work/parties).
- Plan the contents of the page. You can include interviews, descriptions, advice to readers, small items – lists of new ideas with prices.
- Each group member writes ONE article. Share out the articles.
  Remember – Write interesting headlines.
  – Write in short sentences.
  – Use people's words or reported speech.
  – Think about illustrations.

If one of the group is a good artist, get him/her to illustrate the articles.

*Don't forget who your readers are. Write what will interest them.

news
Philippines and the US

IN THE months ahead the major foreign policy crisis facing the US in the Third World is likely to be in America's only former colony: The administration is enmeshed in a deepening crisis there and believe that the coming presidential elections can restore democracy and stability, thereby protecting economic interests. The election, at the end of this month is portrayed by the media as a clash between good and evil. The people's army are preparing for the election too but not with democratic argument, but with the gun.

fashion
Summer in Paris

"I MUST admit I'm starting to panic now. I've got a friend in Paris who says there might be some there, but its pretty desperate." Keith Rylatt is understandably worried. The very last pair of original, red tag, button fly, shrink-to-fit, "Double X" denim Levi 501s with the all-important red stitching on the outside seam, came off the production line in San Francisco in March. The ultimate icon of a revered style has finally become history in the America that Gloria Vanderbilt made famous. It would seem that the only chance of finding a pair in Europe is to head for Paris

★B&B★
FASHIONS
Fashions for all your needs
Credit available
Drop in and see us
21 High Street
Maidstone Kent
(0622-1841622)

PROJECT TASK 4

Make a classroom display of the writing you have done: on the wall or on large sheets of paper with drawings and photographs from other magazines?
Make sure everyone in the class can see everything from all the groups.
Why not write magazines like this again – once or twice a term?

GROUP C ARTS & ENTERTAINMENT

CHOICES is for people in your school/college/workplace, so write about *local* events. Of course you can review national events too.

- Decide what kinds of arts and entertainments you want to write about (for example: live events, records, books, films, TV).
- Plan the contents of the page. You can include reviews, previews, interviews, profiles of famous people, news stories etc. You can also include facts and opinions.
- Each group member writes ONE article. Share out the articles.

Remember: – Write about what *you* have seen, read or heard recently.
– Give facts and opinions; you can write good or bad reviews.
– Write in short sentences.
– You can include more than one item in your article (eg review 2 or 3 books, films or records).

*Don't forget who your readers are. Write what will interest them.

GROUP D SPORTS DESK

- Decide what kind of sports you want to write about. For example:
  Team sports: football, basketball, etc.
  Individual sports: athletics, tennis, golf, skiing etc.
- Decide what type of sport you want to write about: local, national, international.
- Plan the contents of the page. You can include previews and reports of games, interviews with sports people, sports techniques, profiles of stars, tables of results.
- Each group member writes *one* article. Share out articles.

Remember: – Write about something recent that *you* know about.
– Write interesting headlines.
– Write in short sentences.
– Give facts and opinions – make sure that the facts are correct.

*Don't forget who your readers are. Write what will interest them.

GROUP E ADVERTISING

Advertisements help to pay for *CHOICES*. You cannot do without them. Your job is to write the advertisements.

- Decide what kinds of adverts will be in *CHOICES*. Think about the contents of the other pages. Decide on 5 or 6 products.
- Look at the style and content of adverts in other magazines and newspapers. Which adverts do you like and why? Discuss in your group.
- Plan where to put your adverts. (For example: adverts for a watch or for shampoo are best on the Fashion page.)
- Each member of the group writes *one or two* adverts. Share out the adverts.

Remember – Slogans can be very useful (eg 'It's the real thing' – Coca Cola).
– Keep the sentences short and the language simple.
– Make the product sound as good as possible.
– Free gifts often help to sell things.

*Don't forget who your readers are. Write about the kind of things they probably buy.

Language Study 5

Reported speech When someone reports another person's words, this is called **reported** or **indirect** speech. Notice how the verbs change:

Actual words
- 'I always *watch* the TV news.'
- 'People *are spending* more money on magazines.'

Reported speech
- He said he always *watched* the TV news.
- He said people *were spending* more money on magazines.

Note You can use the word *'that'* after the reporting verb:
- 'I usually go to Spain in the summer.'
- He said *that* he always went to Spain in the summer.

Use the verb **tell** to report instructions or commands:
- 'Forget the idea.'
- 'Write to her this evening.'
- *He told* me *to forget* the idea.'
- *They told* him *to write* to her this evening.'

Note the reporting verb **tell** must have an indirect object.

Use the verb **ask** to report requests
- 'Will you marry me?' he asked.
- 'Could you get me a drink?'
- *He asked* her *to marry* him.
- *She asked* me *to get* her a drink.

Relative clauses You can use a relative clause to specify **which** person or **which** thing you are talking about:
- The man who came here yesterday was my brother, but the man who's coming tomorrow is a colleague from work.

Note these are **defining** clauses.

You can also use a relative clause to give extra information:
- My brother, who was 22 yesterday, has just got his first job.
- The Rolls Royce, which you bought for £2000, is worth at least £3000.

Note these are **non-defining** clauses, they do not tell you *which* person you are talking abo[ut]

Who refers to people; **which** refers to things:
- The man *who* . . .
- The car *which* . . .
- The children *who* . . .
- The horse *which* . . .

You can use **that** instead of **who** or **which**
- People that come from Manchester are called Mancunians.

Note You can leave out **that** altogether in some sentences:
- Isn't he wearing the suit (that) he bought yesterday?
- The watch (that) you're wearing looks very expensive.

You can also use **when, where, why** and **whose** as relative pronouns:
- Tomorrow's the day when we're taking our exams.
- That's the restaurant where they serve French food.
- Is that the reason why you came?
- That's the ship whose captain is Australian.

Note whose can refer to people or things.

The Present Perfect There are two forms of the Present Perfect:

Simple: • I've seen your mother.
Continuous: • We've been looking at new houses.

You can use the Present Perfect Simple to talk about experiences:
- I've visited France and Germany, but I've never visited Russia.

or about actions which started in the past and have continued until the present
- They moved to Nottingham in 1953 and they've lived there ever since.

You can use the Present Perfect Continuous to talk about actions which have now stopped, but went on for some time:
- I'm tired because I've been playing football all afternoon.

or about actions which started in the past and are still happening now:
- I've been working here for 6 months.

Note You can use **since** and **for** with both the Simple and the Continuous forms of the Present Perfect. Remember:

Use **since** with points in time:
- since 1963
- since this morning
- since 10 o'clock

Use **for** with lengths of time:
- for 20 years
- for a long time
- for 3½ hours

Modal verbs: 'must' and 'can'

The future of **must** is **will have to**:
- He'll have to see the bank manager

The future of **can** is **will be able to**:
- You'll be able to borrow some money.'

The Present Perfect of **must** is **have had to**:
- He's had to see the bank manager

The Present Perfect of **can** is **have been able to**:
- Have you been able to borrow any money?

Question Tags

Use a negative Question Tag with a positive statement:
- You're the new Theatre director, aren't you?
- You used to work in London, didn't you?

Use a positive Question Tag with a negative statement:
- You aren't the new Theatre director, are you?
- You didn't use to work in London, did you?

'have something done' and 'get something done'

Use **have something done** or **get something done** to talk about actions somebody else does — not you:

- We had the car repaired last year. (We didn't repair it ourselves)
- She's having the house redecorated next year. (She isn't doing it herself)
- I'm getting my hair cut tomorrow. (I'm not cutting it myself)
- Didn't you get your bike mended? (Didn't somebody mend it for you?)

Note **Get something done** is more informal than **have something done**.

EXERCISES

REPORTED SPEECH
- Put this conversation into reported speech: (use **say** and **ask**)
  Jane I'm going to the cinema. Would you like to come with me?
  Mary I'm sorry I can't. I'm working late.
- What does your English teacher sometimes tell you to do? Write four sentences. (Use **tell**)

RELATIVE CLAUSES
- Write sentences with **defining** relative clauses about these people:
  your best friend; your English teacher; your parents.
  (Use **who**)
- and about these things or places: your house, your school, your town. (Use **which**, **that**, **where** and **whose**)
- and about these times: the weekend, birthdays. (Use **which** and **when**)

PRESENT PERFECT CONTINUOUS
- Ask your partner how long he has been . . .
  . . . living in this town.
  . . . coming to this school or college.
  . . . wearing those shoes.
  . . . studying English.
  . . . working in his/her current job.
- Write 5 sentences about your partner. (Use **since** and **for**)

MODALS
- What have you had to do this morning? Write 3 sentences.
- What will you have to do this evening? Write 3 sentences.
- If you win a lot of money, what will you be able to do? Write 3 sentences.
- During the last 2 years what have you been able to do that you couldn't do before? Write 3 sentences.

QUESTION TAGS
- Add Question Tags to these sentences:
  – You were at the disco last night, . . .?
  – He didn't get home very late, . . .?
  – She doesn't watch much TV, . . .?
  – They can come to the party, . . .?
  Now say these sentences as real questions and then as statements.

HAVE DONE AND GET DONE
Somebody has given you £1000 to spend on improving your bedroom, your flat or your house. What would you like to have done to it?
Write sentences like this:
'I'd like to have the kitchen repainted.'
'I'd like to get the dining-room decorated.'

Vocabulary

The number refers to the unit in which the word first appears.

A
a few 13
abroad 18
accent 19
accident 4
account 7
ache 4
acid rain 12
act 18
actually 2
advantage 9
advertisement 3
advertising 14
advice 6
aerial 7
affair 5
affect 9
afford 7
against 9
age group 20
ages 14
aggressive 18
aid 7
airline 6
alarm 20
album 15
alcohol 11
alive 8
allow 9
allowed 12
almost 20
along 3
alternative 12
although 17
amount 12
angry 14
announcement 3
annual 7
antique 6
apart from 9
apologise 3
appear 15
appearance 5
application 6
apply 6
appointment 7
apprenticeship 14
approximately 8
area 2
arrange 3
arrangement 3
arrive 2
art 17
article 20
artist 17
artistic 17
assistant 6
at last 2
atmosphere 12
attack 7
attendant 15
attitude 16
attract 16
attractive 17
aubergine 19
audience 15
avoidable 11
awake 14
awful 15

B
back 11
background 19

badminton 18
ballet 17
ban 7
band 15
bank clerk 14
barely 7
battery 11
beach 8
beard 4
beginning 2
behave 18
behaviour 9
besides 18
best wishes 2
bestseller 11
between 2
bill 7
bitter 17
blood pressure 4
blow 12
bomb explosion 17
bonnet 19
book (vb) 3
boot 19
bore 10
bored 10
boring 10
borrow 7
bothered 9
boyfriend 6
brake 11
breath test 18
brewery 19
brick 13
bridge (game) 19
brilliant 16
broadcast 16
budget 15
build 2
building 6
bullfighter 20
bumper 19
burglary 16
busy 5
by 1
bypass 7

C
calendar 4
calm 15
campsite 14
campus 18
can't stand 10
cancel 14
candidate 14
cardboard 13
career 5
carefully 8
cartoon 11
case study 6
casino 11
castle 2
catch 8
cathedral 2
cause 9
celebrate 19
central heating 7
century 18
certain 8
chairman 7
chance 11
change 3
charge 9
charity 20

charming 7
chart 13
chat 10
check 19
cheek 4
chemical 12
chemist 4
chest 11
chilli 13
chips 13
choice 20
choose 3
cider 17
circulation 20
circus 3
city 1
classical music 15
clean 2
cleaner 14
clear 13
client 3
clinic 19
cloth 2
cloud 8
coal-mining 2
coast 8
cocktail 9
coke 17
colleague 14
collect 9
commercial 16
committee 7
community affairs 17
community 8
company 12
competition 15
completely 12
concert 3
concert hall 17
concrete 13
condition 13
conference 15
confirm 5
congratulations 8
conservation 12
consult 15
contacts 20
contain 12
contemporary 15
continue 15
convenient 16
conviction 7
cope 14
cost of living 19
council 7
council house 1
country 10
countryside 18
county 1
courgette 19
court 13
cover 8
crash 5
crate 4
create 9
credit card 6
crew 5
crime 7
crisps 17
criticise 18
crowd 9
crowded 2
cruelty 7
cult 15
curly 4
current 5

customer 7
cut out 11
cycle 10

D
damage 11
damaged 7
dangerous 6
dark 2
dawn 8
dead-end 14
dead-end job 14
dear sir 9
decide 15
deliver 6
dentist 5
deny 5
depend on 9
depot 4
depressing 14
describe 2
description 2
design 15
desk 19
dessert 13
detail 2
details 6
development 9
diary 2
die 5
diet 11
director 3
dirty 10
disadvantage 9
disappear 7
disappointed 14
discover 8
discuss 20
disease 8
dislike 10
dispatch rider 4
distance 9
diver 8
doorbell 5
double 11
doubt 15
downstairs 13
dozen 6
drama 20
driving licence 5
driving test 5
drown 8
drugs 5
drunk 18
dull 6
during 18
dynamic 20

E
each other 10
earn 2
earring 10
economy 20
edit 20
editor 20
education 20
educational 14
elderly 15
election 8
electrician 14
electricity 20
else 11
emergency 5
emigrant 13
employ 8
employment 1

energetic 20
energy 11
engaged 10
engineering 6
engineer 6
enjoy 6
enormous 8
enough 2
enquiries 16
entertainment 17
entrance 8
environment 12
equipment 14
especially 7
estate 2
estate car 14
estimated 10
ethnic music 17
even 17
evening paper 5
event 2
eventually 6
everywhere 11
examine 4
example 4
exams 1
excellent 1
exciting 6
excursion 3
exercise 11
exhibition 17
exist 20
expand 19
experience 9
expert 11
explain 2
explore 8
extend 19
extension 18

F
facilities 9
fact 1
factory 6
fail 11
fair 3
fall in love 4
famine 7
famous 1
fan 15
far 1
farewell 3
farming 2
fashion 15
fashionable 19
fat 11
fatty 11
favourite 10
fear 7
feature 2
fed up with 10
feel 12
fender 19
ferry 14
festival 15
fewer 11
fight 18
figure 1
figures 9
finance 17
fine 13
firm 6
fit 19
fix 18
fizzy 19
flat 1

flatmate 1
flight 3
flour 7
flu 4
flying saucer 6
foam 13
fog 8
foggy 8
folk 15
forbidden 12
foreigner 9
forename 7
formal 9
freeze 7
fresh 11
friendly 2
frightened 7
frightening 6
furniture 20
further 6

G

gallon 19
gears 11
general 20
get rid of 9
gin and tonic 17
ginger 15
girlfriend 6
give up 11
glad 9
goal 5
government 12
great 1
grow 2
guided 3

H

hall of residence 18
handicapped 16
hardly 14
harvest 19
hate 10
head office 6
headline 7
health 11
healthy 2
heart 11
heat 7
helicopter 9
helpful 2
historical 7
hit 15
hitchhike 7
hold 1
homeless 18
honest 15
hooliganism 9
horse racing 5
hospital 1
host 3
household 15
housewarming party 7
housing 1
human being 8
hunt 7
hurry 4
hurt 11

I

ice 8
ideal 10
illness 4
imagine 18
immediately 3
immigrant 13
impressed 10

improve 11
improvement 11
in charge of 15
in fact 9
in favour of 9
include 17
including 6
income 7
increase 2
independent 6
indoor 1
industry 9
ingredients 19
inhabitant 2
injection 4
injured 5
insect 4
inspector 13
instead of 17
insulation 12
intelligent 14
interval 8
invade 2
invention 16
investigate 13
involved 18
issue 20
issues 16

J

jazz 15
jewellery 20
join 15
joiner 6
joke 6
journalist 9
junction 5

K

keen on 20
keep 11
kind 7

L

labour 19
lager 5
lake 12
lamb 13
landlord 18
large 3
last 6
late 12
launch 20
lead 12
leaflet 18
least 9
lecture 3
leisure 20
less 11
let . . . know 16
librarian 10
library 1
licence 6
lift 6
light 2
light bulb 11
like 1
like the back of your hand 14
likely 11
lip 4
lively 8
loan 7
local 2
logo 17
look forward to 2
lorry 7

lose 6
lovely 3
luck 8
luxury 19

M

madam 9
made of 13
magazine 20
main course 13
main road 7
maintenance 12
major 17
make-up 20
manager 1
manifesto 8
mankind 8
market research 20
marmalade 5
match 3
material 15
matter 7
matters 16
maximum 8
meal 10
mechanic 6
media 20
medicine 4
meet 10
meeting 10
membership 12
memo 15
memory 6
mend 19
menu 11
merchant 9
mess 9
messenger 15
midday 8
middle 1
middle-aged 15
middle-class 19
mind (vb) 9
miss 14
miss (train etc) 7
missing 15
mixture 19
model 15
modernise 19
monthly 20
motorbike 9
motorway 5
move 2
murderer 12
musical 3
musician 15
mystery 18

N

narrow 2
nearly 9
neither 15
nerves 9
newsagent 20
nightlife 9
no entry 12
noise 5
north 2
notice (vb) 13
novel 14
nuclear 12
nurse 5

O

occasional 8
occupation 1
offence 7

office block 17
official 5
on foot 1
on my own 13
on their own 3
onion 13
opera 17
operation 4
optician 16
optimistic 8
order (vb) 20
organisation 10
organise 15
original 3
other 12
otter 12
ought to 16
out of work 6
outdoor 6
outside 2
outskirts 10
over 1
overdraft 11
overweight 11
own (vb) 18
owner 13

P

package 4
packing 3
pain 4
painting 17
palace 9
paraffin 7
part-time 7
particularly 10
pass exams 5
patient 4
pavement 7
peaceful 12
peanuts 17
pedestrian 1
penicillin 4
pensioners 10
pepper 13
per 17
perfectly 19
performer 15
permission 11
permit 6
personality 15
personal 11
personnel 14
persuade 20
phone-in 16
picnic 19
pie 5
pilot 5
pint 4
place 10
play (drama) 20
plenty 7
plumber 14
political 15
polluted 12
pollution 12
polytechnic 13
popular 9
population 1
position 9
post (job) 6
poverty 2
power 12
power station 12
predict 8
prefer 10
prepare 15

prescription 4
presenter 16
press release 17
previous 14
probably 8
processed 11
produce 12
product 20
profits 9
programme 3
programme controller 16
promise 8
promotion 15
properly 14
property 12
proportion 10
protect 12
provide 9
publicity 15
publisher 20
puncture 4
purpose 14
put . . . through 16

Q

qualification 11
quality 6
quarterly 17
queue 9
quickly 12

R

race 5
radio station 16
rag 12
railway line 13
raise (money) 15
rate 11
re-use 12
readership 20
real ale 19
reason 10
rebuild 17
receive 12
recent 10
receptionist 6
recommendation 7
record (adj) 7
recover 5
redecorate 19
reduce 12
reduced 7
redundant 14
reflect 16
region 17
regularly 17
relatives 10
relaxed 2
remember 14
rent 13
repaint 19
repair 6
replace 7
reply 4
report 14
reserve 19
resident 17
resolution 4
restore 6
retain 9
review 20
ride 12
ring (vb) 4
risk 11
river 12

132

roast beef 5
rob 9
robbery 13
robot 8
roof 11
rough 14
round 11
route 7
rude 9
rural 8
rush 5

S

sack 11
safety 7
sailing 3
salary 15
sales 9
sales representative 14
salmon 20
sauce 13
sausage 19
save 12
savings 7
scared 7
scheme 9
scientist 11
score 17
scratch 15
scratched 15
script 15
sculpture 17
seal 12
search 7
season 19
seat (vb) 17
seat belt 16
secret 6
see you soon 2
serious 15
several 2
share 14
shareholder 16
shopkeeper 5
short of 20
shorthand 6
shoulder 4
shout 4
show 3
shower 8
shy 6
sick (of) 10
sightseeing 2
sign 12
signature 6
silent film 8
silver 13
simple 15
slim 7
slums 2
smoke 12
soap opera 19
social life 10
sociology 18
sofa 9
solar 12
solo 15
somewhere 10
souvenir 15
spare time 1
speed limit 7
spelling 20
spices 13
spider 7
spoil 9
squash (drink) 5
staff 5

standard 19
star 17
starter 13
starve 12
state 3
stationery 14
statistics 9
steak & kidney pie 5
steal 7
steel 13
steering wheel 18
still 19
stomach 4
stone 13
store 19
stormy 5
story 14
straightaway 6
strange 9
stranger 11
stretcher 5
strict 18
subject 20
suburb 19
successful 8
such 10
suggest 6
suggestion 3
sulphur 12
sunburn 4
sunny 8
sunshine 8
super 14
support 15
surgery 4
surprising 4
surrounding 16
survivor 5
sweater 18

T

talent 15
talkative 6
task 17
tax 8
telephone directory 7
telex 15
temperature 8
terribly 3
test 19
theft 13
thief 13
through 10
thunderstorm 8
tidy 7
timetable 15
tired 2
tiring 2
toothache 16
topic 15
tour 2
touring company 17
tourism 9
track 15
traditional 15
traffic jam 9
tragedy 8
training officer 14
trend 10
trip 18
trout 20
try 1
turn down 17
twice 8
type 6
typical 18
typing 6

U

underneath 17
unemployed 1
unfortunately 3
unique 17
unless 17
unlock 6
unpleasant 7
unpredictable 8
until 4
unusual 6
urgent 16
used to 18

V

valuable 17
varied 16
variety 17
vegetable 11
vegetarian 13
vehicle 5
venue 15
violence 9
violent 19
virus 4
visit 2
vitamin 11
voluntary 14

W

wait 8
waiter 18
waitress 18
wallet 6
ward 4
warehouse 9
waste 18
wavelength 16
weak 19
weekly 20
welcome 3
well-off 6
well-paid 2
whale 12
what's the matter 7
whether 9
while 18
whole 8
wildlife 12
windy 19
wipe 17
wonder 11
wonderful 18
workaholic 14
worker 2
workforce 7
worried 4
worry 12
worse 7
worst 2
worth 4
wreckage 5
wreck 8
wrestling 3
wrong number 16

Y

yet 19
you see 7
you'd better 11
yours 2
yours faithfully 4
yours sincerely 9
youth leader 5

Irregular Verbs

Infinitive	Past tense	Past participle	Verb + ing
be	was	been	
beat	beat	beaten	
become	became	become	becoming
begin	began	begun	beginning
bend	bent	bent	
break	broke	broken	
bring	brought	brought	
build	built	built	
burn	burnt	burnt	
buy	bought	bought	
can	could, was able	been able	being able
catch	caught	caught	
choose	chose	chosen	choosing
come	came	come	coming
cost	cost	cost	
cut	cut	cut	cutting
do	did	done	
drink	drank	drunk	
drive	drove	driven	driving
eat	ate	eaten	
fall	fell	fallen	
feel	felt	felt	
fight	fought	fought	
find	found	found	
fly	flew	flown	
forget	forgot	forgotten	forgetting
get	got	got	getting
give	gave	given	giving
go	went	gone	
grow	grew	grown	
have	had	had	having
hear	heard	heard	
hit	hit	hit	hitting
hold	held	held	
hurt	hurt	hurt	
keep	kept	kept	
know	knew	known	
learn	learnt	learnt/learned	
leave	left	left	leaving
lend	lent	lent	
let	let	let	letting
lie	lay	lain	lying
lose	lost	lost	losing
make	made	made	making
meet	met	met	
pay	paid	paid	
put	put	put	putting
read	read	read	
ride	rode	ridden	riding
ring	rang	rung	
rise	rose	risen	rising
say	said	said	
see	saw	seen	
sell	sold	sold	
send	sent	sent	
shake	shook	shaken	shaking
shine	shone	shone	shining
show	showed	shown	
shut	shut	shut	shutting
sing	sang	sung	
sit	sat	sat	sitting
sleep	slept	slept	
speak	spoke	spoken	
spend	spent	spent	
stand	stood	stood	
steal	stole	stolen	
swim	swam	swum	swimming
take	took	taken	taking
teach	taught	taught	
tell	told	told	
think	thought	thought	
throw	threw	thrown	
understand	understood	understood	
wake up	woke up	woken up	waking
wear	wore	worn	
win	won	won	winning
write	wrote	written	writing

Tapescripts

Unit 1 Presentation

Now listen to some more Nottingham people. They are talking about themselves and their work.
My name's Alan Elston. I'm 22, and I'm a student in my last year at Nottingham University. I live in a small flat with four friends. At the moment I'm working hard for my final exams – I'm studying to be a teacher. Next year? Well, who knows? I'd like to stay here in Nottingham, and work in one of of the city schools, but there aren't many teaching jobs at the moment. The number of children in schools is going down, and some schools are even closing. I just love the people of Nottingham – they're really friendly.

My name's Charlie Bloom. I work at the Raleigh Bicycle Factory. It's a huge place. I started work here when I was only 14 years old. That's 45 years ago, but I like my work, and I know I'm lucky to have a job. We make really top-class bikes – the best in the world, I think. I'm retiring next year – so I'm going to relax, do a bit of work in my garden, and spend more time with my family.

My name's Judy Kingston, and I work in the Central Library – that's right in the middle of the city. I think Nottingham's a wonderful place. It's full of interesting people. I actually work in the Local Studies section of the library. We keep information about Nottingham – books, newspapers, photographs – that kind of thing. And we've also got a large collection of tape recordings of local people. Today I'm making a recording of a Nottingham miner – a man who started work here in 1935. He's going to talk about his childhood, and his work in the mines.

My name's Harsha Khan. My family comes from Pakistan, but now we live here in Nottingham. I've got a stall in one of the markets in the Victoria Shopping Centre – it sells all kinds of Asian food. In my spare time I work for the Pakistan Centre. That's a sort of club for all the Pakistani people in Nottingham. We help them with their problems – like housing, jobs and money. Many Pakistanis can't speak English very well, so we run language classes for them. And we have lots of fun: parties, concerts, films. And there's a Women's group and a Youth Club.

Unit 1 Transfer 4

Listen to this description of New York.
New York – or the Big Apple, as people call it, is the chief city and port of the USA. It has a population of nearly eight million people, and is the sixth largest city in the world. New York stands at the mouth of the River Hudson in New York State. It has five boroughs – Brooklyn, Manhattan, Queens, Staten Island and the Bronx. All the boroughs except the Bronx are on islands. Manhattan is the oldest part of the city, and is the country's commercial centre. It is well-known for its art galleries, and has two universities. New York is especially famous for its skyscrapers – particularly The Empire State Building and the United Nations Headquarters. The main industries of the city are clothing, publishing, textiles, food processing and luxury goods.
Just a few statistics give an idea of what life in New York is like: for example, the city has a hundred hospitals, ninety-one colleges, universities and technical schools, and over two thousand schools. The city employs forty thousand teachers, twenty-five thousand policemen and thirteen thousand firemen. And in their free time New Yorkers have a choice of fifteen television stations and thirty-nine radio stations.

Unit 2 Presentation

Listen to Harry Shepherd and his wife Sally. They are describing the differences between Broxtowe and Old Radford.

Sally   All the bigger families moved from Old Radford to Broxtowe. In those days we had three children, and we needed a larger house.
Harry   It wasn't only the big families though, was it, Sal? It was the problem families too. That's why Broxtowe got a bad name.
Sally   This place is enough to make us all into problem families. It's a worse slum than Radford ever was. And the people there were friendlier. For a start you knew everybody.
Harry   That's true. People talked to each other. I mean, I know it was dirtier and unhealthier, but you had good neighbours. They helped you. They lent you money, they did your shopping for you when you were ill.
Sally   You're right, Harry. We were happier then. Perhaps it's because we were younger.
Harry   Maybe. But, you know, even the young people here don't seem to enjoy themselves.
Sally   No, I suppose not. Broxtowe may be more modern, but life here isn't like it was in the good old days, is it?

Unit 2 Transfer 3

Listen to this man talking about his first job in the 1920s.
I really liked the telegraph boy's job. They gave me shoes and hat, a smart uniform and a big red bike – it was very big and very heavy. It was an easy job really – sometimes I went as far as thirty or forty miles a day delivering the telegrams. It was a good, healthy open-air job.
The first telegram I took out was a three-mile journey to a farm called 'Biglands'. When I got there, I gave the telegram to the farmer. He took it and said: 'Just a minute!' And I said, 'What is it?' and he said 'Here's three pence for you.'
At that time ten shillings a week was the basic wage. I started work at nine o'clock in the morning and finished at five. I only had half an hour for lunch – that was Monday to Saturday. On Sunday mornings in those days the Post Office was open for an hour and a half. There were telegrams on Sundays, so I worked from nine o'clock to half-past ten. Apart from holidays, I worked every day of the week all the time I was a telegraph boy, and that was nearly five years. And I never had a day off except for holidays.

Unit 3 Presentation

1   Listen to this announcement about tomorrow's football match in Nottingham. Where do you think the announcement is from?
Queens Park Rangers are travelling to Nottingham tomorrow for their match against Notts Forest. Forest are currently seventh in the First Division. In a surprise last-minute change, Mark Smalley replaces Chris Fairclough.
The gates open at 2.o'clock, and the kick-off is at three. The last time these two teams met Forest won three nil.

2 Now listen to this conversation between two men. They are talking about the match.

Mike Are you coming to the match tomorrow afternoon, Dave?
Dave Sorry, Mike. I can't. I'm buying a new car tomorrow.

3 Now listen to some more conversations. People are arranging their future entertainment.

Anita Hello Jenny. Anita here. Are you doing anything tomorrow evening?
Jenny No, I don't think so. Why?
Anita Well, we're all going to the American Circus. Would you like to bring your kids along? It starts at 7.30.
Jenny That's a great idea. Thanks.
Anita That's okay. See you there then.

Andy Do you know, there's a concert of folk music from Rajasthan and Bengal at the Hindu Temple?
Jane Really? I'd love to go. When is it?
Andy Sunday. It starts at 8 o'clock, and it costs £2.

Anne Hi Mary. This is Anne. Paul and I are going to the theatre in a few weeks time. Do you and Mark fancy coming along?
Mary We'd love to come. What's on?
Anne It's a musical called 'Are you lonesome tonight?' It's about Elvis Presley.
Mary That sounds great Anne. When exactly is it on?
Anne It starts the week of June 17th. I'm phoning the theatre on Monday to book our tickets.

Unit 3 Skills

Listen to this phone conversation between Paul and his friend Annie. They are arranging a holiday.

Annie Hello, 62943.
Paul Hello, is that you Annie? This is Paul.
Annie Paul! How lovely to hear from you. How is everything?
Paul Never mind that now. Listen. Are you going away for your summer holidays this year?
Annie No, I don't think so. Why?
Paul I just thought we might go somewhere together. How about it?
Annie That's a great idea, Paul! Where are you thinking of?

Now listen to the rest of their conversation. Paul makes several suggestions for their holiday together. He gives places, dates, costs and means of travel. Listen carefully to Paul and fill in the gaps in the chart:

Paul Well, there's loads of choice. Do you want to write down the details and think about it?
Annie Yes, okay, I'll just get a pen. . . . Right.
Paul Well, first there's a student holiday to Crete – that's from July 11th to 25th. The plane leaves Gatwick at midnight on the Friday. And that costs £300.
Annie 11th to the 25th July – Crete – £300. Gosh, that's terribly expensive!
Paul Yes, I know. We could try Spain. Some college friends of mine are driving to the Costa Brava in a minibus in June. That's a lot cheaper. It's £200 – from June 5th to the 26th.
Annie Mmm . . . three weeks for £200 – that's not bad. But it's a very long journey. Is there anything else?
Paul Yes, there are still two places left on an ordinary tourist package to Rome. That's two weeks for £250 – that includes everything – hotels, meals – the lot.
Annie Mmm . . . I suppose that's quite good really. Is it by plane?
Paul No, unfortunately not. It's a coach trip – you get on in London, and then the coach stays with you for the whole holiday.
Annie What are the dates?
Paul August 23rd to September 6th.
Annie Oh . . . sorry, I can't make that. College starts again on September 3rd.
Paul Of course, we could go camping. That's always cheaper – and we could go wherever we like, whenever we like.
Annie Yes, that's not a bad idea. Why don't we do that? We can decide exactly where we want to go later.

Unit 4 Presentation

Mrs Philips goes to the Health Centre to see Dr Fleet.

Dr Fleet Sit down Mrs Philips. Now what can I do for you?
Mrs Philips It's my head, Doctor. I've got a terrible headache, and my throat hurts.
Dr Fleet I see, and when did these pains start?
Mrs Philips The day before yesterday. Tuesday.
Dr Fleet I'm going to examine you. Could you open your mouth wide please? Thank you. Now I'm going to take your blood pressure. Could you roll up your sleeve for me? Thank you.
Mrs Philips Well?
Dr Fleet Well, Mrs Philips, there's nothing seriously wrong with you. Here's a prescription for some tablets. Take it to the chemist's and come and see me next Wednesday, please.

Unit 4 Transfer 2

Pete and Jenny are at a New Year's Eve party.

Jenny Are you making any New Year Resolutions Pete?
Pete Yes, I'm going to stop smoking.
Jenny Never! I don't believe it.
Pete I decided before Christmas. After midnight I'm never going to smoke another cigarette.
Jenny You certainly sound very definite. How are you going to do it?
Pete Well, for a start, I'm not going to buy any more cigarettes – and I'm not going to take any from other people either.
Jenny Are you going to do anything instead of smoking?
Pete What do you mean?
Jenny Well, for example, are you going to eat sweets or something like that?
Pete Oh no! I don't want to get fat. But I did think of one thing. I'm going to start playing the piano – to keep my hands busy. Oh yes, and I'm going to save all the money I usually spend on cigarettes.
Jenny That's a good idea. Well, Good Luck.
Pete Thanks. Now, what about your New Year Resolution?

Jenny Well, I want to buy a car next summer, so I'm going to learn to drive before then. I'm going to book my driving test tomorrow and start lessons on Tuesday.
Pete I learnt last year. It's quite difficult to start with.
Jenny That's what people say – so I'm going to read all about driving and cars first – you know, the way they work.
Pete And lessons are very expensive you know.
Jenny I know, so my boyfriend's going to give me extra lessons.

Unit 5 Presentation

Now listen to these two newsflashes:
We interrupt this programme to bring you a news flash:
A multiple accident, involving thirty-nine vehicles, has completely blocked the M1 Motorway two miles south of junction 25. Police have so far found the bodies of seven drivers. Ambulances have rushed the many injured to hospitals in Derby and Nottingham. In an on-the-spot interview a traffic policeman said:
'I've worked on the M1 for ten years now, and I've never seen anything like this.'

Now before our next programme here is an important news flash:
We've just heard that a DC10 plane has crashed in farmland near to Heathrow Airport. Here's our reporter David Grant:
'. . . 25 miles west of Heathrow Airport. According to airport officials more than a hundred passengers have died in the disaster – but amazingly at least seven people have escaped with only minor injuries. I've been here since 4 o'clock this afternoon, and I've watched the emergency services at work. They've done a magnificent job. Firemen have just brought an elderly man out of the wreckage on a stretcher, and taken him to one of the waiting ambulances. Now back to the studio.'

Unit 5 Skills

Listen to this interview with Caroline Faber.
Interviewer Miss Faber, you've lived a very full life, wouldn't you agree?
Caroline I sure have, dear. It's been absolutely marvellous. I've done nearly everything I wanted – not many people can say that, can they?
Interviewer And I understand you've been married seven times?
Caroline That's right. I've had seven wonderful husbands. I'm still friends with them all. I've been married to Jack for three years – he's my current husband. Three years – that must be a record for Hollywood!
Interviewer You still live in Hollywood?
Caroline Yes, I do. I've lived there for nearly forty years now.
Interviewer Miss Faber, you've been married seven times, but you've never had any children.
Caroline No, I haven't. I suppose I've been too busy. I've had a very exciting life, you know.
Interviewer Tell me about your career. What have you done?
Caroline Well, I've acted in over sixty feature films – and starred in over thirty. I've co-starred with all the greats – Edward G. Robinson, Clark Gable, James Mason, Paul Newman. I've even been in a film with Robert Redford – as his mother, of course!
Interviewer That's fascinating. And what about your private life? That's been very stormy, hasn't it?
Caroline Certainly not. Anyway that's my affair.
Interviewer Yes, of course. But you have mixed with the famous and the important, haven't you?
Caroline Well, I've had dinner with every American President since Eisenhower, and I've had holidays with some of the world's richest men, like Paul Getty, Howard Hughes, you know, the Legends of our Time – that's what people call them, isn't it?
Interviewer That's amazing. And you've travelled all over the World?
Caroline Yes, I have. But, do you know, I've never been to China. I'd just love to go there – just for a holiday.
Interviewer Miss Faber, you're sixty this week. What is there left for you to do?
Caroline What is there left? My dear, there are hundreds of things I still want to do. Do you know, no-one's asked me to do a play in London. I'd love to act at the National Theatre or the Old Vic – that'd be marvellous.
Interviewer Caroline Faber. Thank you for talking to me, and Happy Birthday.

Unit 6 Presentation

Listen to this interview with Anne Peacock.
Interviewer How did you become a pilot Anne? It's an unusual job for a woman, isn't it?
Anne Yes, I suppose it is. Well, I always wanted to fly, so I went to an Air Training College in Oxford.
Interviewer And then?
Anne Well I got my licence there, and I've flown planes on and off ever since.
Interviewer Did you get a job straightaway?
Anne No, certainly not. Nobody thought a woman could fly planes, so it took me several months to find work.
Interviewer How did you get your first job?
Anne It was quite funny actually. At the time I was on holiday in Jersey, and I can remember walking into the offices of Jersey Airlines and asking for a job. Everyone thought it was a great joke. But then the Managing Director interviewed me and said 'Yes.' That was in 1977.
Interviewer So how long have you worked for Orbis?
Anne I suppose I've worked here for about six years. I came here in 1982, or was it 1983? Anyway I've worked here since then.
Interviewer And have you enjoyed your time with Orbis?
Anne Yes, I have. I've flown all over the world. I've seen most of the countries of Europe, and I've travelled to America, Africa and Asia.
Interviewer What about the men pilots? How have they treated you?
Anne Very well really. Most of them have treated me like any other pilot. Of course there have been the usual jokes, but they've always been very helpful when I've had problems. And I've shown everyone that women can fly planes!

136

Unit 6 Transfer 1

Listen to this interview with Susan Mann, a student at Bristol University.

I've enjoyed every minute of my first year here. I mean, much as I love my family, it's done me good to get away from home. I've learned to stand on my own two feet. In some ways life here is very relaxing. In London I went everywhere by bus or underground. Since I came here I've travelled everywhere by bike – it's made me much healthier. Of course I'm not so well-off. I've had to look after my money very carefully – so I haven't bought many new clothes, and I haven't spent much on entertainment – like the cinema or the theatre. But there's always plenty to do here – I've joined several university clubs, and I've played a lot of sport, like tennis and hockey.
And I've made lots of new friends, particularly my flatmates, Sarah and Judy. And of course Steve, he's my boyfriend – I've seen quite a lot of him.
All in all it's been a great year.

Unit 7 Presentation

2 *Manager* Good morning, Mr Grainger. What can I do for you?
 Peter Good morning. Well, you see, I need to borrow £400. I've got to pay a large car repair bill by the end of the month.
 Manager I see. And do you really have to borrow the money? I mean, can't you use your savings?
 Peter No, I'm afraid not. We spent all our savings when we bought the car.
 Manager Oh well, first you must fill in one of these loan application forms – because we need to know details of your financial position.

Unit 8 Presentation

Listen to this politician. He is talking about his party's election manifesto.
When we become the next government, we will spend more money on all public services. In Education we will employ more teachers and reduce the size of classes.
In public transport we will make sure that everyone has good bus and train services wherever they live. We won't cut rural bus services.
Employment is a most important area. Here the government itself will employ thousands of people on important community projects. Also we will encourage people to start new businesses in all parts of the country. And there's the question of Health. This really is our first priority. We will cut the cost of medicines immediately. And we have just decided to start many new Family Centres. These will offer the usual medical facilities but also a new personal and family advice service.

Unit 8 Skills

We asked people the question: 'What will life be like in the year 2500?' Here are some of their answers. Which of the speakers feels that the future will be better than the present?

Paul Enstone, Scientist
It's quite impossible to say, isn't it? But I'll tell you what I think it'll be like. The Earth will be colder than it is now. Large areas of ice will probably cover most of Northern Europe and North America. People from these countries will move south to get away from the ice – so there'll be too many people in certain areas. That means food will be more difficult to get – and inevitably more people will die of hunger. It isn't a very pleasant picture, is it? I can't say I'm very optimistic about the future of mankind.

Phil Oliver, Politician
That's a very difficult question. I certainly hope that the world will be a better place by the year 2500. Everyone will have enough to eat by then – I'm almost sure about that. And I don't think there'll be any unemployment. I think too that people will probably live longer because we'll be able to cure most illnesses. Unfortunately there's only one certainty: none of us will be alive in the year 2500, so we'll never know, will we?

John May, Student
What will life be like in the year 2500? Well, for a start people won't have to work, will they? Robots and computers will do all the routine jobs, and we'll be free to spend our time doing what we enjoy most. On the other hand some things will be more difficult. People won't be able to move about so easily, because no-one will have a private car. Petrol will be too expensive by then for ordinary people. And I should think that heating for our homes will come from the sun. It'll be a different world altogether.

Unit 9 Skills

Section 1
You know my wife and I, we have students regularly throughout the year and we find it's good, especially for the children, you know, meeting people from different countries – yes, it's interesting.

Section 2
They find the nightlife a bit strange in England. They can go out at 11 o'clock at night and stay out until 4 o'clock in the morning, but in England they close at 11 o'clock at night. That's a bit strange for them but apart from that I think they quite like England, most people – apart from the weather.

Unit 10 Presentation

1 Listen to Joan and Peter. They are talking about where they live:
 Joan We really love living in the country, don't we Pete?
 Peter Yes, everyone's so friendly, and there's such a relaxed atmosphere in the village.
 Joan It's all very different from city life. In Nottingham everything was such a rush. We never had any time to relax and enjoy ourselves, did we?
 Peter No . . . I mean we lived in the suburbs of Nottingham for over ten years. My job was in the city centre; I really hated driving to work every day. Now I get up at eight o'clock and walk to work.
 Joan And I've got a part-time job behind the bar at the local pub. It doesn't pay that much, but I just enjoy meeting people and having a chat.
2 Now listen to what Judy and Dave think about living in the same village:
 Judy I'm really sick of living here, Dave. It's so dead. There's nothing to do at the weekends. We always end up going into town, and then it's so expensive getting back here late at night. I'd really love to move somewhere with a bit more life.
 Dave Look Judy we've been through all this before. I agree about this place, but where could we go? The trouble is there aren't any jobs around.

Judy I know that, but I'm sure you could find something. I'm fed up with sitting in front of the telly or going to the pub every evening. There's nobody else of our age here. They're all middle-aged or old. It's all such a bore.

Dave Okay, I don't mind looking for jobs in Nottingham again, but I'll have to find a well-paid job. We'll have to pay more for a house in Nottingham, you know.

Judy Yes, I know. We'll start saving again. And perhaps I could find myself a part-time job. It's just that I can't stand living here much longer.

Unit 12 Skills

Listen to John talking about the environment. He is explaining why he is a member of Friends of the Earth.
Part 1
There are several reasons why I think the Friends of the Earth are a good organisation, mainly because of their work against pollution. I joined the organisation about 10 years ago, after university, because I was worried about the development of nuclear energy, and the killing of many wild animals.

Part 2
I agree with their ideas about energy – I think we should try to use alternative energy, like solar energy or wind energy, much more than we do.
I don't agree with what the government says about acid rain. I feel we must do something about it – I'm sure the problem starts in British power stations.

Part 3
I think the government should control industry more – I can't agree that pollution and acid rain come only from the millions of cars on the road.
Another thing I like about the Friends of the Earth – they don't just *talk* about a problem, they actually do something about it.

Unit 13 Skills

Paul and Luba are from Nottingham, but they now live in Canada. Listen to Luba talking about their move.
Part 1
Paul and I are both from Nottingham, we were brought up there originally, but we left in 1973, to come and live in Canada. Our parents were quite poor, both our fathers worked down the coalmines, and had a lot of problems with their health. We moved because we wanted a better, safer life for the children – we wanted them to have a better chance.

Part 2
Both our families were Ukrainian – they came to Britain in 1945. Both of us spoke Ukrainian at home, and only learned English when we went to school. After school, we went to Ukrainian clubs, where we learned about our history and culture – we did a lot of folk dancing, too.
One of the reasons we came here to live in Winnipeg was the large number of Ukrainians who live here. You can walk down the streets in the centre of the city, and hear quite a lot of people speaking Ukrainian – that's very exciting for us. We wanted our children to grow up with their own culture, and not be just English kids from Nottingham. Here in Winnipeg there are Ukrainian restaurants, newspapers, and schools for the children to learn about their history. They can be Canadians here, without losing their Ukrainian culture. That's very important.

Unit 14 Presentation

Richard Evans began a new life at the age of 40. He is now a full-time writer with 3 best-sellers to his name. Listen to this interview with him:

Interviewer Richard Evans, can you tell us how you became a writer?

Richard Evans Well actually writing always interested me. Even when I was a child, I used to spend a lot of my time writing stories.

Interviewer But you haven't always been a writer, have you?

Richard Evans No. My first job was in a bank – that was the worst time of my life. Then I spent 8 years as the manager of a shop – that was a dead-end job. After that I got into taxi driving. Actually I really enjoyed doing that. It was a good life. I used to know London like the back of my hand. In those days I used to write in my spare time. I used to work for four days a week and write for the other three. Then, when my first novel became a best-seller, I gave up being a taxi driver.

Interviewer How has this success changed your life?

Richard Evans I don't know where to begin. My life is completely different. For a start, I didn't use to have my own house or car – now I've got both. And I never used to have a holiday. I think also I'm more relaxed now, I mean, when you've got two jobs, you can't really do either of them properly, can you? I used to think about my writing while I was driving around London. When I got home, I used to write down my ideas – and often I didn't use to go to bed until two or three o'clock in the morning. Now I write for eight hours a day and then relax.

Interviewer Is there anything you miss about your past life?

Richard Evans Yes, there is, actually. I used to meet lots of interesting people. Now I meet hardly anyone at all. Writing is a very lonely occupation – but I'm certainly happier than I used to be.

Unit 14 Skills

Listen to the cassette. You will hear Colette talking about how she got her first job.
Well, I actually come from Stockport. I went to college in Widnes just outside Liverpool for a year's training on reception. From there, obviously, I started writing off for jobs – about the March time, I was due to leave in the June – started off writing for jobs, and it was actually my lecturer at college (who) knew the front-of-house manager here at the time, so I wrote to him asking if any vacancies became available in June, would he consider me – I got a reply saying my letter was on file – the usual – (you) think you('ll) never hear anything else. Then one day they just rang up and asked if I could come for an interview – a vacancy had arisen. I came here for the interview on . . . it was a Thursday – took me ages to find the place – Nottingham all a one-way system and that – and the following Thursday they rang me up to say that I'd got the job if I wanted it, could I start on the Monday. So I arrived here on the Monday (or) on the Sunday evening 'cause I live in the hotel – (they) provide accommodation. That's how I came to be in Nottingham.

Unit 15 Presentation

Now listen to this conversation.

Anne Do you want me to buy you a weekend ticket for the Folk Festival, Mike?
Mike Who's on this year?
Anne It's a really good line-up. There's The Chieftains, Lonnie Donnegan, the Pogues and . . .
Mike I love watching the Pogues.
Anne So do I, but I prefer the Chieftains. They sound more Irish to me. Anyway, would you like me to get you a ticket?
Mike Okay, but just a day ticket. I haven't got enough time to stay for the whole weekend, and I don't like queuing for drinks at festivals.
Anne Neither do I. There are never enough bars. So – Friday, Saturday or Sunday?
Mike I'd rather come on the Sunday – then we can see the Pogues and the Chieftains.

Unit 16 Presentation

1 Chris Hughes is the programme controller at Radio Trent, one of Nottingham's two local radio stations. Listen to what he says about the station:
The idea is to provide a radio service which – most importantly of all – people enjoy listening to, that reflects life in Nottingham and the surrounding area, and also makes a profit for the shareholders and the directors of the company. Radio Trent broadcasts twenty-four hours a day – we never stop. It's a music-based station and we find that playing music attracts the most listeners. But we can't just do that – we have to provide a news service to let people know what's going on in the area, and that's broadcast every hour, twenty-four hours a day.

2 What do you like about Radio Trent?

I like the local news programmes. I listen to all of them.

We never miss Careline. It's a wonderful programme.

I like the music, of course, and I always listen to the local weather and traffic reports when I'm driving around Nottingham.

Have you any suggestions for improvements to Radio Trent's broadcasting?

They shouldn't play so much pop music. It's boring. They should play other kinds of music as well – like jazz and classical.
A local radio station ought to make local people feel important. There ought to be more interviews with local personalities.
I know they have to have advertisements – but they shouldn't have them so often. Every half hour is too much.

Unit 16 Skills

1 Radio Trent jingle/song and people's comments:

Song	Comments
Your kind of music Your kind of people	I dunno you just turn it on – it's sort of an (h)abit you know what I mean.
Radio Trent and you	
You turn us on and we'll be here.	The fact that it's local.
	I like the music what they play.
Relax and your troubles disappear.	It's easy to listen to. I have it on in the car. I just like it. It's varied.
Playing your favourite songs. We're Radio Trent on 301. Or 96 point 2. Your kind of people every day. Radio Trent.	All the music and the news. Funny sometimes.
	Well you can play records for people over Trent where some radio stations don't like you doing it.
	I like it because it's in stereo.
	Because it's brilliant.

Radio Trent adverts

2 Nottingham University concerts
In celebration of their centenary, Nottingham University in association with Radio Trent present the Hall Music Series. A programme of concerts for all musical tastes. On Sunday the seventeenth of January at 8 pm in the University's Nightingale Hall the Harry Beckett Quintet present an evening of Modern Jazz. Admission free. Just one of the concerts to look forward to in the Hall Music Series.

3 Barry Austin Men's Clothes Sale
Chris Hello there, Dave. What you having, then?
Dave Oh, well. I'll have a pint then please Chris. Say, you're looking smart. Won the pools, have you?
Chris Oh, no such luck . . . I've been down to Barry Austin – he's got suits, shirts, trousers and jackets all at unbelievable prices. And the quality – well, you can see for yourself. And there's plenty for the missus too.
Dave Where is this Barry Austin, then?
Chris Well the nearest one to you is Arnold, but there are others at Beeston, Bulwell and Hucknall. Why don't you get down there? You don't need to have won the pools to dress well with Barry Austin.

4 Estate Agent advertising house
Hello, David Sale speaking.
Harrow Road, Woolaton, stands adjacent to the open space of Woolaton Park and offers a most attractive tree-lined street close to shops and good schools and yet within one mile of the city centre. This south-facing, three-bedroom home offers much style and character with not just the usual lounge and dining room, but playroom and study as well. Priced at a competitive £38,500 – and that has to be reasonable for this location. Details from me, David Sale, Nottingham 46296.

5 Mavericks – Restaurant
Darn it, missed again
Breakfast at Mavericks is one thing you can't miss. Mavericks are now serving breakfast every day between 8 and 10 am.
Eat in or take-away.
Orange juice; Mavericks own special bacon and egg burger; hash brown; and as many refills of tea, coffee or hot chocolate as you like.
Mavericks – on the corner of Exchange Walk and Wheelergate.
The fastest, friendliest food in town.

6 East Midlands Airport – Intercity Airlines
Attention businessmen and secretaries.
Intercity Airlines operate a day return to Brussels from East Midlands Airport.
Contact your travel agent or phone Derby 812177.

7 East Midlands Electricity Sale
Hello, it's me SuperTed at the great East Midlands Electricity Sale.
And how's this for a bargain. Fifteen, yes fifteen pounds off the Lec T241 fridge freezer. Down to £144.95 with free delivery. And that's just another of our fantastic bargain offers.
Pop down today and see for yourself. SuperTed Sale is on now at your East Midlands Electricity Shop.

Unit 17 Presentation

Michael Prochak talks about the Colchester Arts Centre
We do a lot of things really, a very varied sort of programme which includes theatre, music, dance, community affairs, art exhibitions and even lunches. We have a number of resident events which happen regularly, like the Folk Club, which happens once a week, the Jazz Club, which happens once a month, and an Alternative Cabaret, which is a quarterly event now. And besides that, then each weekend usually has a major concert which can be either classical, folk, jazz, or some sort of ethnic music – or a drama event, a touring company, touring theatre, touring dance, or a community affairs type programme.

Unit 17 Skills

Harry is talking about the band he plays in:
Part 1
It's a 5 piece band, we're called Eastwind, and it's quite difficult to describe, but I think the best way to put it is we play an original blend of rock and pop. We try and play as much as we can around Colchester, although at the moment there aren't that many venues around.

Part 2
As for money, we don't really charge too much, just petrol money, or we'd rather do it for free and for the fun of it, than sit at home and not play at all.
We've all got daytime jobs, which again poses a problem because we can't do anything too big, as we're all working already. Ideally what we'd like to do is to get good enough to get rid of our daytime jobs, maybe tour, get some money behind us for a single perhaps, who knows?
How much does it cost to make a single?
Difficult to say, depending on who you know – contacts in the music business are always a good thing to have. Around two or three hundred pounds, I suppose, for just the tape alone, and the pressing's extra.

Unit 18 Skills

Kim is talking about her life in Nottingham, studying at Nottingham university.
Part 1
You were a student at Nottingham. What did you study there?

I studied American studies and English, with a component of drama.
It's a beautiful university with an enormous campus, and woodland, and there's a big lake. The buildings are very grand, and castle-like. You can go rowing on the lake in boats, there are beautiful gardens and parks. You can go for lovely walks and not see a building for quite a while. Most of the students live on campus. There are 12 halls of residence, some for mixed sexes, some for just men, some for just women. And there were many dances, and competitions, and there's a good theatre on campus, and the students do a lot of productions. There's also a big sports hall with a bar – very important.

Part 2
Nottingham is a superb town to live in. Geographically it's very interesting, because it has a real old town centre, in the old sense of the word, and all the facilities are in the centre. There are 2 very successful theatres, there are concert halls, the council has just spent a lot of money on providing facilities for everybody in the centre of the town. There are alternative fringe theatre groups, there are lots of different pubs where there's music played, there are night clubs. Nottingham is famous for its nightclubs. People come from all over the region to Nottingham at the weekends. Consequently on Friday and Saturday nights there are a lot of people in the centre. Quite exciting.

Part 3
You can't go to the cinema at 11 o'clock at night. I think – no – there are more advantages than disadvantages, because it's really a lot cheaper to live in Nottingham than London. The people in the North, I still think, are friendlier, much more friendly than people in London, and I like the atmosphere of a Northern town. Near to the Peak District of course, near to Derbyshire, near to beautiful countryside.

Unit 19 Skills

Anita is talking about life in America. She is describing what people do on national holidays:
Part 1
Can you tell us what is special about the 4th of July in America?

4th of July is a national holiday when we celebrate the Declaration of Independence, signed in 1776. This was a time when the people in the colonies in America decided that they wanted to be independent of the British.
On the 4th of July, some people have the day off, well, all of the people who work for the government, in post offices, for example, have the day off, banks close and some businesses close for the day. It's a real family day, students and schoolchildren finish school in June, so they have the day off . . .

Part 2
What sort of things happen on the 4th of July? What do people do to celebrate their holiday?

Well, most people in America get together and have a barbecue, either roast chicken or hot dogs, hamburgers, and of course we eat outside. Most towns and local city governments get together and organise some sort of parade, which people will go out and watch together, or they'll organise a fireworks display in the evening.

Part 3
Thanksgiving is celebrated in November. It's always on the 3rd Thursday of the month. This day we celebrate the end of the harvest season. It started when the first people came from Europe to live in America, and after their first harvest they got together with the American Indians, who helped them with their harvest, and had a big meal together.
And what do people do nowadays?
Well, nowadays we get together and cook a big meal, or we go out and watch parades through the streets, or go and see special football games.
And do you have fireworks displays, that sort of thing?
No, no, fireworks are only on the 4th of July.
And what do people eat when they have their big Thanksgiving meal?
Well the big Thanksgiving meal is mainly as many different foods as you can come up with. Turkey is the main feature of the meal, we also have all different types of potatoes, or

yams, corn, macaroni, peas, sometimes even sauerkraut. Dessert is traditionally pumpkin pie, with whipped cream, or we can have a mince pie, or sometimes even apple pie. Oh, and for drink, a special drink is warm apple cider.

Unit 20 Presentation

My alarm usually goes off early, at about 6.30, although I'm not a morning person. I actually prefer to stay up late at night, but not when I'm working the next day. Yesterday was fairly typical.

My working day started at about 8 o'clock, although the office doesn't really open until 9 o'clock. I like to get in before everyone else, because it's the only time of the day when I can work quietly.

My secretary came in at 9, and I answered letters and prepared for the day's meetings and appointments.

We had an editor's meeting at 10.30, when we talked about stories and articles for the next issue of Lifestyle. We discussed everyone's work and decided on new ideas for the reporters and writers to work on. That took about two hours. Then I went out to lunch with a television producer – it's important for me to make contact with people in the media.

In the afternoon I read several new articles and rewrote two of them in my own way. I really enjoy writing, although all my teachers at school said I was terrible at English!

Acknowledgements

The publishers would like to thank the following for permission to reproduce photographs, illustrations and text. Every effort has been made to contact copyright holders and apologies are made for any omissions.

Canadian High Commission: Camera Press, London: Nottingham Evening Post: The Albany Hotel, Nottingham: Pan Books: The Health Education Council: East Anglian Tourist Board: Topham Picture Library: Rank Theatres: Friends of the Earth Ltd: Cambridge Evening News: National Trust: Greater London Council: Sally & Richard Greenhill: National TV Licence Records Office: Cambridge City Council: Radio Trent: Chris Hughes: Oxfam: Times Newspaper Ltd: London Features International: Living Magazine: Nottinghamshire County Council: Labour Party: Manpower Services Commission: London Transport: Milk Marketing Board: British Tourist Authority: Dateline: The Mansell Collection Ltd: Manos Holidays: Sealink UK: Collins & Hayes: PGL Young Adventure Ltd: The Observer: Colorific Photo Library/Louie Psihoyos.

Designed by Stephen Raw, Letterforms.

Illustrations by Pantek Arts, Swanston Graphics, Oxford Illustrators, Piano Graphics (Mike Mosedale), Linda Rogers Associates, Andrew Warrington.

Typeset by Rowland Phototypesetting Ltd in 10pt Palatino Origination by Colorcraft Ltd, Hong Kong

Printed in Hong Kong by Colorcraft Ltd
for Hodder & Stoughton Education, a division
of Hodder & Stoughton Ltd, Mill Road, Dunton Green, Sevenoaks, Kent

Copyright © 1986 Michael Carrier and Simon Haines

First published 1986

ISBN 0 340 33401 0

All rights reserved. No part of this publication may be reproduced or transmitted in any form or by any means, electronic or mechanical, including photocopy, recording or any information storage and retrieval system, without permission in writing from the publisher or under licence from the Copyright Licensing Agency Limited. Further details of such licences (for reprographic reproduction) may be obtained from the Copyright Licensing Agency Limited, of 7 Ridgemount Street, London WC1.